CENTRAL
COPENHAGEN
~ 1945 ~

THE GIANT-KILLERS

JOHN ORAM THOMAS

The Giant-Killers

THE STORY OF THE DANISH
RESISTANCE MOVEMENT
1940-1945

TAPLINGER PUBLISHING COMPANY

NEW YORK

First published in the United States in 1976 by
TAPLINGER PUBLISHING CO., INC.
New York, New York

Copyright © 1975 by John Oram Thomas

Library of Congress Catalog Card Number: 76-11049

ISBN 0-8008-3258-2

To
the Mothers and Wives
of the
Danish Resistance

CONTENTS

Acknowledgments   10

Introduction   11

1   THE PRINCES   28

2   THE MOONSHINERS   43

3   'DENMARK CALLING...'   53

4   LOTTE   70

5   THE PRESS   81

6   THE STUDENTS   92

7   EXODUS   108

8   THE TRANSPORTERS   121

9   FORCHHAMMERSVEJ 7   142

10   KNUD   156

11   BOPA   169

12   HOLGER WAKES   192

13   CITRONEN   213

14   FLAMMEN   226

15   AMALIENBORG   245

16   THE HIDDEN EYE   253

17   THE CHURCHILL CLUB   261

18   THE RECEIVERS   270

19   PRIEST MILITANT   279

20   DAY OF VENGEANCE   287

21   UNDERGROUND ARMY   302

Index   314

ILLUSTRATIONS

Between pages 48 and 49

Ebbe Munck, L. A. Duus Hansen and Edith Bonnesen
(Lotte)

John Oram Thomas with some of the *Nonsuch* crew
on *Operation Moonshine*

Commodore Brian Bingham with Captain 'Ginger'
Stokes

Community singing in Frederiksberg Gardens,
September 1940

King Christian X taking his morning ride on his
72nd birthday

Sandbags and 'Spanish rider' barricades near
Amalienborg Castle

Barricade built across Nørrebrogade in Copenhagen

Between pages 112 and 113

Arne Sejr, Ib Mogens Bech Christensen (Knud), and
Pastor Harald Sandbæk

G. F. Duckwitz

A party of Jews escaping to Sweden

Tuborg Harbourmaster Johannes Johannesen

Kim Malthe-Bruun

The Elsinore Boys

Between pages 240 and 241

Svend Otto Nielsen (John), Bent Fauerschou-Hviid
(Flammen), and Jørgen Haagen Schmidt (Citronen)

Unpacking a container of arms dropped by the R.A.F.

Illegal manufacture of weapons

At a group meeting before an action, explosive issued
to the saboteurs

Saboteur roadsweeper

Railway Sabotage

Sabotage of Langebro by Bopa

The French school in flames after the disaster during
the R.A.F. raid on Shellhus

Two photographs of the Gestapo headquarters after
the raid on Shellhus

Between pages 304 and 305

Special issue of *De Frie Danske* commemorating the
fifth anniversary of the German occupation

Police-Constable Frank Zorn on guard at Sorgenfri
Castle

Fighting at Amalienborg Castle on the morning of
5 May 1945

The Police and the Royal Life Guard changing guard
at Amalienborg Castle, 10 June 1945

The same occasion; 250 police marching away from
Amalienborg

Montgomery arriving in Copenhagen

Three Copenhagen freedom fighters reading the news
in the *Berlingske Tidende*

5 May 1945: Happy girls parading through
Copenhagen

*A diagram of the R.A.F. raid on Shellhus is on
page 294*

ACKNOWLEDGMENTS

To all my good friends of the Danish Resistance Movement who through the years have helped so unsparingly to compile this chronicle, my heartfelt thanks. To name them individually would entail another book, but I must record special debts of gratitude to Dr. Jørgen Hæstrup for his invaluable advice and guidance to a lesser scribe; to *adjunkt* Hans Snitker for a wealth of information on the illegal Press; to *Frihedskampens Veteraner*, to *Amelienborg-Klubben*, to Bopa, Holger Danske and the transport groups, to *Muséet for Danmarks Frihedskamp* and to Minerva Film for opening their archives to me; to Detective-Inspector Frank Zorn and to Hans Gjerløv for permission to use photographs from their private collections; to Eiler Hansen for generous help with translation; and to Barbara and Michael Thomas, who helped to prepare the manuscript.

In the chapter on the Moonshiners, I have drawn considerably on the story I wrote for the *Hull Daily Mail* shortly after the conclusion of the operation. Again, my thanks to that bright newspaper.

The title was inspired by the story of David and Goliath in the First Book of Samuel, chapter 17, particularly verses 44–51.

INTRODUCTION

Denmark's foreign policy before the outbreak of the Second World War was one of neutrality and total adherence to the principles of the League of Nations. Germany's growing militancy following Hitler's rise to power had no effect on this traditional attitude. In 1939 Denmark was the first and only Scandinavian country to sign a non-aggression pact with Germany; yet on 9 April 1940, with neither warning nor official declaration of war, she was attacked.

At 4.25 a.m. German troops crossed the frontier at Krusaa, in Jutland, and five minutes later the Danish naval command reported that units had landed at Middelfart, Assens, and Nyborg in Funen. Shortly came news that more Germans had disembarked at Korsør, in South Zealand, and that paratroops had been dropped on Masnedø. Meanwhile a German merchant ship carrying an assault battalion had managed to pass the coastal forts unchallenged and had moored at the Langelinie Quay in Copenhagen. By 5 a.m. Kastellet (the Citadel), headquarters of the Zealand Division and the residence of General W. W. Prior, the Danish commander-in-chief, was in German hands.

The Danes were caught completely unprepared. On the morning of 9 April their entire active army strength comprised some 3,300 trained soldiers and 4,250 recruits in Zealand; about 3,300 trained men and 3,000 recruits in Jutland; and about 685 recruits in Funen. Only in South Jutland was any attempt made to stem the invasion. The German soldiers, who had been told that their mission was to 'protect' Denmark against a British assault, drove into heavy machine-gun and rifle fire at Haderslev, Tønder, and Søgaard. But the gallant, hopeless resistance was overwhelmed. In Zealand the fighting was confined to a short-lived engagement in the streets around Amalienborg Palace by a party of the King's Guard and an abortive defence of Værløse, the military airfield near Copenhagen, in which one Danish fighter plane was shot down and the rest destroyed on the ground.

Copenhageners awoke that morning to find the streets crowded with German troops while squadrons of aircraft circled above with orders to bomb the capital if resistance continued. Similar shocks awaited the inhabitants of towns and villages throughout Denmark. To avoid further useless sacrifice of life King Christian X, after conferring with his ministers at Amalienborg, ordered the troops to lay down their arms. All fighting stopped. Under protest Denmark was occupied. More than five years were to pass before the Germans were finally driven out of the country. The occupation was to cost 10,000 million Danish kroner and about 4,000 lives.

The first reaction of the Danish people was confusion and bewilderment. They heard and read proclamations from their own government insisting on non-resistance and the maintenance of law and order. In the face of well-drilled troops, equipped with tanks, bombers, and all the might of the German armouries, what could anybody hope to do? The military defence had collapsed and nobody had ever thought of a civilian resistance movement in case of occupation. There was no precedent for such action. Yet, in hindsight, it was inevitable that resistance in Denmark should be born and grow. The Danes were traditionally hostile to Germany. That hostility stemmed from the centuries-old struggle for Schleswig, culminating in the Danish-German war of 1864; it stemmed from the abominable attitude of the German government towards the Danes living in North Schleswig between 1864 and 1914; and it increased after 1933, when Hitler came to power, because the strong democratic traditions of Denmark were completely antipathetic to the Nazi creed and policies.

The coalition government of Social Democrats and Radicals, led by Thorvald Stauning, were absolutely democratic and absolutely anti-Nazi but on 9 April 1940, they found themselves with no alternative to capitulation. Behind their decision was a consideration of the military weakness of Denmark, of the geographic impossibility of fighting, and of what would happen in North Schleswig if the struggle continued. Denmark had regained North Schleswig under the Versailles Treaty. If a state of open war were declared and the Germans denounced the treaty as it applied to North Schleswig, some 200,000 Danes would become Germans overnight and would become liable to conscription into the armed forces while the civil population could expect nothing but brutal repression. For all these reasons the government decided to give in and even the Conservative opposition, who had been pressing for rearmament, agreed that they had no choice.

The problem, then, for government and people, was what to do after capitulation. Uncertainty, helplessness, even in some circles despair, prevailed into the summer of 1940. Yet already the first seeds of resistance were being sown.

First to act were 'the Princes', a group of junior officers of the army and navy intelligence services. Because Denmark was not at war with Germany they were able to continue their normal work, and, in the course of their duties, collect unofficially a great deal of information of value to Britain. In July 1940, they made contact with Ebbe Munck, a Danish newspaperman, and it was agreed that he should go to Stockholm as correspondent for *Berlingske Tidende*. There he would receive information from the Princes, which he would pass to the British legation for transmission to London. That service started in October 1940, when the first batch of information went to Sweden, and it was to continue until the end of the occupation. It grew to such proportions and was operated with such efficiency that if the intelligence service had been Denmark's only contribution to the Allied war effort, for that alone the Resistance would have been worthwhile.

The first shock passed. People listening in their homes to the calm voice of the BBC—which the Germans were never able to suppress—realised that Hitler's threatened invasion of Britain had failed to take place. Perhaps, after all, he was not invincible, hope spread and with it indignation at the increasing German interference in Danish internal affairs. Hitler's original idea had been to make Denmark into a model 'Aryan' protectorate. His government had promised that there would be no intrusion upon the kingdom's territorial integrity or political independence and that the Danish state's sovereignty would remain intact. The German forces were ordered to be 'correct' in their behaviour to the Danes. The Nazis wanted to be friends, and in the beginning—though friendship was never evident on the government's side—the official Danish policy was to conform.

But the people said no; many rejected the government's policy and openly demanded 'Norwegian conditions' (a complete break with the Germans). The first signs of widespread passive resistance came in a revival of the national spirit, notably fostered by Arne Sørensen and his *Dansk Samling* party. Eminent Danes like the historian Vilhelm la Cour published books and lectured on Denmark's proud history. Community singing of national songs in halls and parks became popular throughout the land. Boys and girls took to wearing knitted caps in the pattern of the RAF's red, white and blue roundel. Cyclostyled 'illegal' news-sheets and pamphlets began to appear in increasing numbers. On 26 September 1940, King Christian's seventieth birthday, hundreds of thousands of Copenhageners swarmed into the streets and gathered at Amalienborg Palace to cheer him as a symbol of national unity.

The king himself played his part in strengthening the country's morale. He left the palace at eleven every morning to ride through the streets of the capital. Bolt upright in the saddle, blue eyes gazing firmly ahead, he never acknowledged the salutes of the German soldiers who sprang to attention as he passed. There is a story that one puzzled trooper asked a boy standing beside him on the kerb: 'Who is this old gentleman who rides past here every day?'

'That is our king,' the boy replied.

'So! If that is your king, where is his bodyguard?'

The boy drew himself up proudly. 'We are *all* his bodyguard,' he said.

On another occasion, a communist greeted the king with a clenched-fist salute and a cry of 'Red Front!' The king smiled and returned the salute. Then he turned back the flap of his military tunic to show the scarlet lining. 'Red front,' he said amiably.

Resistance in Denmark gained its initial impetus from a multitude of small groups of friends scattered throughout the country finding other groups in a common aim to show that though Denmark had been occupied, she had not been conquered. At first the actions of the resisters were aimed more against their own government than against the occupying forces. They were hunted by the Danish police and, when caught, punished as criminals, but not a single section of the populace remained unaffected as the first dim sparks of the resistance fanned into a steady flame. Even schoolchildren were active in the struggle and the exploits of the Churchill Club, a group of teenage boys at Aalborg's Cathedral School, have become a part of Denmark's folk history.

What singled out Denmark among other European occupied countries was the very high level of organisation behind all resistance activities. Denmark was highly developed culturally and educationally and the comparatively small population— some four and a half million—were thoroughly organised in political, military, industrial, agricultural, craft, and athletic associations. When the occupation came, this was to be of inestimable importance. As early as 12 April 1940, the leaders of the political party *Dansk Samling* met and agreed it was their duty to try to create a just anger in as many Danes as possible and to induce them to decide for themselves that they wanted, when the time was ripe, to take up arms and liberate their country. To this end they organised meetings in private homes, halls, and schoolrooms for discussions and the singing of national songs; they published broadsheets and books on Danish history and its relevance to the current situation; they even issued Christmas cards carrying patriotic quotations from great figures of the past. The activity developed with amazing speed and within a year they had thousands of helpers throughout the land—not a single section of the populace remained unaffected. Meanwhile, during the summer of 1940, numerous Danish youth associations had combined to form the nationwide *Dansk Ungdomssamvirke* (Danish Youth Cooperation) to counter any attempt by the Danish Nazi party to infiltrate the individual clubs and associations. *Ungdomssamvirke* did not engage in active resistance. They went along with the official government policy between 1940 and 1943 believing that the policy of negotiation with the Germans could be useful to Denmark, and could spare the population many miseries. Nevertheless, in conjunction with the meetings, community singing and similar activities, they played a notable part in strengthening the national morale. It must be said, however, that there is still considerable debate in Denmark whether in fact *Ungdomssamvirke* were a help or a hindrance to the Resistance Movement. Some Resistance veterans claim that too many youngsters thought that by joining the organisation they had done all that was required of them and that valuable potential recruits for the Press, sabotage, and other active groups were lost. It is a matter of opinion.

In July 1940, the government was transformed completely when Erik Scavenius replaced Dr. P. Munch as foreign minister. The conservatives mistrusted Munch, who had been against rearmament and who, although he was anti-Nazi, had followed a policy of reconciliation with Germany. It was generally felt within political circles that Scavenius would be the better man in the existing situation. It was thought that he knew how to deal with Germans. He had been Danish ambassador in Berlin and as foreign minister during the First World War he had succeeded in maintaining Denmark's neutrality. If Munch were to resign, it appeared there was no other choice but Scavenius, though he was disliked by the Danish people. Scavenius was not pro-German but he was a very realistic politician who believed at the time that there was a distinct possibility that Germany was going to win the war and that therefore it was best for Denmark to reach agreement with Hitler's government before it was too late.

The Danes disagreed. The events of 1941—the German attack on Russia and the entry of the Americans into the war after Pearl Harbour—gave them increased hope and stiffened their will to resist. Following the attack on Russia, the Danish communist party was banned and as many members as the police could arrest were interned. The others went underground and linked up with the active resisters. While the brilliantly organised 'illegal' Press stirred and kept the public accurately informed, sabotage grew from isolated 'nuisance' actions into better-planned, though still sporadic, operations.

Morale was boosted further by the magnificent work of the British Broadcasting Corporation. One of the reasons why the Polish resistance failed was that it was cut off from all outside aid and encouragement. Denmark was nearer geographically to Britain and had a very close relationship with her. Thanks to an excellent grounding at school most Danes understood and spoke English to some extent. If they knew no English in 1940 they learned very quickly during the years of occupation. So they were kept well informed several times a day both by the BBC's Danish Service and by the British Home Service, which was less affected by 'jamming'.

An instance of this was given to me by the eminent Danish historian and Resistance veteran Dr. Jørgen Hæstrup. He said: 'On Saturday, 21 June 1941, my family had gone down to a little fishing village on the south coast of Funen for a holiday. I was to follow by bicycle next day. In the morning, when I got up, I listened to the BBC and heard that Hitler had attacked Russia. I was confused. I knew I could not go on living without the BBC, especially in that situation, and I was afraid I should be unable to listen to the broadcasts in that holiday village. When I got there at 6.30 p.m. I went restlessly out into the street just as the BBC's Danish news bulletin was going on the air. From every one of the small houses where the fishermen lived, through the open windows one could hear the news-reader's voice. I stood there for about two minutes; then a fisherman came out and said: "Come inside and listen with us." I went in. The living-room was filled with fishermen, farmers, and holiday-makers. We were a happy lot. We met every evening in that house throughout the summer, listening to the BBC and discussing the situation among ourselves. Eventually the fisherman became a Resistance man. He worked on the escape routes over the Øresund, he collected intelligence, he served on arms reception committees, and he was a saboteur.'

The efficiency of the 'illegal' Press was due to three main factors: first, the well-organised Danish social structure, which made it easy to find people who could write, print, distribute the finished newspapers, and finance the whole operation;

secondly, the accuracy of the news, owing to the fact that the papers were served by *Information*, an illegal press agency which provided a service of precise information gathered from the BBC, from Swedish sources, from the Danish ministries, and from uncensored reports flowing in to the legal newspapers; and thirdly, the important link between *Information* and the Danish Press Service in Stockholm, created by Ebbe Munck and managed by the Danish journalists Erik Seidenfaden and Gunnar Næsselund. Three or four times daily, bulletins were sent across the Øresund by *Information*, enabling the Danish Press Service to send out from Stockholm to all parts of the world news of what was happening inside occupied Denmark.

Radio communication between Denmark and the free world was better than in Norway or any other occupied country. The Secret Intelligence Service and later Special Operations Executive organised radio communication by means of telegraphists trained in England and parachuted with equipment produced in Britain into the countries where they were needed. Many of the telegraphists were very badly trained and their transmitters and receivers were poor. Very often the equipment was lost or smashed on landing, something which happened in Denmark in 1941-2; the telegraphists had to make their way to Copenhagen and ask the radio engineer Duus Hansen for help. Hansen helped the first pair to land, Thomas Sneum and Sigfred Christophersen, sent over by SIS in the autumn of 1941, and later the SOE parachutists who landed in the spring of 1942. From 1943 onwards, having finally won the full confidence of SOE, he was allowed to build up his own radio communication system, using his own equipment and employing only Danish professional operators.

In the spring of 1942 the Resistance Movement began to get into its stride and throughout the year tension rose. On 26 September the king received the usual fulsome birthday telegram from Hitler. He replied coldly and formally: 'My very sincere thanks—Christian X.' Hitler was furious. He immediately recalled the German ambassador, C. von Renthe-Fink, and sent the Danish ambassador in Berlin, O. C. Mohr, back to Copenhagen. For two months there were no diplomatic relations between Denmark and Germany. Then, in November, Scavenius was called to Berlin to negotiate with Ribbentrop, who demanded that the Danish government be reconstituted with Scavenius as prime minister. He refused. The Germans then said that the new government must be allowed to act without putting their proposals or decisions before parliament. When Scavenius returned to Copenhagen with the German demands there was a general feeling in Danish political circles that they could not be fulfilled but eventually, after a few days of debates and negotiations the Danish politicians yielded to the demand that Scavenius should replace Vilhelm Buhl as prime minister. This put the Danish government in a very peculiar situation with the public who were unable to accept the fact that for the first time they had a prime minister not elected by parliament but installed by German command. On the other hand the Scavenius government had a parliamentary majority behind it because none of the politicians was anxious for a clean break with Germany.

In the spring of 1943 the situation changed decisively. The illegal Press had grown up and had become a powerful instrument. Throughout Denmark people listened to the Swedish radio and the BBC; the real truth about the progress of the war was common knowledge. With news of Stalingrad, El Alamein, and the North Africa landings, there was every reason to believe that the Allies would be victorious. SOE had opened their offensive in Denmark, sending over instructors, equipment, explosives, and weapons. From April sabotage had become effective and action by tough, well trained groups like Bopa and Holger Danske was spreading from German transports and installations to Danish factories and shipyards working for the German war machine. Many people who had not believed in sabotage came to realise that it could be effective and changed their attitude. In the beginning Resistance 'terrorists' had been opposed not only by the Germans but by Danish collaborators and lukewarm 'patriots' who dreaded the reprisals. Their propaganda worked on the lines that it was a useless waste of men and effort to resist the *Herrenvolk*. But when, with the full approval of the Resistance, the RAF bombarded Burmeister

& Wein, a Copenhagen shipyard working for the Germans, the resultant damage and casualties helped to convince people that sabotage by the Danes' own underground forces was less costly for the population. In August 1943, an illegal Gallup-type poll indicated that seventy per cent of the Danish public were 'for' sabotage.

Tension grew and throughout Denmark, wherever there was a German garrison, there was fighting, rioting, and more and more antagonism between German soldiers and the Danish army and civil population. One incident followed another—and all affected the German morale.

In October 1942, just before Scavenius became prime minister, the Germans had ordered a new general, Hermann von Hanneken, to Denmark to secure the country against invasion. Hanneken feared the Danish Resistance because he realised that from the spring of 1943 it had been linked closely with the activities of SOE; therefore sabotage and resistance could be connected, in his opinion, with British plans to invade. He repeatedly urged the German government for authority to disarm the Danish forces and to step up the fight against the Resistance.

During July and August 1943, there were nationwide strikes. The first began on 28 July at Odense, where a German minesweeper was being built. Two days before the vessel was due to leave the shipyard it was sabotaged. The Germans were furious. Troops marched into the shipyard and all the workers walked out. The strike of the shipyard men led to similar action in the town. The workers at every Odense factory and industrial plant downed tools. A few days later there was trouble at Esbjerg. There the walk-out at a fish warehouse developed into a 'folk-strike'. Everybody in the town, fishermen, factory workers, police, firemen, office workers, civil servants, and council officials, stopped work and all the shops closed their doors. The Germans ordered a curfew. The people ignored it. They crowded into the streets and there were clashes with the soldiers. After five or six days the Germans were forced to yield and lift the curfew. It was too late. A couple of days later another strike began in Odense. Thence trouble spread to Aalborg, Aarhus,

and practically all the towns in Jutland and Funen. At Odense
the directors of the foreign office and the ministry of justice,
the minister of labour, the burgomaster, even the union leaders,
had implored the workers to go back to their benches—but
their pleas were in vain. The Copenhagen government realised
that they had lost all popular support. If the Germans were to
make one further demand they would have to resign.

News of the strikes had been reported to Hitler, including one
special incident which had occurred at Odense. A German
officer had gone there by train to investigate the disturbances.
As he walked out of the station he was met by a jeering mob.
Frightened, he drew his pistol and fired into the crowd. After
he had fired six shots and wounded a few people, including a
young boy, he was overwhelmed and beaten almost to a pulp.
That incident, with others, led Hitler to impose on Odense,
capital of the island of Funen, a fine of one million kroner,
which was to be paid to the German *Wehrmacht*. Meanwhile,
increasing sabotage was adding to the problems of the occupying
forces. On 24 August 1943, in broad daylight, a team of five
men from Holger Danske blew up the Forum, Copenhagen's
largest public hall. It was the last straw.

Four days later the Danish government were faced with the
following ultimatum from the German government:

The Danish government must forthwith proclaim a State
of Emergency throughout the whole country. The State of
Emergency must proclaim the following measures:

(1) Public meetings of more than five persons are prohibited.

(2) Any form of strike or any form of support of strikers
is prohibited.

(3) Any form of gathering or meeting in a closed room
or in the open air is prohibited.

There will be a curfew between the hours of 8.30 p.m. and
5.30 a.m. All restaurants will close at 7.30 p.m.

(4) All weapons and explosives will be surrendered before
1 September, 1943.

Any encroachment on the rights of Danish citizens as a

result of their own or their relatives' cooperation with the German authorities, or relationships with Germans, is prohibited.

(5)   There will be a censorship of the Press under German control.

(6)   Summary courts will be set up to deal with cases where the above-mentioned decrees are violated to the prejudice of security and order.

Violation of the above-mentioned decrees shall be severely punished under the laws which empower the government to maintain order and security.

Any sabotage and all assistance in sabotage, any defiance of the German *Wehrmacht* and of its members, as well as continued retention of weapons and explosives after the first of September, will be subject to the death penalty immediately.

The German government expects the Danish government to accept the above-mentioned demands before 1600 hours to-day.

The ultimatum was rejected. No Danish government could take responsibility for giving in to the German demands and the politicians had no choice. On 28 August 1943, the government resigned and the Germans declared a state of emergency. On 29 August the Danish forces were disarmed and interned and the navy's ships were scuttled, though a few smaller craft managed to escape to Sweden.

From 29 August Denmark was *de facto* in an open state of war with Germany and got similar treatment to that of the other occupied countries. The Gestapo and their Danish jackals, the *Schalburgkorps*, hunted the freedom fighters relentlessly. Captured saboteurs were shot or deported to German concentration camps. Sabotage was answered by the wanton destruction of such well loved Danish institutions as Copenhagen's beautiful Tivoli Gardens. Each time Resistance liquidation squads killed a German or Danish informer the Germans retaliated by shooting a well known Dane. On 4 January 1944, the murder of Denmark's great priest, poet, and dramatist, Kaj Munk, horrified the free world. His body was found in a ditch on Hørbylunde

Hill, near Silkeborg, in Jutland. His face had been battered savagely and he had been killed by five pistol shots, fired at close range. The murder was carried out by the notorious 'Peter Group' at the command of the highest German authority.

Towards the end of September 1943, to the anger of the entire Danish people, Jew-baiting began. It was a dismal failure. There is a widespread myth that King Christian expressed his sympathy with his Jewish subjects by insisting on wearing the Star of David on his military tunic. It is a pretty fable, but in fact no Jew in Denmark was ever made to wear the yellow Star. As far as I have been able to discover, King Christian's sole recorded comment on the matter was his terse message to Hitler: 'We have no Jewish problem. We have only Danes.'

The Germans had been preparing the action against the Jews for some time. The membership lists and the archives of the synagogue in Copenhagen had been seized and used to compile lists of 'wanted' victims. On the evening of 30 September all telephones were disconnected while the German 'prairie wagons' raided the addresses. Luckily, very few Jewish families were in their homes. Thanks to good contacts inside the German headquarters, warnings had gone out in advance through the Resistance Movement and some politicians. The German move sent a new wave of indignation and determination throughout the country. With the help of the greater part of the people (and, let it be said, not a little sympathetic 'blindness' in *Wehrmacht* quarters), within a few weeks almost all of Denmark's Jewish population—more than 7,000—had been helped to escape across the Øresund to Sweden. Only 474 fell into Gestapo hands, half of them during abortive attempts to get transport to Sweden. They spent the rest of the war in the German concentration camp Theresienstadt and, by sharing Red Cross food parcels with their guards, managed to save themselves from the gas chambers.

Denmark's Resistance Movement during the following two years of occupation was to earn high praise from Field-Marshal Montgomery, who rated it the best in Europe.

The Freedom Council came into existence on 16 September 1943, to become the supreme leaders in the fight against the

Germans. Reporting to the Freedom Council were the K-Committee, the general staff co-ordinating important sabotage and the distribution of supplies from the Allies. Denmark was divided into six regions, each with headquarters in direct radio communication with London and responsible for major sabotage actions, particularly against the railroads. During the Battle of the Ardennes the Danish saboteurs were able to delay a German division for three days on its way through Jutland. Also reporting to the Freedom Council was *Information*, the central news-gathering service which furnished the illegal Press with so much useful material. Reception committees were responsible for receiving and storing guns and ammunition dropped by aircraft from Britain or sent from Sweden by sea. The transport groups handled illegal traffic and helped Danes and Allied servicemen who were wanted by the Gestapo. Special sabotage groups—they could justly be called suicide squads—included many communists who showed patriotism, ability, and keenness which earned the great respect of all who worked with them. Last, but certainly not least, an efficient intelligence service reported to headquarters in Stockholm and direct to London. Thanks to these men and women and the superb radio service, the movement of every German ship and every military unit in Denmark was known to London in advance.

In the summer of 1944 a general strike was called as a protest against the German oppression. In Copenhagen and the provincial towns and cities all work stopped and all factories and shops were closed. The Germans cut off food supplies to the capital, together with water, gas, and electricity, but the workers refused to yield. In protest they burned huge bonfires throughout the city during the blackout hours. On the last night of the strike five thousand fires were blazing in the streets and open spaces. Eventually, fearing the effect of the loss of production on their war effort, the Germans had to abolish the curfew and withdraw the terrorist troops and Schalburgmen from the city.

On 19 September 1944, the Germans rounded up the Danish police, many of whom were Resistance sympathisers. About 2,000 men were sent to Buchenwald and other German concentration camps but 7–8,000 went underground, in some cases to become active members of the Resistance fighting groups.

By this time some 5,000 Danes had been interned in German and Danish concentration camps and all the prisons were crowded. German terrorism intensified. Prisoners were murdered and their bodies thrown into the streets. Men and women were tortured diabolically in the Gestapo headquarters and in the camps. Many were shot down in their homes and in the streets. Murder ran riot, with the infamous Hipokorps (*Hilfspolizei*) even more brutal than its German masters. So the will and spirit of the Resistance was strengthened.

Meanwhile, equipped with weapons dropped by aircraft or smuggled from Sweden, an underground army of 45,000 men were preparing for the day of liberation. Another well-armed force of 5,000, many of them seasoned fighters badly wanted by the Gestapo, were training in Sweden. The illegal Press were publishing more than 225 newspapers and periodicals to keep the public informed about the true situation in Denmark and the free world. Liquidation squads brought swift justice to the *stikkers*, foul creatures who wormed themselves into Resistance groups to betray their countrymen to the Gestapo for a handful of kroner. And still, despite every German effort, the transport routes continued daily to carry hunted saboteurs and other refugees to Sweden and to bring back vital supplies. The Germans grew more helpless and the worsening situation in the Fatherland further sapped their morale. In Denmark their enemies were everywhere. Even behind the windows of Christiansborg staid civil servants were planning their destruction with smooth efficiency.

After the resignation of the Danish government on 28 August 1943, the civil servants had taken upon themselves the administration of the country's affairs. They had no official right to do so; they had mandate neither from parliament nor people; but they assumed automatically all the functions of the former government. With the formation of the Freedom Council and the consequent intensification of Resistance activities, nobody in the free world could doubt that outright war was being waged against the Germans; therefore the civil servants could continue their work without doing any harm politically to Denmark. On

the other hand they could and did help the Resistance Movement because it is always easier to carry on resistance in a
country where, on the surface at least, the civil administration
is functioning fairly normally. Mao Tse-tung once said: 'The
resistance man is like a fish in water. If there is no water, there
will be no fish.' There was water in Denmark—a certain kind
of normality created by the civil servants who, without harming
Denmark's political face, helped the people through the ordeal
of occupation and at the same time directly aided the Resistance
Movement. They ensured, for example, that all the men and
women who were deported to German concentration camps and
prisons received an adequate supply of Red Cross parcels, paid
for by the Danish State. Again, despite close supervision by the
German authorities, they managed with bland official minutes
and skilful bookkeeping to smuggle millions of kroner out of
the Danish budgets for the direct benefit of the Resistance.
Indeed, during the latter part of the occupation the Resistance
Movement was financed largely by the Danish civil servants'
'government'. Sometimes they took an active part in more
dangerous and exciting activities. During the final months of
the occupation the most important sabotage actions were
planned in consultation between the saboteurs and the directors
and officials of the factory or installation to be 'hit', the object
being to procure the utmost immediate disruption of production
with the minimum permanent damage to the buildings and
plant. Several of these discussions took place in government
offices. The famous South Harbour bridge sabotage in Copenhagen was arranged in the Ministry of Trade, where the Bopa
leaders sat down with ministry officials and harbour executives
and worked out the whole operation.

At 9 o'clock on the evening of 4 May 1945, the news reached
Denmark that Germany had capitulated. Within minutes
candles were burning in the windows of every Danish home and
the nation hailed its liberation in a blaze of light. By the morning of 5 May, when the first British troops marched in, the
Resistance men and the underground army had taken control
throughout Denmark.

That is the bare outline of the story of Denmark's five finest years. It is one of the least known to English-speaking peoples of all the tales of heroism and endurance to come out of the Second World War but it is undoubtedly one of the greatest. It is a story of high adventure, of grim tragedy and, at times, of blatant comedy, for the Danes defeated their enemy as much with laughter as with guns. This book makes no pretence of being a full history of those stirring times. I have tried only to tell the stories of some of the men and women who played their part in the fight for freedom and, through them, to pay tribute to the many who suffered and died.

1 : THE PRINCES

If, as some aver, the Danish high command in 1939 were not acutely sensitive to the German menace, their complacency was not shared by a group of junior officers in the army and navy intelligence services. Long before the outbreak of war they had established close and friendly relations with their opposite numbers in the Swedish intelligence services, giving and receiving a great deal of useful information. They appreciated that if trouble came to Denmark, Sweden could be a very useful neighbour.

Following the German occupation on 9 April 1940, these young men, who had always worked closely together, combined to form a group known as *Prinserne* (The Princes), led by Lieutenant-Colonel E. M. Nordentoft, Captain of Horse H. M. Lunding, Captain V. L. U. Gyth, and Captain Per Winkel, of the general staff intelligence section, in close cooperation with Commander P. A. Mørch, of the naval staff intelligence section, who at that time was not even known to the British authorities. Since until 1943 there was no interference by the Germans in the affairs of the army and navy they were able, with the utmost caution, to continue their intelligence work, keeping a particularly close watch on the movements of German troops and ships and the building of fortifications. The information they collected, obviously of the greatest importance to the Allies, was transmitted regularly through Stockholm to London. They also maintained links with the Polish, French, Dutch, Norwegian, and Belgian intelligence services, although to much lesser effect.

The group had no direct contact with the British but they knew that the latter were setting up an organisation, Special Operations Executive (SOE), which could be used in the occupied countries. One of the Princes, Captain Volmer Gyth, had a friend, Jutta Graae, a young woman who worked in a savings bank in Copenhagen and who had very good British connections, largely through her brother-in-law, the journalist Ebbe Munck. In the years before the outbreak of war she had received several visits from British contacts who were working on plans for connections with the Continent in wartime. In July 1940, a meeting was arranged between the Princes and Ebbe Munck, who had just returned from Finland, where he had been covering the Russian-Finnish war. It was agreed that Munck should get himself appointed correspondent for the Copenhagen newspaper *Berlingske Tidende* in Stockholm. There he was to make contact with Captain H. Denham, the naval attaché at the British legation, and begin a regular delivery of all the information collected by the Princes. The first message to England was sent by Gyth, who on 13 April 1940, saw some British legation people in a train at Fredericia station and handed them a letter describing the current position in occupied Denmark; but the first really important report was transmitted through Munck in October 1940. It was a review of everything that had happened during the summer, seen from the army, naval, and political points of view—a sort of general estimate of Denmark's present situation and probable future. From that time until the German capitulation Britain was to receive a constant flow of information of all kinds, military, naval, air, political, commercial, industrial and social, from the Princes and their associates. It has been estimated that from November 1943, until May 1945, there was a daily transmission to London through Stockholm of some thirty reports—a total of about fifteen thousand. The tally for the five years of occupation was probably double that figure.

The information gathered for the Princes by agents throughout Denmark was typed, micro-filmed, and sent by courier to Ebbe Munck in Stockholm. The couriers were Danish businessmen and others who had German visas for Sweden. The microfilms were smuggled across the Øresund inside shaving brushes and hair brushes, in soap tablets, even in anal containers, and none went astray. Munck passed the messages to Denham, who sent them on to London. The work was carried out entirely by Danes and financed with Danish money, and the reports were so comprehensive that soon the British were able to call a halt to their own espionage in Denmark. There were also Swedish officials who crossed the Øresund regularly with messages from the Princes to the Swedish defence staff.

In November 1940, Sir Charles Hambro, a British banker, met Ebbe Munck in Stockholm to discuss cooperation between activist circles in Denmark and SOE. They agreed that the existing intelligence network should remain completely in Danish hands but Hambro emphasised that the British were interested in fostering a resistance movement which, when the time was ripe, could begin widespread sabotage. He promised that SOE would give full support to any properly organised resistance movement and would provide the necessary explosives, weapons, and instructors. As a result of this meeting a former Press attaché at the British embassy in Copenhagen, Ronald Turnbull, was sent from London to Stockholm in February 1941. His official post was Press attaché at the British legation but his real job was to organise and control SOE activities in Denmark and Sweden. Thereafter, throughout the occupation, he worked closely with Munck.

It was through the Princes that London first received accurate information concerning the V1 'flying bomb'. It was already known that German scientists and engineers were working at Peenemunde on some kind of secret weapon which, Hitler boasted, would bring Britain to her knees, but its exact character was a matter of surmise. By a lucky chance one of the missiles, test-fired on the east coast of Germany one day in August 1943, went off course and landed on the Danish island of Bornholm. A small crowd of fishermen and farm workers gathered to look at it. They were accustomed to mines drifting on to the beaches but this was plainly no mine. Among the first on the scene were a local policeman, Johannes Hansen, and the naval intelligence officer on the island, Lieutenant-Commander Christian Hassager Christiansen. While Hansen took photographs of the missile, Christiansen made sketches and detailed notes of its construction. They had barely finished when a German officer arrived.

'Have you taken photographs of this object?' he asked Christiansen.

Christiansen quite truthfully replied: 'No.'

The officer accepted his word. German soldiers took the missile away and the crowd dispersed. (When, later, Commander Mørch proposed that Christiansen should be awarded the Distinguished Service Cross, his main argument to the British authorities was: 'He said "no" at the right moment').

Hansen developed his negatives and they, with the drawings and notes, were sent to the right people in Copenhagen. A Danish civil air pilot who had been among the crowd also sent photographs to the capital. Eight copies of the pictures and documents were made and distributed for transmission to Sweden by various routes, including the ferry between Elsinore and Halsingborg. The mate of the Danish ferryboat, Benny West, a former navy man, normally took charge of material going to Sweden, but that day, as it happened, he was on leave and his deputy had not been briefed sufficiently on how to handle such matters. He hid the package clumsily and a German patrol found it while making a routine search of the vessel. The Germans knew that the photographs, sketches, and notes must have been made on Bornholm and Christiansen, as the most likely suspect, was arrested. The Gestapo tortured him mercilessly but he remained silent. West was arrested and interrogated but he, too, gave nothing away. Christiansen was sent to a hospital to await trial and almost certain execution. He was rescued by a military team who specialised in such jobs and eventually taken to Sweden, where he worked for the intelligence service in Malmø until the end of the occupation.

Despite this mischance the pictures and description of the V1 missile were passed to London by Munck and Turnbull a full year before the Germans were ready to use the weapon against Britain.

On 29 August 1943, the smoothly-working intelligence system was temporarily disrupted. The Danish army were disarmed and interned and the Princes had to go underground. Mørch and Gyth, together with Jutta Graae, escaped to Sweden, where they were joined later by Nordentoft and Winkel. Lunding was less fortunate. He was arrested in his office, having made no attempt to escape. After withstanding steadfastly many days of intensive interrogation and torture he was deported to Germany, where

he remained, first in a convict prison and afterwards in a concentration camp, until the spring of 1945. In May of that year
he was on his way to execution with a party of condemned men
who included Leon Blum, Hjalmar Schacht, Schuschnigg and
Martin Niemüller, when the transport was captured in the
South Tyrol by American troops and the prisoners released.

Long before the events of 29 August the Princes had begun
an operation which was to have a crucial effect upon the course
of the war. Early in 1943 SOE in London sent them through
Turnbull an inquiry whether the world-famous Danish physicist
Niels Bohr would be willing to accept an invitation to work in
Britain. Bohr at that time was allowed to work quite freely at
the Institute of Theoretical Physics on Blegdamsvej, Copenhagen, because despite his overt antagonism to the Nazi regime
his laboratories were frequently visited and used by German
scientists. Gyth went to see him at his mansion of honour at
Carlsberg and passed on SOE's message but the professor was
unwilling to discuss the matter without written confirmation.
Three open postcards to three cover-addresses in Stockholm
conveyed this information to Turnbull, the messages being
hidden under one 10-øre and two 5-øre stamps. On a second visit
to the mansion Gyth brought the conversation around to the
feasibility of making an atom bomb but Bohr said he did not
believe it could be done, although he knew that the Germans
were working on the project.

Towards the end of March the Princes received another
message from Turnbull:

To Peter
From Jarlen

Most Important

We intend sending to JUSTITSRAADEN in the near future a
bunch of keys which contain a very important message from
the British Government to Professor Niels Bohr. We would
be very grateful if you could see that Professor Bohr gets the
keys and also if you or someone appointed by you would
explain to him how to find the message.

The following diagram shows the position in keys A and A1

of the message which has to be extracted. Key A1 is the one with the number 229 on it and key A is the *long* key next to it.

A small hole to a depth of 4mm has been bored in the two keys. The holes were plugged up and concealed after the message was inserted. Professor Bohr should gently file the keys at the point indicated until the hole appears. The message can then be syringed or floated out on to a micro-slide. The message is a very very small micro-film and is repeated in duplicate in each key. It should be handled very delicately.

I do not myself know the contents of the message except that I do know is *very important*. Will you kindly warn JUSTITSRAADEN and tell him to expect the bunch of keys. We will send the keys through to him by separate courier as soon as we know that this sending has reached you and that you have had time to warn JUSTITSRAADEN.

Next day Jutta Graae rang Gyth and told him that Count 'Bobby' Moltke had brought from Sweden a bunch of keys which 'somebody or other had forgotten'. Gyth bought a file and vice and borrowed a microscope from a doctor. He collected the keys and took them to the Princes' headquarters. A guard was posted outside the door to ensure complete security, then Gyth and Winkel got down to work. They clamped the first of the keys into the vice and began to file very carefully at the indicated point. Before long a hole no bigger than a pin's head appeared. The two men tied handkerchiefs over their noses and mouths to prevent blowing away the film, which plainly could be no larger than a grain of sand. Gently removing the key from the vice, they shook three specks of film on to a glass slide, which they placed under the 600-power lens of the microscope. The films were identical but some of the words were so indistinct that all could not be read in any one copy and they had to compare all three to get the complete text.

The message was from Bohr's close friend Professor James Chadwick, of Liverpool University, a leading figure in British nuclear research. It was typed on the university's paper, signed by Chadwick himself and invited Bohr to go to England, where he would receive a hearty welcome. 'There is no scientist in the world who would be more favourably received, both in our university circles and by the general public,' Chadwick wrote. He assured Bohr that he would be able to continue his own work without hindrance but that there were certain special problems on which his cooperation would be of the greatest value. 'However, I do not wish to influence your decision,' Chadwick continued. 'Only you can weigh all the different circumstances and I have the fullest confidence in your decision, whatever it may be.' He added that Bohr would be told how help could be given for his escape to Britain.

Gyth took a copy of the message to the professor and called at the mansion next day for his answer. It was a refusal. Bohr felt that his place was in Denmark. He expressed his gratitude that his friends in Britain had not forgotten him and said that he wished fervently to contribute to the common cause for freedom and human dignity. But he continued: 'I feel it my duty in our desperate situation to help resist the threats to our free institutions and to protect the refugee scientists who have sought sanctuary here. However, neither such duties nor the danger of reprisals against my colleagues and relatives would weigh sufficiently to keep me here if I felt that I could be of real help in other ways, but that is scarcely likely. Especially I feel convinced that regardless of what the future may hold, immediate use of the latest wonderful discoveries in atomic physics is scarcely possible.'

Gyth reduced the typewritten letter, which took up a half-folio sheet, to a 2mm × 3mm film. Engineer Duus Hansen, who operated radio transmissions for the Princes, had a travel visa for Sweden and agreed to act as courier. Wrapped in silver foil the film was hidden under a plug in his denture and the next morning was in Stockholm.

A few weeks later Bohr rang Gyth and asked him to go to his home. It transpired that he wanted a second letter sent to England. He emphasised that the matter was urgent and that at all costs the letter must not fall into German hands. Bohr had heard reports that the Germans were making preparations for the extensive production of uranium and heavy water. In his second letter to Chadwick he told of these reports and discussed the possibility of using chain reactions with slow neutrons to produce a nuclear bomb but he remained sceptical about the potential use in warfare of atomic energy. He believed it would be impossible to separate U235 on a sufficiently large scale.

Gyth took the letter back to headquarters, photographed it, placed the undeveloped negative in an envelope with a black lining and addressed it to Munck in Stockholm. The negative would be ruined if it were taken out of the envelope by a German interceptor and exposed to normal light. That evening Duus Hansen sent a radio report to Stockholm about '213'—code-number for Niels Bohr—and Gyth drove to Elsinore to contact Benny West, the mate on the Halsingborg ferryboat. West agreed to drop the letter, franked with Swedish stamps, into a mailbox on the other side of the Øresund. It reached Munck in less than twenty-four hours and a few days later Gyth was able to tell Bohr that his letter had been read with great interest by Chadwick.

Towards the end of September 1943, Niels Bohr and his brother Harald were warned that they were to be arrested in the drive against the Danish Jews and it was decided that the whole family should try to escape to Sweden. With the aid of a Resistance group the professor and his wife were taken by fishing-boat to Limhamn on 30 September and their two sons followed next day.

Gyth was in Stockholm when Max Weiss, a Danish police sergeant working with the transport groups in Sweden, rang from Malmø to say that there was consternation and fury among the Germans over Bohr's flight. The Gestapo agents in Sweden had been ordered to prevent him at any cost from reaching Britain or America. Swedish intelligence officers arranged a meeting for Gyth with an inspector in the Swedish secret police, to whom he expressed his fear that the professor might be kidnapped or even murdered. The inspector said sceptically: 'My dear fellow, this is Stockholm, not Chicago.' Gyth retorted that Chicago at that moment was on the other side of the Øresund and that no American gangster could compare in cunning, ruthlessness, and brutality with the Gestapo. 'I have told you the unvarnished truth,' he warned. 'Now it is your responsibility. If anything happens to the professor it will be a disgrace to your country.'

From that time on Bohr was guarded ceaselessly by at least three armed men of the Swedish secret police. For safety's sake Gyth personally escorted him by train to Stockholm and at the station got him away from his old friend Professor Oskar Klein, who had come to meet him. The pair were too easily recognisable. Professor Klein put Mrs. Bohr and her sons into a taxi and Gyth gave them orders to change cabs at a point where they were unlikely to be recognised and pursued. Gyth took Bohr in another taxi to a house which was used by the Swedish intelligence service and hurried him through the attics to the further side of the building, where a third cab was waiting. Superfluous as they might seem in a neutral capital city, these cloak-and-dagger tactics were grimly necessary. Stockholm was swarming with German agents and an attempt on the professor's life could not be ruled out. For that reason very comprehensive security arrangements were imperative. Armed guards were always posted at the houses where he stayed, first with Professor Klein and later with Emil Torp-Pedersen, an official at the Danish legation, and he never went out unaccompanied. Unfortunately, Bohr was not security-minded. Though Gyth had warned him repeatedly to be careful about what he said on the telephone, whenever anyone rang and asked for him by his cover-name he would reply amiably: 'This is Bohr.'

Throughout his brief stay in Stockholm he exerted all his personal influence to get the Swedish government to intercede with Germany for the good of the Danish and Norwegian Jews. He had talks with Crown Prince Gustav Adolf and the Swedish foreign minister and, through the good offices of Princess Ingeborg, King Christian's sister, he even obtained an audience with King Gustav. Always accompanied by Gyth, he tirelessly visited the offices of the Swedish ministries but his efforts met with only limited success. When he saw that he could do no more he agreed to accept the British invitation, which had been reinforced by a telegram from Lord Cherwell, Churchill's personal adviser on scientific matters. His departure by air was arranged for 10 p.m. on 11 October.

The professor was then living in the home of Torp-Pedersen, who drove him to Bromma airport in his own car, followed by a Swedish police car. Half an hour after Torp-Pedersen and Gyth had returned home, congratulating themselves on the completion of a difficult assignment, the front door bell rang. Torp-Pedersen opened the door, and there stood Bohr. The aircraft had taken off on time but had been forced to turn back because of a leak in the oil system, so the professor had taken a taxi back to Stockholm. He seemed quite unaware of the danger this had involved. Since the Swedish police guard had been withdrawn, Gyth had to spend the rest of the night on watch before the professor's bedroom door.

On the following evening Bohr was driven to the airport and put aboard the Mosquito which was to take him to Britain. According to Torp-Pedersen, he was too busy talking to listen to the instructions of the pilot while he was being fitted with flying suit, oxygen mask, and Mae West. He certainly does not seem to have appreciated that as he was to travel in the bomb bay of the aircraft, he would be able to communicate with the pilot only through headphones.

The Mosquito took off and headed for Scotland. When it neared the Kattegat, where there was a considerable risk of attack by German night fighters, it rose to an altitude of ten thousand metres and the pilot warned Bohr to put on his oxygen mask. There was no reply. The professor had forgotten to plug in his earphones. The pilot was more than a little worried. Without oxygen his passenger, an elderly man, would certainly pass out and might even die. He put the aircraft into a dive and flew over the North Sea at low level. When the plane landed in Scotland he hurried to the bomb bay to let Bohr out.

'How did things go, Herr Professor?' he asked nervously.

'Excellently,' said Bohr. 'I slept beautifully most of the way.'

A full month before the Bohr affair Mørch and Gyth had begun to investigate the possibility of organising a Danish free corps in Sweden on the lines of the police force which had already been established by the Norwegians. Through one of their Swedish intelligence contacts, Major C. af Petersén, they were put in touch with Inspector Harry Soedermann, a specialist in scientific crime-fighting techniques, who had been chosen by the Swedish government as their main liaison with the Norwegians. Soedermann invited Mørch and Gyth to spend a few days at a Norwegian camp outside Stockholm. As a result of their visit they decided to organise a force of armed police capable of being developed into a fighting brigade who could take over in Denmark if a state of chaos arose following liberation. Initial recruitment was to be from the twelve hundred Danish male refugees already in Sweden. An interview was arranged with the Swedish minister for foreign affairs and, through Soedermann, Mørch and Gyth put forward their requests. The minister was extremely kind and helpful. He promised that the Danes should be allowed similar facilities to those accorded to the Norwegians, with camps each to house about five hundred men, equipped with Swedish weapons and with trained instructors. He said there need be no problem about money to buy arms; that could be settled between the Swedish and Danish governments after the war. But he insisted that before any action could be taken King Christian must give his official sanction to the formation of a police corps. Mørch and Gyth asked Swedish friends to go to Denmark with a letter for the king, who at that time was ill following a riding accident. If he could not be seen, Crown Prince Frederik's agreement was to be obtained. The letter was handed to Prince Axel, who took it to the king, and the royal assent went back through the same channels.

Recruitment for the police force began but so many refugees were arriving in Sweden that the plans had to be modified. Before long the refugees included about five thousand fit and strong young people, students and the like, many of whom were wanted by the Gestapo for their exploits as saboteurs or as members of the illegal Press and transport groups. They were now chafing in enforced idleness and it was plainly advisable to register them and get them under discipline, so that their needs could be attended to without risk of trouble. It was arranged, therefore, that senior officers should be brought from Denmark to Sweden to take control of the new force, for example, to take over administration of the arms (a point on which the Swedes were worried) and also to get more weapons of all kinds. On 10 November 1943, Major-General Kristian Knudtzon arrived in Stockholm, accompanied by Lieutenant-Colonel F. L. Hvalkof and other officers. Later they were joined by Captain F. Kjølsen, of the Royal Danish Navy, and Lieutenant S. Thostrup (now Admiral Thostrup, commander-in-chief of the Danish armed forces). A general staff was formed, comprising General Knudtzon, a chief of army staff, a chief of naval staff, aides-de-camp and various specialists, and work began immediately. A camp site was provided at Sofielund, Konga, deep in the forests of Småland, and the initial force, mainly officers, began building barracks for some five hundred men. As soon as the buildings were habitable the call-up of the younger volunteers commenced.

As the Swedish minister had promised, there was never any serious problem in financing the Danish Brigade. The Danish minister could draw from the Swedish National Bank almost any amount he wanted. That was agreed behind the scenes between the Danish and Swedish governments. The biggest difficulty was to find money for the purchase of weapons from the private munitions firms, who insisted on payment in hard cash. (Later all the money for the Danish intelligence services in Sweden went through General Knudtzon and not through the Danish minister, who was always sceptical about their usefulness.)

Eventually three more camps were established, at Sätrabrunn, Sala, north-west of Stockholm; at Håtunaholm, Sigtuna; and at Ronneby, in Blekinge. By the spring of 1945 the brigade, under the command of General Knudtzon, with Hvalkof as chief of staff, had grown to five fully-equipped battalions with an estimated strength of three thousand, five hundred officers and men, together with various auxiliary corps. There were four light battalions and a heavy battalion with machine-guns, mortars, and 20mm and 37mm guns; a pioneer commando, trained in the use of explosives, in the laying and clearing of minefields and in the use of flame-throwers; a motor service company staffed by expert drivers and mechanics; a field ambulance company, with doctors, surgeons, nurses, and stretcher-bearers; and a women's corps trained in every job from first-aid to field cookery. In addition there was a fire-fighting company, a military police company specially trained to deal with traitors and informers, and a company of ordinary camp constabulary. At the command of the brigade there was a naval flotilla of one patrol vessel, three minesweepers and eleven smaller craft, manned by a hundred and fifty officers, petty officers, and ratings. The Swedish air force also arranged that a few fighter planes should be at the disposal of Danish crews in the event of open warfare in Denmark.

The question arose how this force was to be used. Originally, in 1943, Mørch and Gyth had discussed with the Swedish authorities a police force to be used in a chaos situation in Denmark. Now it was evident that this larger, highly trained and well-equipped Danish Brigade could be a useful adjunct to SHAEF's strength and could be used to advantage in any Allied operations in Denmark. There were also internal disciplinary problems. Most of the volunteers had a good education—they were probably the best-educated Danish force in modern times; they were well-fed and well-clothed; but they were getting a little bored with the constant parading and drilling to no apparent purpose. Were they to be in at a fighting finish, they wanted to know, or would they be sent home tamely after all the shooting was over? The suggestion was made that the name of the brigade should be changed to Danforce and that its members should be assured that they would be front-line fighters when the day of liberation came. The change of name proved of great psychological importance and did much to boost morale, but would the Swedes give free rein to a military force in their country, and if so, when? Those were questions discussed during many months between the Danish intelligence chiefs and the Swedish authorities. It was certain that no matter what their true inclination, the Swedish government would not prejudice their neutral position by permitting any of their own troops at any time to go to Denmark. It proved equally certain that they would not allow Danforce to move until official permission had been received from Denmark.

The dilemma was resolved by Ebbe Munck. He went to London in August 1944, and insisted that the British high command should acknowledge Danforce as a fighting force to be incorporated in their over-all plans for the liberation of Denmark. He urged them to put pressure on the Swedish government to release Danforce if and when fighting seemed imminent. His mission succeeded. General Dewing, who was to command operations in Denmark, went to Stockholm in December 1944, inspected Danforce, and decided that the brigade would be strong enough to play a major role. Consequently, Danforce were incorporated into the Danish-British strategy and the Swedish government agreed to a swift release of the brigade when the need arose. Formally, Danforce were still under the command of the Freedom Council, but since the general agreement between the council and the British authorities was that the British should take over all Danish units in the case of actual fighting in Denmark, Danforce in fact were due to come under Dewing's command.

By the beginning of May 1945, Danforce were trained, in high fettle, and eager to go into action. Headquarters were established at Häckeberg, in southern Sweden, and there five thousand men and women waited for the order to embark. In Stockholm Mørch waited impatiently by his telephone. Shortly after nine o'clock on the evening of 4 May Nordentoft called with the message which had been sent across the Øresund and relayed to him from Danforce headquarters: 'Hans er rask' ('Hans is all right'). Those were the prearranged code-words which meant that the Danish 'shadow' government now wished Danforce to be sent to Denmark. 'Hans' was, in fact, Hans Hedtoft, a leading social democrat who had been active in Danish-Swedish relations. Mørch immediately rang the Swedish prime minister, Per Albin Hausson. 'Good evening, sir,' he said. 'Hans er rask.' The prime minister replied: 'Good, my boy. I will take the necessary steps. Good luck to you all.' He telephoned General Ehrenswärd, of the Swedish defence staff, who made the necessary arrangements. Five minutes after the word reached Häckeberg Danforce were on their way to Halsingborg. The transports were ready. In the early hours of 5 May the

brigade reached Elsinore and thence proceeded to Copenhagen.
Except for a few clashes with street snipers, the men were not
to get the fighting they had hoped for, but they did an honour-
able job as military controls in the towns and on the Jutland
border as the dispirited *Wehrmacht* took the long road home.

2: THE MOONSHINERS

After General Knudtzon had taken command of the Danish Brigade in November 1943, Mørch and Gyth withdrew to concentrate on their real work with the intelligence services. Gyth insisted on going to England, where he hoped to talk with General Alan Brooke. He wanted to work with the Secret Intelligence Service in London. Nordentoft, Winkel, Mørch and Jutta Graae decided to remain in Sweden. They knew that SIS were interested in Denmark only as an intermediate station for agents working in Germany and preferred to continue their association with SOE, with whom they had cooperated well for two years. A group was formed comprising Ebbe Munck as 'first among equals', Erling Foss on the civil side as representative of the Freedom Council, Nordentoft and Mørch on the military and naval side, Turnbull as SOE representative, and an American, Viggo Albertsen, for the U.S. Office of Strategic Services (OSS). These six men became co-opted supreme controllers of all Danish resistance activities in Sweden. They were responsible for the intelligence services, for the Danish Brigade, for the communication lines (*Ruterne*), for the provision of weapons, and for maintaining communication with the Swedish government and the Swedish armed forces. Their relationship with the government was, to say the least, remarkable. They were on the friendliest terms with the Swedish prime minister, the minister of the interior, the minister of justice, the foreign minster, and the minister of defence, with all of whom they could meet secretly in their offices or even in their homes if circumstances made it necessary.

An extraordinary example of their relationship with the Swedish authorities was given to me by Commander (now Commodore) Mørch.

'Some time after I had gone over to Sweden,' he said, 'the British naval attaché, Captain Denham, asked me: "What about the German minefields at the southern end of *Store-Bælt*?"

'I said: "You have had many messages and maps from us. We have been following the mine-laying very closely."

' "Yes," he said, "but those papers are now lying in the Admiralty. I can never get them out. Tell me the position."

'I said: "Wait until tomorrow."

'I went to our contact on the Swedish general staff and told him: "The English naval attaché wants some information about the German mine-laying. Can you find our latest report to you on the subject? You'll have to go to the defence staff and tell them that I want to see my own report."

'Next day I went to his office and he had the report ready for me. It showed the location of the German minefields, the number of mines laid, and so on. I went back to Denham and told him: "You can have this for twenty-four hours. You must guarantee that I shall get it back then."

'On the following day I returned, picked up the report and gave it back to the Swedes. I think this is the finest example I know of cooperation between three countries—one in a full state of war, one neutral and one in a state of semi-war with Germany.'

The group had an excellent system of communication with Denmark and Britain. Apart from the radio facilities provided so brilliantly by Duus Hansen, whose work is dealt with in another chapter, they had a beautiful link with Denmark in the form of an officially dead line in one of the telephone cables between Malmø and Copenhagen. This was reactivated by co-ordinated work by friends in the two cities. Then, with the connivance of Swedish officials in *Telegrafverket* and the navy, members of the group could sit at the top of a tall tower in Malmø and talk with intelligence people in Copenhagen every week-end for long periods, exchanging news from the free world to Denmark and from Denmark to the free world. The Germans never discovered this use of the cable, which continued un-interrupted until the end of the occupation.

After 29 August 1943, the intelligence service formerly con-trolled in Denmark by the Princes was taken over by Svend Truelsen, a reserve lieutenant in the Royal Life Guard who in civil life had been secretary to the Agricultural Council. He had been designated by Nordentoft to take on the job if the Princes were arrested or had to leave the country. With outstanding energy and ability he swiftly reorganised and extended the network with headquarters in Copenhagen, Aarhus, Aalborg, and Kolding and with hundreds of agents spread throughout Denmark and down into northern Germany. Information flowed in concerning the location and numbers of German troops, the movements of warships and road, rail and sea transports and work on fortifications, airfields, and harbours. The appearance of any new German aircraft or weapons was noted and the technical details sent to regional headquarters and thence to Copenhagen. To deal with the ever-swelling flood of reports the radio service was expanded and improved. High-speed transmissions were introduced to handle urgent messages to and from London, while less urgent or lengthier messages continued to go out through Stockholm in processed form. In June 1944, Truelsen was called to London to head the intelligence division of SOE's Danish section, where he did equally brilliant work. He was succeeded in Copenhagen first by F. Busenius Larsen and, after the latter's arrest in September the same year, by O. Blixen-krone-Møller and P. V. Hammershøy, with F. Tillisch, I. Bruhn Petersen, and others as local sub-leaders, all working on the army and on the naval side with naval contacts like H. Bundesen, H. Nyholm, P. Prom, and K. Lundsteen. Under the leadership of these officers the hazardous work performed by hundreds of anonymous men and women throughout the country, together with their comrades in Sweden, was so efficient that at the time of liberation Field-Marshal Montgomery was to declare the Danish intelligence service second to none.

One of the most important and successful tasks of the service was to organise and maintain, with the cooperation of friends in the Swedish government, a constant supply of weapons to Denmark from Swedish and Allied sources. The practical operation was directed by Commander F. C. S. Bangsbøll from headquarters in Malmø and sub-offices at Torekov and Klakshamn. Arms and ammunition were smuggled from Malmø, Halsingborg, and other convenient places along the Swedish south and west coasts under the deck cargoes of sailing boats hired at great expense. Unloading and distribution in

Copenhagen were the business of a group led by Captain H.
Bundesen, of the navy, and Lieutenant Jørgensen, of the army.
Almost incredibly, not a single round of ammunition was ever
found in transit by the Germans. Thousands of guns of different
types and calibres, including bozookas furnished by the British
and Americans, were landed safely.

The operation code-named 'Moonshine' had its origin in the
first dark days of 1941, when Britain stood alone. There was an
urgent need for fighter planes to replace the losses sustained in
the battle against the *Luftwaffe* but a bottleneck in the supply
of ball bearings to the aircraft factories was holding up production. Sir George Binney, then on the staff of the British
legation in Stockholm, went to London to suggest a potential
solution. There were, he pointed out, large British merchant
ships lying at Gothenborg with full cargoes of ball bearings. If
the Germans marched into Sweden as they had invaded Denmark and Norway (a distinct possibility), both ships and
cargoes would be lost. If the ships made a run for England and
were sunk on the way, the ball bearings would be lost to the
Germans while Britain would be no worse off. But if the
ships got through, their cargoes would ensure an appreciable
increase in aircraft production. The logic of this proposition
was accepted and in March 1941, Binney organised the first run
across the Skagerrak. All five ships reached port safely. A second
attempt with a larger number of ships in March 1942, was
moderately successful. The third attempt was a costly failure.
Undeterred, Binney put forward another proposal. The operation, he said, called for light, fast craft of shallow draught and
with a reasonable cargo capacity, which would stand a sporting
chance of outrunning or evading patrols from the German fleet
based at Kristianssand and which, in emergency, might even
take refuge by heading for the middle of a minefield, where
heavier ships could not follow.

By great good luck suitable vessels were available. Delivery
of five motor gunboats built for a foreign navy had been prevented by the outbreak of war and they were now lying idle in
a British shipyard. The ships were taken over by the ministry of
war transport, converted to accommodate a cargo of fifty tons

each, and given an impressive armament of twin Oerlikon guns fore and aft, twin Vickers machine-guns on the bridge wings, and a quadruple Vickers on the chart-house. The flotilla was to sail under the red ensign of the merchant service and Immingham, near Hull, was chosen as its home base. The commodore was Sir George Binney, later succeeded by Brian Bingham (Brian Russell); the masters and other officers were Ellerman's Wilson men; and the crews were Hull and Grimsby trawlermen and merchant seamen. All of them were volunteers. By the winter of 1943 Operation Moonshine was ready to be put into effect.

In August 1944, Ebbe Munck went to London to discuss with the British authorities a number of matters including the future of the Danish Brigade. While he was in the city he happened by chance to hear that his old friend Binney was running a service to Gothenborg to collect ball bearings. He got in touch with Binney through Kaj Winkelhorn, of OSS, and proposed that since the Moonshine ships were running empty to the Swedish coast they should fill their holds with weapons for Denmark. Binney liked the idea but Munck could not get the British authorities to agree. He spoke to Winkelhorn, who said: 'If the British won't do it, we will.' Binney was told about this and exerted his own pressures to get the deal through. It was now a matter of national pride and Moonshine was not prepared to take second place to any American operation.

In Stockholm Mørch was told by Turnbull to arrange with the Swedish authorities a suitable landing point on the western coast. After some difficulty he found that the Swedish social minister, Gustav Möller (the man who had to be approached before any major enterprise was started) was at a small town called Tidaholm, where he was to make an election speech. Mørch went there, met the minister at breakfast in his hotel, and told him frankly that a place was needed on the west coast where Moonshine could land arms strictly for the use of Danish forces. Möller said he needed time to think about it. 'Meet me at the railway station at 4.15 this afternoon,' he said. 'We can go together to Gothenborg and talk things over on the train. Meanwhile I will arrange what can be done.' They met as agreed and the minister said: 'I have arranged that some high Swedish officials will be at Gothenborg station when our train arrives. There I shall present you and your wishes to the *landshövding*, Professor Malte Jakobson, to the police chief, and to another top official.' When the train reached Gothenborg the three men were waiting. Möller made the introductions and said: 'Commander Mørch will be sending a representative here to make preparations. You must ensure that complete security is maintained.'

Some days later Mørch was called to the minister's office in Stockholm and told that everything had been arranged. Preparations were being made to discharge and load the Moonshine ships at Lysekil, a small port a few miles north of Gothenborg. But at the last minute a snag arose. It was discovered that among the customs staff at Lysekil there was a Nazi sympathiser. An effort was made to have him transferred to another port but the chief customs officer would not agree. Möller applied pressure and, much against his will, the man was removed. With this threat lifted, the operation could proceed. The first delivery of fifty tons of weapons was made in January 1945, and another consignment followed. The arms were loaded on to a train on a special track and taken to Gothenborg. There a party from the Swedish army boarded the railway trucks and rode with the crew down to the south coast. At that point Swedish police took over and saw the consignments through to Malmø, Halsingborg, Landskrone, and other ports, where they were loaded into Danish ships for transport to secret depots in Denmark.

For two bitter winters the Moonshiners ran the close blockade of the Skagerrak and Kattegat to fetch essential supplies for the British war factories and on later trips to take arms to the Danish Resistance. The North Sea crossing in winter is seldom a pleasure cruise but in those tiny ships—not much bigger than river launches—it was often an ordeal demanding from all on board almost superhuman physical and mental endurance. Even in moderate weather the motion of the ships was violent beyond the ken of the most seasoned fishermen; in a prolonged spell of bad weather it was not unusual for half the ship's company to be completely 'flaked out' with seasickness and fatigue. Able

Above: Ebbe Munck and L. A. Duus
Hansen.

Edith Bonnesen (Lotte)

Operation Moonshine: John Oram Thomas (centre) with some of the *Nonsuch* crew. Stanley Close, the irrepressible steward, is at extreme right

Commodore Brian Bingham (nearest camera) on bridge of *Nonsuch* with Captain 'Ginger' Stokes. *Hopewell* overtaking in the background

Community singing in Frederiksberg Gardens, September 1940

Greetings from his people as King Christian X takes his morning ride
on his 72nd birthday in 1942

Sandbags and 'Spanish rider' barricades near Larsens Plads at the corner of Toldbodgate and Amalienborg Castle

Barricade built across Nørrebrogade in Copenhagen during the Folk Strike

seaman Charlie Walmsley, a Hull trawlerman sailing in *Nonsuch*, once said: 'When I first joined, they asked me if I was ever seasick. "Me?" I says. "I've been thirty-odd years in trawlers up around Bear Island. Never was sick in my life." But half the first trip I spent laid out on the deck. I never knew nothing like it.'

Racing through the blackness of the storm-swept Skagerrak, hunted by enemy surface craft and reconnaissance planes, the crews were subjected to long-drawn hours of almost unbearable strain. Sometimes the weather beat them and with as much as half the voyage accomplished they had to turn and run for home. Once they battled for more than sixty hours before admitting defeat. More often, in the teeth of wind and seas in which it seemed incredible that a little ship could live, they made port. Each trip called for a combination of careful planning, courage, bluff, and magnificent seamanship, together with more than average luck. Sometimes bluff succeeded when disaster seemed inevitable. There was the time, for instance, when the 'Met' men boobed. They had forecast the kind of foul weather which the Moonshiners liked best; instead, as the little ships neared Sweden they found themselves on a millpond-like sea under a cloudless sky lit by a brilliant full moon. Then, following the sighting of suspiciously innocent fishing vessels, enemy planes were seen heading for the commodore ship, *Gay Viking*. Desperate measures were called for if capture or sinking were to be evaded. The skipper ran up the German ensign; the planes dipped in salute and flew off, and again the ships made port successfully.

Since, characteristically, the Moonshiners discharged their cargoes under the windows of the German consulate, many ruses were employed to mislead the consul and Gestapo agents. Occasionally, in spite of all precautions, information filtered through to the enemy and a race developed between the blockade-runners and the forces sent to intercept them. Sometimes the luck failed. It failed the *Master Standfast*. She was captured by German patrol boats after a grim struggle and her master, Captain C. R. W. Holdsworth, was killed. On another run *Gay Viking* went down in the Skagerrak. Fortunately all hands were saved.

The Moonshiners had unusual ideas about what constituted fair weather. In the later stages of the war I found myself briefly in *Nonsuch*, which had taken over as commodore ship from the ill-fated *Gay Viking*. Johnny Marrow, the mate, greeted me with the comforting information: 'We *live* in these ships. Six meals a day, three down, three up!' Some hours out of Hull we ran into a belt of fog. Visibility was reduced to a cable-length. *Hopewell*, astern, became merely a voice on the radio-telephone. On the open box-bridge Captain David 'Ginger' Stokes, inevitable cigarette-holder clenched between his teeth, peered ahead into the clammy white blanket. Beside him Brian Bingham huddled in his padded jacket. Behind them stood the signals officer, Dick Wray. The mate was busy with his instruments in the hutch-like chart-room. On deck the lookouts were motionless, dimly visible figures. I had an eerie, helpless feeling that we were cut off from the world.

Suddenly Bingham spoke. 'Lovely weather, Ginger.'

'Grand,' the skipper replied.

'This is the kind of weather we like to get in the Skagerrak,' Bingham told me. 'We can go full out without bothering about Jerry's patrols. We're hard enough to spot in ordinary darkness. This makes it a piece of cake.'

Stanley Close, the steward, appeared with mugs of scalding tea and Bingham asked: 'What will we do for rations if we have to stay out in this fog for a week?'

'Well, sir,' said the imperturbable Stanley, 'there's an old sea-gull following us. He'd go down well with some sage and onions.'

The steward was the recognised humorist of the *Nonsuch* and he took his role seriously. His round, cheerful face was crowned by an ancient beret obviously designed to attract ribald comment. 'Lucky Skag' gumboots were another essential of his wardrobe and a murderous butchery knife was his badge of office. Unlike most of the crew, he had come to blockade-running from the deep seas and his stories of the China coast rivalled the best efforts of Baron Munchausen. A superb cook, he had a particular liking for the fish he called Jumbo haddock, which he caught on a line baited with the foil top of a tobacco tin. Pointing to cloudy marks on the flesh he would observe: 'Those smudges are the thumb-prints of our Lord. He made 'em when he broke the fishes to feed the Multitude. Or so,' he would add thoughtfully, 'the lee-gend says....'

His mild demeanour was deceptive and when action was called for he became a very efficient Oerlikon or Vickers gunner. It was he who once asked 'Ginger' Stokes cheerfully, as an enemy fighter roared in to attack: 'Shall I shoot him down, sir, or shall I just cripple him?'

Another licensed character was 'Cream Cake' Charlie Walmsley. His nickname was given to him by his crew-mates. 'They reckon,' he said, 'that I only go to Sweden to get at them cream cakes. Eh! but they're grand stuff.'

After one trip ashore in Sweden with Dick Dibnah, the *Nonsuch* motorman, he met an Estonian captain who insisted on taking them to dine at Gothenborg's most swagger restaurant. 'It was a lovely place,' Charlie said, 'but we felt a bit awkward-like. We were just as we had come off the ship—jerseys, seaboots and all—and all these chaps were in swallowtail coats and the women in long dresses, and a string band going. Eh! but it were a "do". Anyway, this captain made us go in, and the waiter chap took our duffel coats most politely, and the band played English tunes as we walked to our table. You'd have thought we were dukes or summat. But,' he shook his head, 'we didn't have any cream cakes that time. It were all fish.'

Sleeping and feeding in cramped quarters, often soaked to the skin and half-frozen, but always light of heart, the Moonshiners carried on their dangerous work until the German capitulation. Their spirit was reflected in the christening of their ships: *Gay Viking, Gay Corsair, Nonsuch, Hopewell*, and *Master Standfast* are names which will be golden forever in the annals of the port of Hull.

It says much for the security-consciousness of trawlermen that few if any of the Moonshiners ever knew that another arms delivery service to the Resistance was proceeding simultaneously with their own. 'Operation Hiccup' began in the summer of 1944. Weapons were loaded into Danish and British trawlers at

St. Andrew's Dock, Hull, and transferred to Danish vessels fishing on the Dogger Bank, which took them to Esbjerg and other harbours on the west coast of Jutland. From there they were distributed throughout Jutland by Anton Toldstrup's organisation. Since most of the air droppings were in northern Jutland, weapons delivered through Esbjerg went to the southern part of the peninsula, where they were most needed. From the summer of 1944 until January 1945, Hiccup delivered 224 containers of arms, a number of packages, two thousand Danish kroner and, as thanks to the skippers and crews, many 'comfort' parcels of whisky and cigarettes. In April 1945, there was a further delivery of four tons of material. A later consignment of ten tons never reached Denmark because capitulation came before it could be delivered.

All told, the weapons deliveries to the Resistance from Britain amounted to one thousand tons—seven hundred tons from the air, two hundred tons by Hiccup, and one hundred tons by Moonshine.

3: 'DENMARK CALLING...'

From the Resistance point of view, engineer Lorens Arne Duus Hansen was a classic example of the right man in the right place at the right time. As a youth he had trained as a radio-telegraphist at the Navigation School in Svendborg, on the island of Funen, and later he had gained five years' practical experience at sea. After graduating as an engineer he had joined the Danish radio firm of Bang and Olufsen, rising to become chief engineer. In that position he had access to all the technical advances in radio throughout the world and he had many friends in the major electrical firms of Europe. He had, additionally, an uncompromising hatred of Hitler and his Nazi regime in Germany.

One day in 1939 a man claiming to be a radio 'ham' called at his office in Copenhagen and asked whether he could supply a hundred-watt modulator for use with a radio transmitter. The man gave such a detailed technical description of the instrument that it was clear he could build one himself. Duus Hansen's suspicions were aroused. Modulators were used in radio-telephony, not radio-telegraphy, and the authorities certainly would not permit the use of such high-powered equipment by an amateur. The modulator must be required for some illicit purpose. Duus Hansen reported the interview to the police. They investigated and discovered that the transmitter was being used illegally by a gang of Danish Nazis. That and a similar incident later in the year turned Duus Hansen's thoughts seriously to the role which radio could play in the event of an invasion of Denmark.

Almost immediately after the German occupation began, he was approached by some people (he does not know, even today, who they were) who asked him to build a small set and make some transmissions for them. 'Just send the messages and they will be received in Sweden,' they said. No return messages were ever received and soon the transmissions ended.

Nearly a year was to pass before Duus Hansen again became involved in illegal radio work. In June 1941, Lieutenant Thomas Sneum, who had already done useful intelligence work on the island of Fanø, 'borrowed' a privately-owned aeroplane and with a brother-officer, Lieutenant Kjeld Petersen, flew across the North Sea from Denmark to Britain, taking with him invaluable films of the German radar installation on Fanø. Sneum's aim was to join the British army but SIS sent him home to continue his intelligence activities. In September 1941, he was parachuted into Denmark with a telegraphist, Sigfred Christoffersen. They landed safely near Holbæk but their mission was doomed from the start. They were an ill-assorted pair and neither man had been adequately trained. Their transmitter had been damaged on landing and Christoffersen failed to make contact with England. Sneum's efforts to operate the set were equally inept. Between them they succeeded only in making the apparatus unusable. After some time, when it was clear that they could not get along together, they parted in Copenhagen and tried to establish their own contacts. Eventually Sneum got in touch with Duus Hansen and asked for help.

Duus Hansen was not impressed by the transmitter with which the men had been provided by SIS. It was bulky, heavy (about twenty kilogrammes), not easy to operate, and it could be used only with alternating current. The power was weak (7.5 watts) and a good aerial was essential for effective transmission and reception. Duus Hansen built a new transmitter of greater power, using the SIS crystals which were essential for the determined frequency for connection with London. As Sneum had not sufficient Morse training, Duus Hansen repeatedly operated the set for him.

Through the Princes, with whom by this time he had established contact, Duus Hansen sent a report via Stockholm to London, in which he expressed his opinion of the transmitter and suggested technical improvements. He urged the conversion of the apparatus to all-mains (AC and DC) working, since more than half of Copenhagen was served with direct current. He also stressed the desirability of greater power, to obviate the need for special aerials and special locations to obtain reasonably sure communication.

Meanwhile the difficulties of Sneum and Christoffersen continued. The Princes, who were cooperating with SOE and who (with the exception of Gyth) had no confidence in SIS, considered the pair a danger and refused to work with them. The Germans knew of their presence in Copenhagen and were hunting them relentlessly. Finally, in March 1942, they escaped to Sweden across the icebound Øresund. Sneum returned to London, where he received a cold welcome. Indeed, Commander F. N. Stagg, of the Danish section, SOE, has put on record: 'The treatment of Siem (Sneum) on his return to England in May 1942, is a disgraceful chapter in the English handling of one who had given us what radar specialists then called "the most valuable piece of intelligence yet received".' During the remainder of the war Sneum served with the Norwegian air force in Britain.

The Princes, whose only radio link with Britain in the first years of the occupation was the BBC, wanted to establish their own transmitting and receiving station, with Duus Hansen as telegraphist, but London would not agree. SOE had an inflexible rule that nobody could be given their secret codes and act as a telegraphist unless he had been trained in England. The problem was solved when Duus Hansen procured a German travel visa for Sweden and went to Stockholm. There he met Turnbull and Munck and his credentials were accepted. He was given a transmitter of the standard British type, but because he was a highly-skilled professional it produced much better results in his hands. However, he was not satisfied. He built himself an AC–DC transmitter and receiver which, though smaller and lighter than the British equipment, were more powerful and had a much greater range.

On the night of 27 December 1941, Dr. Carl Johan Bruhn was sent by SOE in a Wellington bomber to contact the Resistance forces in Denmark. With him went Mogens Hammer, a mechanical engineer, as his telegraphist. They were dropped near Haslev, a small town in southern Zealand. Dr. Bruhn's parachute failed to open and he was killed. Hammer landed safely but his transmitter was lost. He went on alone to Copenhagen and succeeded

in making contact with a Resistance group. Eventually, with
the help of a director of Bang and Olufsen and Stig Jensen,
a newspaper editor working with the illegal *De Frie Danske*, he
was put in touch with Duus Hansen, who built him a new
transmitter. Unfortunately, he was not allowed to use it. Orders
came from SOE in Stockholm that he was to lie low and refrain
from any action until further notice. The transmitter he had
brought from England was found by the Haslev police and sent
to police headquarters in Copenhagen. There, thanks to his
friendship with police officers sympathetic to the Resistance,
Duus Hansen was allowed to inspect it and abstract the invaluable crystals before it was handed over to the Germans.

In 1942 SOE sent more parachutists to Denmark. The first to
arrive were Captain C. M. Rottbøll, who was to replace Bruhn,
with two telegraphists, Max Mikkelsen and Johannes Poul
Johannesen. On the night of 16 April the three landed in the
woods outside Jyderup, west of Copenhagen, and made their
way to the capital. From the moment of touching Danish soil
they were constantly in peril. The discovery of Bruhn's body
had alerted the Germans to the fact that a British-directed
resistance movement was being organised in Denmark. Their
counter-measures included the building of a highly efficient
direction-finding service to pinpoint illegal transmitting stations.
That increased the risk for the telegraphists. Only a few
messages could be sent and the senders were always in danger.
Their apparatus was low-powered and, since they had been
insufficiently trained before being sent into the field, their Morse
was weak. Consequently there were frequent requests to and
from London for repetition of words, and transmissions were
correspondingly slow. Duus Hansen gave the men technical
assistance and supplied them with information about the German and police methods, including the German direction-
finding methods on which his friends at police headquarters kept
him well posted. He repeatedly cautioned the telegraphists about
the risks implicit in protracted transmissions, particularly when
the operator worked continuously in one house and without
guards. He was deeply worried by the rashness of Poul Johannesen, about whose transmissions he had received alarming

reports from his police contacts. They had shown him reports from the DF cars indicating that the Germans knew the address (an apartment on Vinkelager in the district of Vanløse) which Johannesen was using, and were waiting only for another transmission to begin before raiding the place. On 4 September 1942, a party of Gestapomen and more than 150 Danish police surrounded the apartment block. In the shooting that followed a policeman was killed. Johannesen took a cyanide pill before he could be arrested and died on the way to police headquarters.

Disaster also awaited Johannesen's fellow-parachutists Rottbøll and Hammer. Both had been warned by Stockholm to take things easy and do nothing but plan future work. SOE were under great pressure from the Princes at that time to abstain from encouraging sabotage and similar activities. Hence, for the parachutists, the summer of 1942 was both dangerous and depressing. After Johannesen's death the Resistance men and the police came to a gentlemen's agreement through Duus Hansen that both sides should exercise caution and avoid shooting, since it would benefit only the Germans if a war broke out between them. This at least relieved the tension slightly. Then the Germans discovered Rottbøll's hideout and ordered the Danish police to raid the building. Unluckily, the squad who carried out the assignment on the night of 26 September had not been told about the no-shooting agreement with the Resistance. Two policemen went up to Rottbøll's apartment and hammered on the door. Rottbøll had been asleep and was in his pyjamas. He opened the door and one of the policemen grabbed his arm. As he did so, Rottbøll's pistol went off and the bullet hit the policeman's belt buckle. The two policemen immediately opened fire at point-blank range and Rottbøll fell, riddled with twelve bullets.

After this incident a message was sent to police headquarters, saying that the Resistance considered the agreement to have been broken by the other side. In future firearms would be used without hesitation in all cases where police tried to interfere in matters of importance.

Hammer had been so closely hunted by the Gestapo and police that he had to leave the country. On 20 September with

E. Borch Johansen, he crossed by kayak from Gilleleje to Sweden and went immediately to London. There he heard that Rottbøll was dead and that SOE were without a leader in Denmark. He had to go back. On 19 October he was dropped, in a specially-made rubber suit, in the sea off Tisvilde in northern Zealand. He landed safely and set out for Copenhagen to take command of SOE. His job was desperately difficult—to keep the organisation ticking over until the spring of 1943, when things could get going seriously with the arrival of new people and supplies of arms and equipment. Meanwhile he was ordered to remain passive, to avoid direct contact with SOE comrades, and only through intermediaries to maintain contact with a few Resistance men like Professor Mogens Fog. He was to be, in fact, a kind of faceless caretaker-manager with direct access neither to his employers nor his staff. It was an almost impossible task but somehow he kept going throughout the winter, and in March 1943, handed over the organisation intact to his successor, Flemming B. Muus. Hammer left Denmark in April 1943, and for the rest of the war served as an officer in the British army.

Following the raid at Vinkelager, Duus Hansen in his reports to London stressed again and again the need for revision of the radio operation. The work, he said, could be done properly only by professionals who could send fast Morse and who would be able to listen through disturbances during reception and thereby shorten the time of transmissions. He pointed out that the German DF service was developing so efficiently that the cars could fix a sender's location and be on the spot within minutes of picking up the signal. He urged London to stop sending parachutists with clumsy British equipment and allow him to organise his own service with properly-trained Danish operators and home-built transmitters which would work on AC and DC. By the spring of 1943 he had a third edition of his all-mains combined transmitter-receiver ready. He had succeeded in reducing the size of the set to the dimensions of a Copenhagen telephone directory, so that it could be fitted into an ordinary briefcase like that carried by almost every Danish office worker and student. (The cumbersome British suitcase was well-known to the Germans from its use in other occupied countries.) The weight was reduced to one and a half kilos and the power increased to twenty watts, compared with the British set's twenty kilos and seven and a half watts. Further, the 'telephone book' was made from components and valves used in every domestic radio, which therefore could be used to provide spare parts.

On 29 August 1943, the Princes had to leave for Sweden. They asked Duus Hansen to go with them but he refused. He sent a message to London, saying that he proposed to remain in Copenhagen and keep the radio communications open. At that time only he and a well-trained parachutist, Gunnar Christiansen, were still working as telegraphists. Poul Johannesen and Gøtrick Andersen were dead and the others, for various reasons, had left the service.

SOE in London, who earlier had been hesitant, now accepted all Duus Hansen's proposals. Because of the greatly increasing activities of the Resistance Movement they badly needed a new radio organisation in which all regional groups and other important service branches, such as intelligence, sabotage, arms reception, and financial administration, would have their own individual codes and operators. They agreed to stop sending parachutists with suitcase transmitters; instead they would supply Duus Hansen with crystals, transmission schedules, and individual codes for the different groups. Recruitment and the manufacture of equipment would be the Danish responsibility.

It was not difficult for Duus Hansen to make contact with willing and qualified radio-telegraphists from the merchant service and navy. They were already skilled in Morse and it was necessary only to give them a short course in procedure, the use of codes and schedules and technical control of the 'telephone book' transmitter-receiver. To protect the operator against the ever more effective German direction-finders, every man was given a bodyguard of several helpers. It was the latter's job to take the set to the sending point and keep watch to warn the telegraphist if a DF car were seen in the neighbourhood. After the transmission the guards took the set to the next selected 'safe house'. In the case of perilously close German activity the group scattered, leaving the set behind to be picked up when the danger had passed. It was necessary, therefore, to put more sets at the groups' disposal, so that one was not dependent upon what might be disastrous recovery action. Danish engineers and technicians undertook to manufacture 'telephone books' in the required numbers. Up to the end of the occupation about sixty sets were made. Denmark was the only occupied country which provided its own equipment and trained its own operators independent of London. At its peak the radio service had about one hundred members— telegraphists, code handlers, and guards—covering the whole country.

The telegraphists were Duus Hansen (cover-name Napkin), Gunnar Christiansen (Mat), and Tage Fischer-Holst (Joseph) in Copenhagen and Zealand; Poul Jelgren (Sam) in Aarhus, P. Nielsen (Moses) (attached to Anton Toldstrup's headquarters), P. Rønnelin Møller (Saul), Willy Jepsen (Isak) and J. Bergh (Cain) in mid-Jutland; T. F. Stotz (Noah) in north Jutland; J. Albret (Matthew) in west Jutland; J. Holbach (Jonas) in south Jutland; J. Jacobsen (Bisquit) in Malmø, Sweden; and H. Kj. Duus Hansen (Robert) in Funen. Thanks to brilliant organisa- tion and first-class security, casualties were few. Christiansen was arrested in May 1944, but survived the horrors of a German concentration camp. Thomas Friederich Stotz was taken by the Germans on 16 November 1944. Next day he was forced to transmit to London but he slipped into his message a pre- arranged code-word which warned SOE that he had been arrested. He took his own life in his cell at Aarhus to avoid further interrogation.

Duus Hansen had early pointed out to London the danger that lay in keeping a telegraphist on the air to acknowledge messages which could have been sent 'blind' if transmitted at a fixed time by a powerful British station. The blind sending method was introduced towards the end of 1943 and came to be used in all occupied countries. The telegrams were numbered 1 to 100 and there was no need for repetition or acknowledg- ment. Every night, in the so-called 'night broadcast', an agreed number of telegrams was sent to each country. One or more of these was a dummy, indicated by a special introductory word or phrase, so that the Germans should not be able to judge from the number of telegrams the actual number of genuine messages. A similar arrangement governed 'cross-reports' from the BBC's Danish news broadcasts.

From the British side there was no limit to the number of telegrams which could be sent but in Denmark the telegraphists were continually hampered by security considerations and had to make the best possible use of extremely short daily sending times. A telephone connection, 'Minestrone', which had been set up between Snekkersten on the north Zealand coast and the American consulate 'annexe' in Halsingborg, Sweden, and which was used for the least urgent messages and Press material, never lessened the problem. London therefore asked whether it would be possible to establish high-speed telegraphy, so that about seven or eight times as many telegrams could be sent in the same transmission period.

Duus Hansen succeeded in acquiring two 'transmitters' and a hand-perforator. A 'transmitter' is an automatic key which is set in motion by a paper strip in which holes are punched to represent the separate letters in a word or sentence. The telegrams had to be transferred to the strip with the hand-perforator, a slow and difficult job. When the strip was placed into the electrically-driven transmitter, transmission speed could be stepped up to six to eight hundred letters per minute, compared with one hundred letters sent with the conventional Morse key. Messages transmitted at such high speeds could not be received in the ordinary way and written down by hand; the signals were recorded in England on wax plates and afterwards reproduced at a slower, readable rate. This type of automatic sending was first introduced in the Copenhagen district and later used in Jutland with a single operator. High-speed telegraphy made possible a considerable increase in the number of messages transmitted, a possibility which was turned to the fullest account.

Curiously, the German direction-finding police for a time showed no interest in the high-speed transmissions. They evidently assumed that such a technique was beyond the capabilities and resources of the Resistance; but they soon changed their minds and the hunt for the telegraphists was intensified, resulting sometimes in street battles between the radio groups and their pursuers. Duus Hansen, it should be said, always discouraged the guards from attacking the DF cars. He believed it was better for the groups to avoid a confrontation than to wreck one or two cars and cause the Germans to use new methods or to carry out reprisals in the district.

Even with the high-speed transmissions the radio network gradually became loaded to full capacity because of the steadily rising amount of traffic, and a breakdown at a power station in one or more of the areas could have had very unfortunate consequences. For that reason a few battery-operated transmitter-receivers were made to take care of the most urgent messages in the event of a power failure.

The service ran smoothly until 1944, when an indiscretion by a parachutist working with Flemming Muus, the SOE leader in Denmark, and another parachutist bringing crystals from London, almost led to catastrophe. The newcomer had been told to report to Muus on Raadhuspladsen (the City Hall square) in Copenhagen. For certain reasons Muus did not want to meet the man and sent his assistant instead. The parachutist arrived with a parcel and told Muus's representative: 'I have been instructed to give this package to you. You are to give it to a man called Napkin.'

The other replied: 'Take it to him yourself. His name is Duus Hansen and his office is over there in Jernbanegade, only fifty metres away.'

The man went to Duus Hansen's office and said: 'I have a parcel for you from England.'

The engineer stared at him blankly. 'I have no connections with England and I'm not expecting a parcel of any kind,' he said. 'I think you must have the wrong man.'

'Isn't your cover-name Napkin?'

'No.'

'Oh! come on. You can rely on me.'

Duus Hansen repeated: 'I have no connections with England. I haven't sent for any parcel. You're talking to the wrong fellow.'

The parachutist went away, but the damage was done. Shortly afterwards he was arrested by the Germans and under interrogation revealed Duus Hansen's identity. The Germans were delighted. They had never been able to understand the developments which had taken place in the Resistance radio-communications system. Now that they knew the leader was one of Europe's foremost radio-engineers, all was made clear. They raided the Bang and Olufsen offices but Duus Hansen was not there. He had seen the danger signals and had gone underground. All the searchers found was a couple of crystals. Fortunately for the office staff, they had collected all the materials the engineer had left and put them into a box labelled 'Private property of Mr. Duus Hansen', thus avoiding arrest as his accomplices.

That same afternoon the Germans raided Duus Hansen's house in Klosterrisvej on the outskirts of Copenhagen. They arrested Mrs. Duus Hansen and took her to Dagmarhus, in the centre of the city, where many Resistance men and women were already imprisoned. They said: 'You'll have to remain here until your husband reports himself to us'; but two or three days later they released her and sent her home. Duus Hansen telephoned her and told her: 'Don't stay in the house. You may be arrested again. Take our son and go off to our relatives on Funen.' But she was reluctant to leave her home. She was again arrested and again set free. Probably the Germans hoped that on release she would get in touch with her husband and give them the chance to trap him.

Duus Hansen said: 'One evening a young man called at our house. He pretended he was a Resistance man and identified himself as XY999 or some such number. We never used such cover-numbers. It was the kind of thing he'd read about in thrillers. He said that he'd just returned from Sweden and that it was absolutely vital that he should make contact with me. He said: "It's life or death for a lot of people." My wife said: "I can't put you in touch with him. I have no contact with him." That was true. She couldn't get in touch with me though I could contact her.

'The man acted very nervously and insisted: "But surely there's some way you could help. Could you take a message for me or tell me where I could leave a letter for him?" He played his part so well that my wife was uncertain, but I'd told her: "If anybody comes here and asks for me, don't believe him."

'The man said: "Try by all means to get in touch with your husband. I'll come again on Friday afternoon, just in case you get a message through for me."

'My wife got rid of him and eventually I learned about the visit and the arrangement that he would call again.

'On the Friday afternoon a team from Holger Danske or Bopa, I'm not sure which, were waiting at the corner of Klosterrisvej. When the man showed up they stopped him and said: "We want to talk to you."

'He said: "I'm all right." He must have thought they were Gestapomen or Hipos.

'They said: "What do you mean, you're all right?"

' "I'll show you," he said, and he produced a pistol permit signed by the Germans.

' "Yes," they said. "That's what we're looking for. You'd better come with us." And at that moment it became clear to him that he was talking to the wrong people.

'They took him to a house and called me. I saw the man and asked him: "What were you going to do at that house in Klosterrisvej?"

' "I wanted to talk to the owner."

' "About what?"

' "Some information."

' "For whom?"

' "For my employers."

' "I know who your employers are," I said. "I know them well. Have you ever seen the man?"

' "No."

' "You have a written description here. Could you recognise him?"

'The description he was carrying said the wanted man had side whiskers and walked with a rolling gait, like a sailor.

'I said: "You say you have to deliver a message to this man."

' "Yes."

' "Then you can deliver it to me. I'm Duus Hansen."

'He went white. He said nothing for a minute or two; then he asked: "If I tell you everything, will you let me go?"

'I said: "That's the only chance you have." (I didn't say: "Yes, you can go if you tell me everything".)

'He asked: "Would you let me go for an hour or so? I have a very important message to give to my sister."

' "No. If you have a message, write it on a piece of paper. We guarantee that it will reach your sister."

'The other men said: "That's enough. Come on, you. Follow us."

'They took him away—and I've heard nothing of him since...'

After that incident Duus Hansen arranged a meeting with his wife at a safe-house on the Zealand coast. He told her to telephone the Germans at Dagmarhus and ask them to keep all visitors away from her home. He said: 'Tell them you don't agree with your husband's activities and that you just want to live in peace. Say that they would be doing you a great service if they kept all Resistance suspects away from you.' She hesitated but at last she picked up the telephone and asked to be put through to Dagmarhus.

The officer to whom she spoke was very polite. He said: 'We didn't realise you felt so strongly about your husband's activities. If that's your attitude, of course we'll do our best to keep all intruders away from your house. We'd appreciate it greatly if you'd call in here one day for a chat about these things. You could give us some information and we could protect you.'

She promised that she would think about it, but that night she left with her son for Funen, where she remained until the end of the occupation.

The hunt for Duus Hansen continued. A party of Gestapomen went to his office in Jernbanegade and asked his successor to show them the books. 'You're still paying wages to that man Duus Hansen,' they said. 'You are putting the money into his bank regularly.'

'Well, of course. He was the boss here and that's the way he wanted it. We only do what he tells us to do.'

The Germans interviewed Mr. Olufsen, a director of the firm. 'Have you sacked Duus Hansen?' they asked.

'No, we haven't fired him,' he replied. 'He just left us.'

'Then why are you still paying him?'

'We aren't paying him.'

'Your bank says that you are. Have you no control over such matters? Don't you have a pay roll? Haven't you noticed that he's still on it?'

Olufsen said: 'There are about a thousand people in this company. If their names are on the pay roll, we pay them. We don't ask every month whether a man's still with the firm. If he's on the pay roll, he gets his money.'

'But you've ordered his monthly cheque to be paid into the bank.'

'No. He was in charge of the office and he made that order himself.'

The Gestapo leader shook his head. 'We don't believe you,' he said. 'There can be no doubt that you are supporting Duus Hansen directly with money and materials. At the same time you've refused to work for the German war effort. You've never supplied us with any equipment or parts. You've always found some excuse to refuse an order from us. Now this is your last warning. If we see the slightest attempt again to support this terrorist or to evade an order from us, we'll blow up either your factory or your Copenhagen office.'

Olufsen did not think the firm's office was in danger. It was immediately behind Dagmarhus and wall to wall with the Gestapo office. He got in touch with the German OKW (*Oberkommando der Wehrmacht*) and asked: 'How seriously should we take a threat that the Gestapo will blow up our factory?'

The German laughed. 'The Gestapo have no authority to order such an action,' he said. 'Only the military people could do it.'

The factory was blown up five days later. At the same time Duus Hansen's house on Klosterrisvej was blown up. The Gestapo chief had ordered that the destruction should be complete, so a charge of one hundred kilos of dynamite was used. The little house was blown to pieces and the roofs of the surrounding houses were also blown off. Duus Hansen's grand piano landed in a garden about two hundred metres away. Luckily, there were no human casualties.

Meanwhile Duus Hansen was busier than ever. In addition to transmitting, building new equipment, organising new communication lines and writing reports to England, he was doing practically all the micro-photography for the Resistance groups in Copenhagen. He always made two negatives. One was hidden and the other sent to England undeveloped. Panchromatic film, which is sensitive to red light, was used and the parcel of undeveloped negatives was marked *'Open in red light only'*. If it were seized by the Germans it would be taken to a darkroom, opened in red light, and the negatives would be ruined.

In the winter of 1944 Duus Hansen was invited to England to discuss with SOE communication plans which, among other things, took into account possible developments in Denmark before a German capitulation. He was told: 'We have a new system—the Marker system—which we should like you to consider. At present you can call England only at fixed times, according to your schedule. With the Marker system you could call at any time. An operator would always be listening to certain frequences and you could maintain connection throughout the twenty-four hours. There's now so much traffic all day between Denmark and Britain—Resistance leaders, regional leaders, sabotage and intelligence groups, and so on—that we simply can't cope. With the activities of the German DF cars making difficulties, we can't handle the traffic. If you could organise another line to relieve it, working on frequencies it would be difficult for the Germans to monitor, it would help us very much and it would also help you.'

Duus Hansen said that Minestrone, the telephone connection between Snekkersten and Halsingborg, was working well but it was too slow and the messages were sent in plain language. It would not solve the British problem. A high-speed telegraph line between Copenhagen and Malmø was needed.

'Yes,' said SOE, 'but Sweden is a neutral country. We should like such a line but you couldn't put it in with our consent. We can send you the materials, but what you do with them is your affair.'

Duus Hansen went to Stockholm and talked to the American authorities, who agreed to establish a 'consulate annexe' in a nine-storey building in Malmø. This, since it had extra-territorial status, could be used by the Danish radio group without fear of Swedish interference. An ultra-short wave trans-mitting and receiving station was installed on the top floor of the building and a similar station was put up at No. 4 Strandvej, the coast road between Copenhagen and Elsinore. The connec-tion, code-named Badminton, worked perfectly. Telegrams sent from Denmark were received and transcribed in Malmø with the aid of an undulator, which converted the Morse signals into a wavy line on a paper strip. The messages were coded and handed to the American vice-consul, who had the right to use the Swedish state telegraph service, and forwarded by him to Lon-don as diplomatic express telegrams. London replied daily with a number of dummy telegrams which went straight into the waste-paper basket.

The Badminton line obviated direct transmissions from Copenhagen to London but Duus Hansen found it politic to maintain a limited traffic. A complete stoppage would have led the Germans to examine all other possibilities of communica-tion, whereas a weak activity could give them the impression that their counter-measures had been effective.

Towards the end of the war Duus Hansen devised an ingenious remote-control system of communication. A 'tele-phone book' transmitter could be connected to a telephone and operated by a telegraphist with a key at the other end of the line. In this way a man could sit in a house at Roskilde, for example, and operate a transmitter in Copenhagen. The difficulty was that frequencies could not be changed because nobody was sitting at the transmitter. By coupling a 'telephone book' to the Badminton line in Malmø it was possible to establish direct communication between Copenhagen and Lon-don. The German direction-finders could determine that the messages were being sent from Malmø but they could not interfere. Although the system was free from risk, it was used only to a very limited extent. It required the cooperation of a telegraphist in Malmø and it was troublesome when London wanted a change of frequencies because of disturbances.

Before Duus Hansen left London to return to Denmark in

the spring of 1945, he went to say goodbye to Lieutenant-Commander R. C. Hollingworth, head of Danish Section, SOE.

'Go back and prepare a big celebration,' Hollingworth said. 'We'll be over to share it with you in July or August.'

'I'll do that,' Duus Hansen replied, 'but I may have been arrested and hanged by the Germans before you arrive.'

'Hanged by the Germans?' Hollingworth repeated. 'You must refuse to be hanged. You are a British officer. It is your right to be shot!'

Duus Hansen remembered that conversation on the day of liberation. During the war he used to lunch at a little restaurant on Strandboulevarden. A party of German officers from the Citadel always ate at a neighbouring table. After the capitulation he thought it would be interesting to see how they would react if he walked in for luncheon in his British uniform. He put it on and went to the restaurant. The Germans stared; then one of them walked over, clicked his heels and saluted smartly. He asked: 'Are you the man who used to come here regularly?'

'I am,' said Duus Hansen.

He said: 'Of course we didn't know who you were. If we'd known, you wouldn't be here today. But you won the war. I congratulate you.' He clicked his heels, saluted again, and marched back to his table.

4: LOTTE

Female agents seldom measure up to the standards of beauty and wit demanded by Hollywood and by the writers of sensational fiction. Edith Bonnesen (cover-name Lotte) was a notable exception. A tiny, blue-eyed natural blonde, she was quick-thinking, resourceful, and further blessed with an irrepressible sense of humour. In 1940, when the Germans invaded Denmark, she was a civil servant on the staff of the ministry of transport in Copenhagen. During the course of her work she saw many letters and reports of potential interest to Britain. She took them to her apartment in Hellerup and made copies, which she passed to friends in the intelligence service. In 1941 she began work with the illegal Press and her apartment became a meeting-place for Resistance men and parachutists. Mogens Hammer lived there for several nights before he left Denmark. Inevitably, the Germans got wind of Lotte's activities. Good friends in the Danish police told her that people she knew had been arrested and had given names. They warned her: 'Be careful. You are next on the list.'

In the summer of 1942 the blow fell. Mogens Hammer's brother, Svend Erik, a member of *De Frie Danske*, went to Lotte's apartment at 3 o'clock one morning and told her that a captured Resistance man had given her name. He was convinced that she would be arrested the following day. But Lotte said: 'That's all right. I know what has been said and I can adjust my story accordingly.'

The Germans arrived at the apartment but Lotte would not open the door to their knocking and they went away again. On the following day she was arrested in the office of her departmental chief at the ministry. She was taken to Dagmarhus and interrogated by the Gestapo for many hours. Bullying and threats failed to shake her. She maintained indignantly that she was an innocent civil servant with no interest whatsoever in undermining German authority. Two Danish policemen then escorted her to police headquarters, where they tried to make her tell the truth about her activities. They promised that they would not repeat what she told them to the Gestapo, but Lotte knew that they were working hand-in-hand with the Germans. She insisted that she had already told the Gestapo all she knew, and at last they sent her home.

Eight days later she was arrested again. The same two policemen went to her office, took her to Vestre Fængsel prison and put her into a cell. After a few hours, having been refused permission to speak to the Danish police authorities, she asked the guards to ring Major Drescher, the German commander in Dagmarhus. Much to her surprise he arrived at the prison with a Danish interpreter. Then the comedy started over again. Drescher said that since Lotte had sent for him, she must have something to tell him. Lotte retorted that she wanted only to know why she had been thrown into a German prison without having been brought before a Danish court. Drescher was courteous but very persistent and finally Lotte told him a story which she knew would cover whatever he had been told by the others who had been arrested. Afterwards he gave orders for her release and drove her to the railway station. He said he was not satisfied that she had told him all she knew and that this would not be the last time she would see him. 'Very well,' she said. 'You're welcome to come again. Meanwhile, goodbye.'

Some weeks elapsed and then the two Danish policemen went to the ministry again. This time they took Lotte straight to Vestre Fængsel. They told her that Drescher was very angry with her and did not wish to see her. She could stay in jail until she was ready to tell the truth. Lotte said: 'Lovely! I need a holiday. That's wonderful.'

After eight days a Gestapo man went to the prison and asked her if she were ready to talk. She said that she was quite ready to repeat what she had told them but that she had nothing new to say. 'That's not enough,' he snapped. So Lotte continued her 'holiday' for a few more days. Finally she was taken before a Danish court and was set free.

Once more the two Danish policemen visited Lotte. 'May we speak to you as friends?' they asked.

'After the war,' she replied. 'I've nothing to say to you now.'

'Well, will you call us if you meet any of those Resistance people?' they persisted.

'Of course,' she said. 'I'm a good citizen.'

Shortly afterwards a Dane who was known to be a collaborator rang Lotte's best friend and asked whether she were at his apartment. He said: 'No, but I'm expecting her.'

'I think she's a wonderful girl. Do you think I could meet her?'

'Sure. I'll fix it for tomorrow afternoon.'

The friend rang Lotte, told her about the conversation and described the collaborator. Lotte said: 'Right! Make the appointment. I'll be there.'

She rang the two Danish policemen and said: 'You asked me to call you if I were contacted by the illegal people. Well, one of them is trying to get in touch with me. I'm meeting him tomorrow afternoon and I should like you to be present.'

The Danes arrived at the rendezvous with Gestapomen and a couple of Alsatian police-dogs. They recognised the *stikker* but they could not admit it. They were forced to arrest him and take him back to Dagmarhus, there to face a tongue-lashing from Drescher.

On 29 August 1943, Lotte went underground. She left her apartment and her job and, equipped with false identity papers, began work with the saboteurs and other groups. She was working at one time with a Bopa team when they received word that a goods train was to leave Copenhagen for Germany with a consignment of ammunition. They got hold of a time-table which told them when the train would start and the route it would take. They held up the train and got away with the entire load of ammunition.

Eventually Lotte met Duus Hansen, who asked her to supply him with a list of apartments occupied by reliable, childless Danes from which the telegraphists could operate. She got the apartments, with keys, and from then on she worked exclusively with the radio group.

Apart from his radio activities, Duus Hansen was involved with Flemming Muus, the SOE leader, in work connected with the transports to Sweden. The first transport committee had been broken by the Germans and a new one had been set up. On 14 August 1944, the leaders asked Duus Hansen to go to their office, an apartment on Nytorv, to discuss arrangements for sending an operator to Jutland. There was also a parcel of crystals and other radio components to be collected.

Duus Hansen said: 'I'm sorry but I can't get there. I'm up to my eyes in work. If there are questions you want to ask, I'll send my secretary, Lotte, down to you. She can bring your queries back to me and she can pick up the parcel at the same time.'

'As it happened, Duus gave me the wrong job,' Lotte said. 'I hadn't been in the office more than ten minutes when the telephone rang. The caller wanted to know whether I or Citronen (Jørgen Schmidt) was in the office. He wouldn't give his name. That made us nervous and I said: "Give me the crystals and I'll get out of here."

'At that moment somebody started hammering on the door. We looked at each other but there was nothing for it but to open up. A party of Gestapomen armed with sub-machine guns burst in. They seemed to be more frightened than we were. They rushed around the room, pulling out drawers and turning things upside-down, while we stood and looked at them. I had a bunch of telegrams in my pocket and I took them out and ate them. I took the crystals out of my bag and put it down. The Gestapomen were so hysterical that they didn't notice.

'As we were standing there with our hands up, one of the men asked me: "Where are your suicide pills?" I said that I had no pills but he wouldn't believe me. He saw that I was chewing something and said: "You're eating a pill." I said: "No, I'm not." I could hardly tell him I was chewing the last of the telegrams.

'They ordered us down into Nytorv and followed us. One or two stayed up in the office, where there was quite a lot of stuff. They bundled us into cars and took us to Shellhus, the Gestapo headquarters on the corner of Farimagsgade and Kampmannsgade. All the others in our group were handcuffed. I was the only one with hands free. They took us into Shellhus.

Inside the door a huge German soldier stood on guard. He looked at me very hard and I had the feeling that he wouldn't forget my face in a hurry. There was a Gestapoman armed with a sub-machine gun on each side of me. They took me to a room on the fourth floor, where a crowd of Germans and Danish *stikkers* came to look at me. They said jubilantly: "That's Lotte, all right. That's the one we've been after." They had a bottle of vermouth and began to drink from it, passing it from hand to hand. They were ever so happy that I had been caught.

'A Dane in German uniform started to ask me questions. I told him I had nothing to do with the office in Nytorv. I said I had gone to see a man in the apartment next to it and had opened the wrong door. The Dane took me into another room. One of the Gestapo leaders came in and asked: "Has she said anything?"

' "No. Nothing at all."

' "Well, take her down to the cellars. Don't waste any more time. We know all about her activities during the past few years and she must talk."

'The Dane took me to a big room on the second floor and told me to sit down. He went into another office and spoke with another man about me. He was gone a long time. I walked up and down the room, thinking: "Why should I stay here, waiting to be taken down to the cellars?" I knew what would happen down there and it wouldn't be funny. And I knew too much about the Resistance organisation—too many names and all that was going on. I thought: "Lotte, my girl, you must take a chance. Nobody can see you here."

'A man and woman were sitting on a bench on the other side of the room, looking very dejected. Probably, like me, they were waiting for a trip to the cellars. I felt that they wouldn't interfere, so I walked out through the doorway. The corridor was empty. Everything was quiet. I decided that if anybody came along I'd ask for the lavatory, but nobody came. From where I was standing I could see the doors of the elevator but I knew it would be too risky to try that route. I made my way to the stairs and went very cautiously down to the first floor. Two Gestapomen, with briefcases under their arms, came out of an office and walked towards me. They glanced at me but they didn't speak. I suppose they took me for a secretary. I walked along, close behind them, hoping that anybody who saw us would think we were together. Then, to my horror, I saw the big soldier standing by the elevator. He stared at me, puzzled. He obviously remembered seeing me being brought into the building under guard. I expected him to grab my arm and ask: "Where are you going?" I thought that if he did, I'd say: "I've been spying on some of those illegal people and now I'm going out on the next job." He made no move to stop me but he followed the three of us down the next stairs, step for step. When we came to the front door, the two Gestapomen stood aside politely to let me pass. I smiled sweetly and said: *"Danke schoen."*

'I walked on out, but then I saw the barbed-wire barricade. I'd taken the wrong turning. I had to nerve myself to turn around and go quietly back the way I'd come and so out into Farimags-gade. That was the most difficult thing of all; my heart was thumping like a steam-hammer. But if the big guard had been standing in the entrance and had seen me running, it would have been the end. I was quite certain that I wasn't going to make it over the railway bridge into Hammerichsgade without getting a bullet in my back but I thought it was much better that I should be shot than that I should be recaptured. I knew too much.

'When I got over the bridge and around the corner into Studiestræde I knew I had a chance. An ambulance was stand-ing by the kerb. I opened the door of the cab and told the Danish driver: "I've just escaped from Shellhus. Will you help me?"

'He went pale and shook his head. "I'm sorry. I can't."

'I said: "Thanks a lot. You're one of the good ones." I slammed the door and started to run down Studiestræde. God! that was a long street. I dashed across H. C. Andersens Boule-vard, back on to Studiestræde, and tore left around the corner into Vester Voldgade, where I managed to board the streetcar to Nørreport station. Only then did I begin to feel safe.'

When Lotte got back to the radio group's headquarters in

Østerbrogade Duus Hansen was in a vile humour. 'Where the devil have you been?' he demanded. 'You've been gone for hours.'

Lotte said meekly: 'Yes, I know, but I'm sure you'll forgive me when you know where I've been.'

'Well, where?'

'In Shellhus.'

'WHAT?' roared Duus Hansen. 'Then how on earth did you get here?'

'I walked out,' said Lotte.

Later on Flemming Muus telephoned Duus Hansen. He said: 'Our girl friend has gone on a trip with our friends.'

'I know.'

'You're very calm about it. Don't you understand what I'm telling you?'

'Yes. I understand, but she's back here now.'

'But I mean...'

'I know what you mean, but it's all right. She's come home. She didn't like the smell in the bakery.'

After twenty minutes Muus called again.

'Are you sure you understood what I said?' he asked. 'You know our girl friend went on a trip?'

'Yes.'

'Well, aren't you worried about it?'

'No.'

'You still don't understand.'

'Yes, I do. She's here. Would you like to speak to her?'

There was a long pause. Then Muus said: 'No. I'm satisfied. But after this, I'll believe anything.'

His incredulity was forgivable. To the best of my knowledge, Lotte was the only Resistance fighter ever to get out of Shellhus alive.

Ironically, within a few days it was her own comrades who almost put an end to her career.

She had reported to Duus Hansen and Flemming Muus that the man responsible for the raid on the Nytorv office was the *stikker* known as Søren. He had been seen to meet a Gestapo-man by the newspaper kiosk on Vesterbros Torv and had been heard to protest that his payment of five hundred kroner (about £25) was too little for betraying such important Resistance people. The story was confirmed and Muus ordered the Holger Danske group to get rid of the informer. Lotte, who knew and could identify Søren, was asked to accompany the liquidation squad. She was to meet them at an apartment in central Copenhagen.

There followed an incredible comedy of bungling and misunderstanding which could well have ended in tragedy. It began when the Holger Danske leader entrusted with the operation was somehow persuaded that Lotte might have been allowed to leave Shellhus because she was really a double-agent working for the Germans. He believed this sufficiently to order his squad to shoot her down if she arrived at the rendezvous in the company of one or more men.

Lotte kept the appointment and was hustled into the apartment by a youth carrying a Sten-gun. In the living-room another youth was sitting behind a writing table; two more stood by with Sten-guns at the ready. Lotte looked from one to the other, more amused than angry, though she did not like the nervous way in which they fingered the triggers of their weapons. 'What's going on?' she asked the youth at the table. 'Is this some kind of joke?'

'No joke,' he replied unsmilingly. 'We have orders to take you up to North Zealand and execute you.'

'Well, that shouldn't be difficult,' she said. 'I'm unarmed, so can't put up a fight. But first let's get on with the job I've been given by Jørgen (Flemming Muus). After that, you can do what you like.'

'We'll take care of that *stikker* later. Now you must come with us.'

Lotte sighed. 'All right,' she said, 'but I hope you know what you're doing. I don't know how you dare disobey Jørgen's orders.'

She was hustled downstairs, with a raincoat hooding her head, and put into the back seat of a car. The youths piled in after her, shoved the muzzles of their guns through the windows, and the car roared away, taking corners on two wheels. It was all like a very bad B-movie, Lotte thought. 'Take it easy or you'll get done for speeding,' she warned the driver. 'I've just come out of Shellhus and I don't want to be picked up again by the Gestapo.'

A few kilometres out of Copenhagen she pulled the raincoat from her head. 'I don't mind being shot,' she said, 'but I'm damned if I'll let you smother me.'

The youth who appeared to be in charge of the party said: 'You're taking this very coolly. Aren't you scared of what's going to happen to you?'

'Why should I be?' she retorted. 'I know you're my own people, even if you are acting like a bunch of idiots. Germans don't carry Sten-guns. Now stop at the next automat. I want to make a telephone call. You're welcome to listen to what I say.'

He looked at her uncertainly. 'Well ... all right, but don't try any funny business.'

The car pulled up outside a public telephone box on a deserted stretch of road. Lotte got out, accompanied by the leader, and put a call through to the radio group's new headquarters on Damhussøen. She said: 'Tell the boss that I've been kidnapped. The orders we were given haven't been carried out. I don't know where I'm being taken or whether I'll be coming back. These children are trigger-happy. He'd better do something about it.'

When she got back to the car she could see that the youths were confused and not a little worried. Lotte was not acting like any *stikker* they had ever encountered. The leader held out the raincoat and said apologetically: 'I'm afraid I'll have to ask you to put this thing on again. Honestly, you really aren't supposed to see where we're going.'

For the rest of the long drive they were friendly and listened with interest to Lotte's account of her escape from Shellhus. The journey ended at a small week-end cottage on the north Zealand coast. As Lotte was shepherded through the front door she saw a letter lying on a side-table and slipped it into her pocket. She was taken into a room with picture-windows looking out over the Øresund and told to sit down. She settled herself comfortably in an armchair and said: 'I'm glad you brought me here. It's always been one of my favourite places.'

'You know where you are?'

She took the letter from her pocket and pointed to the address. 'If you wanted to keep it a dark secret, you shouldn't leave things like this lying around,' she said. 'As a matter of fact, the owner of this house is a friend of mine.'

The youths were plainly shaken. They held a low-voiced conference for a few minutes and then the leader said: 'Look, we're beginning to think there's been a bit of a mistake somewhere. I'm going back into town to get further instructions.'

'I think you're wise,' Lotte said, 'but I hope you know whom to contact because you'll get no names from me. And hurry, please. I'm very busy and I have a lot of appointments today.'

The leader and another youth left immediately for the capital. It was evening when they returned. Anders And (Major F. B. Larsen) came with them, full of apologies and bearing a huge bunch of flowers as a peace-offering. He personally drove Lotte and the youths back to Copenhagen but she made him drop her some distance from Damhussøen. 'I'll find my own way home,' was her final insult. 'I'm afraid I couldn't trust you boys with my underground address.'

Some days afterwards Flemming Muus and Duus Hansen met to discuss Lotte's future. They agreed that she could not remain in Denmark. She was too well-known to the Germans. If she were arrested again and subjected to torture in the Shellhus cellars she might disclose too much and endanger key circles in the Resistance. She knew the identities and functions of too many leaders and the contents of too many vital telegrams. It was left to Duus Hansen to persuade her to leave the country. He told her that she would be sent to Stockholm with a letter of introduction to Ebbe Munck, who would certainly take care of her and find her a job in which she could continue to help the Resistance. But Lotte protested violently. She refused point-blank to go to Sweden and insisted that she should be allowed to continue her work in Denmark—if necessary, alone. She pointed out that many important lines would be broken if she crossed the Øresund. She was involved not only with the radio group but with the sabotage and illegal newspaper groups; she was helping with the supply of ration cards and false identity papers to men who had gone underground; and she was collecting thousands of kroner every month to take care of families whose husbands and fathers had been arrested. Further, she admitted, she had nothing but contempt for the Danes who had taken refuge in Sweden; she thought they should have remained in Denmark and done their duty.

Duus Hansen heard her out patiently. Then he said: 'Lotte, there's no room for discussion. You must go. That's an order.'

'And if I refuse?'

'You'd get a draught in your skull. You know that. You know it's too risky to let you stay here, so please be ready for transfer.'

'When?'

'As soon as possible.'

Duus Hansen escorted her to the boat a few nights later. After a long interrogation by the Swedish police (they had heard about her escape from Shellhus and thought she must be a German spy), she was taken by the Danes to Stockholm. When the Minestrone line was completed she was sent to Halsingborg to operate it from the American consulate 'annexe', where she could work protected by extra-territorial status. During the spring of 1945 she also worked for a few days each week with the Badminton operator in Malmø.

Typically, while in Halsingborg, she managed to get herself appointed temporary American consul, in which capacity she was able, *inter alia*, to assist in the safe passage to England of a party of RAF pilots who had been shot down over Denmark and taken to Sweden by the Resistance transports.

5: THE PRESS

It was to be expected that following the occupation one of the first German moves would be to institute strict control of the Danish State Radio, the newspapers, periodicals, books, and all other potential media for anti-German propaganda. It was equally to be expected that the highly literate Danes would take immediate steps to counter these measures. But the most optimistic prophet could not have foreseen that within five years, from a handful of amateurishly typed or cyclostyled leaflets and chain-letters, there would grow a powerful, nation-wide network of hundreds of illegal newspapers far exceeding in circulation and influence the organs of the authorised Press.

From 9 April 1940, control of radio services and newspapers was exercised through the Press division of the Danish foreign ministry; direct German censorship was not imposed until 29 August 1943. But from the first day of occupation news stories were doctored or suppressed, free public expression of opinion was prohibited, and all infringements of the regulations were punished by Danish courts and later by German tribunals.

Nevertheless, truth could not be entirely suppressed. Swedish newspapers were smuggled into Denmark by ferries crossing the Øresund and passed from hand to hand. People listened in their homes to the news broadcasts of the BBC and the Swedish radio. Posters carrying hand-printed anti-German slogans and caricatures were pasted by night on walls and shop windows. Chain-letters and pamphlets made public such important matters as the secret discussions about a currency and customs union between Denmark and Germany. The political party *Dansk Samling* organised closed 'sitting room' meetings, with members of parliament and other prominent Danes as speakers, for the discussion of topical questions and published the excellent pamphlets of the historian Vilhelm la Cour, which were printed in large numbers and sold readily throughout the country.

The importance of the nationwide 'meetings activity' during

1940 and 1941 can hardly be over-estimated. The lead of *Dansk Samling* was followed by many other organisations, including the different political parties, with *Dansk Ungdomssamvirke* particularly effective in that field. The meetings, closed and public, were held regularly in almost every village, town, and city, and hundreds of thousands of people participated. Some of the speakers, like Professor Hal Koch, chairman of *Dansk Ungdomssamvirke*, attracted huge audiences. For example, early in 1941 it was arranged that Koch should go to Odense to speak about Denmark in 1157, a critical year during which the Danes had gone in fear of German domination. The whole thing seemed quite innocent, but the topic afforded the opportunity of impressing the audience with the need for national unity against the new oppressors. Dr. Jørgen Hæstrup, who was planning Koch's visit with the barrister Ernst Petersen, suggested for the meeting a hall with a capacity of two hundred people. Petersen disagreed. He insisted that the town's largest hall, which could hold three thousand, should be booked. He got his way and the building was packed to the last seat on the last bench. Even so, many had to be turned away and the lecture was repeated for their benefit some days later.

Only two illegal newspapers, with a total print of twelve hundred copies, made their appearance during 1940; by the end of 1941 there were no fewer than eighteen. This enormous increase followed the banning of the communist party on 27 June 1941, a step which resulted in the appearance throughout the country of pamphlets and news-sheets carrying protests against the persecution of the party and its members and calling for a united front against the Germans and their Danish collaborators. The most important of these publications was *Land og Folk* (Country and People), first printed in October 1941. Published monthly and later fortnightly from a secret address in Copenhagen, it attained almost from the start a nationwide circulation of 125,000 to 130,000 copies.

De Frie Danske (The Free Danes), the creation of a Copenhagen group including several professional journalists, appeared in December 1941. In its first issue it scathingly attacked foreign minister Erik Scavenius for signing the anti-Comintern pact and called upon its readers for unanimous defiance 'next time a demand is made upon us by the enemy'. The paper's lively style and accurate news coverage made it popular immediately and its circulation grew from an initial two hundred copies to eight thousand in its first year and eventually to twenty thousand.

The phenomenal growth of the illegal Press continued throughout 1942 and by the close of the year at least forty-nine newspapers, with a combined circulation of three hundred and one thousand copies, were spreading the gospel of resistance. Of the newcomers the most influential and widely read was the monthly *Frit Danmark* (Free Denmark), first published in April. Its leading spirits were the chairman of the communist party, Aksel Larsen, and the former conservative minister, John Christmas Møller, backed by an editorial committee representing all shades of political opinion from the right to the extreme left. The circle included Professor Ole Chievitz, senior surgeon at the Finsen Institution, Copenhagen; Thomas Døssing, director of the Copenhagen Library; Professor Mogens Fog, doctor of medicine; Børge Houmann, business manager of the communist *Arbejderbladet* (*Daily Worker*); Ole Kiilerich, editor of *Nationaltidende* (National News); the barristers Rud Prytz and Ernst Petersen; director Karl V. Jensen; and Henry Christophersen, an official of the Danish Workers Union. Their aim, in which they succeeded brilliantly, was to produce an all-party, opinion-moulding periodical which should become a powerful factor in extending and strengthening national resistance to German domination. The first print in April was five thousand copies but an efficient organisation of distribution groups in all parts of Denmark, similar to that of *Land og Folk*, boosted the circulation to twenty thousand copies by the end of the year and later to a total of one hundred and forty-five thousand.

Another important arrival was *Studenternes Efterretningstjeneste* (Students' Information Service). Meanwhile the communists were increasing their efforts and their new publications during the year included *Folkets Kamp* (People's Fight) at Aalborg; *Aarhus Ekko* (Aarhus Echo), Aarhus; *Vestjyden* (West Jutlander), Esbjerg; *Stjernen* (Star), Silkeborg; *Trods Alt*

(Despite Everything), Odense; *Ny Tid* (New Time), Hillerød and Elsinore; *Gry* (Dawn), Næstved; and *Tiden* (The Time), Maribo.

The difficulties and dangers faced by the illegal newspaper pioneers were many. Most of them were in their teens and early twenties and few had previous experience of printing or journalism. Generally their only equipment was a typewriter or a second-hand duplicating machine of ancient vintage and erratic performance. They had constant problems in finding money and materials and in recruiting trustworthy helpers for production and distribution. Above all there was the problem of finding a safe location—an apartment, a cellar, or the back room of a shop—in which to work. Few indeed were the places where a group could operate for long without fear of detection or betrayal. Often the equipment had to be dismantled and hurried from one house to another literally one jump ahead of the police or the Gestapo. The personal risk was great. Capture meant at best imprisonment and at worst a session in the cellars of Shellhus and almost certain death. Finance was always a difficulty. A paper's circulation figures were no guide to the number of cash customers. Only a minority of readers subscribed to any illegal newspaper, though the public were so avid for uncensored news that many copies circulated from hand to hand until they were illegible. Production was financed mainly by the groups themselves and by gifts from parents, friends, and other sympathisers.

In the late autumn of 1942 Danish police raided the headquarters of *De Frie Danske* and arrested a number of the staff. At the subsequent trial two men who in addition to their illegal newspaper activities had aided British parachutists were sentenced respectively to six years and eight years in jail; the others were jailed from two months to two years.

On 5 November Aksel Larsen was arrested by Danish police and handed over to the German authorities. After a year in Vestre Fængsel he was sent to Germany and held in concentration camps at Sachsenhausen and Neuengamme until the capitulation. Chievitz, Døssing, Prytz, and Ernst Petersen were arrested on 9 December. Fog, Kiilerich, Houmann, Karl Jensen, and Christophersen, who had been warned in time, went underground. Kiilerich escaped via Sweden to England, where he became a member of the Danish Council in London. Chievitz was sentenced by a Danish court to eight months in jail. After his release he continued his Resistance activities and in 1944 became a member of the Freedom Council. Thomas Døssing received four months jail and forfeited his post as director of the Copenhagen Library. After serving his sentence he was interned by the Germans for five weeks. In 1944 he was appointed 'Fighting Denmark's' minister in Moscow.

The *Frit Danmark* affair caused an immense sensation but the trial had a boomerang effect, for the revelation that so many respected figures in medicine, literature and the law were engaged in illegal activities gave the lie to the official contention that only communists, fanatics and irresponsible youngsters supported the Resistance movement. Neither *De Frie Danske* nor *Frit Danmark* was seriously affected by the arrests. New people came forward to carry on the work of those who had been taken, production went on as before, and the circulation of both papers steadily increased.

Throughout 1943 the illegal Press continued to attack the German-dominated administration, to expose the collaborators and informers, and ever more strongly to advocate the case for sabotage as an effective weapon in the fight for freedom. The work of the journals like *Frit Danmark* and *Land og Folk* was ably reinforced by the many regional and local newspaper groups, who rendered particularly important service in fostering and reporting the events of the great folk-strikes which hit the provinces in August. Many new publications saw the light during the course of the year, bringing the strength of the free Press to the astonishing total of 166 newspapers with a combined circulation of some 2,600,000 copies. They were never short of topical material. News flowed in from the editorial staffs of the legal newspapers, from the official Ritzau Bureau news agency, from the BBC and Swedish radio transmissions, and from contacts within the government departments, the political parties, and the police. In the summer of 1943 the Illegal Press Coordinating Committee and the Illegal Press Joint Association Newsroom combined to issue duplicated news bulletins to underground editors in all parts of Denmark through the Copenhagen publishing firm of Frit Nordisk Forlag. The bulletins were issued twice weekly during June, July, and early August but, as tension increased between the Danish and German governments, they began to appear almost daily. After 29 August, the day of the official break with the Germans, the organisation changed its name to *Nordisk Nyhedstjeneste* (Nordic News Service).

Among the regular contributors to the Joint Association Newsroom was Børge Outze, 31-year-old crime reporter and sub-editor of the frankly anti-German Copenhagen daily *National-tidende*. As crime reporter he received most of the news, including police reports, which could not be printed; as sub-editor he automatically 'spiked' it. Then, privately, he passed on the information to the editors of the Newsroom bulletins and to a few of the illegal papers direct. In August 1943, Outze inaugurated a confidential daily news summary for newspaper editors and their boards, a service which was legal even under German regulations. To prevent confusion with copy intended for use solely in *Nationaltidende*, the summaries were headed *For Information*, soon abbreviated to *Informatión*. By a curious chance many more copies were produced and circulated than there were people officially authorised to receive them, and the illegal papers benefited correspondingly. By the end of September *Informatión* had developed into a fully-fledged illegal press agency which gave Outze little time for attending to his normal daily work. Reporters on other Copenhagen newspapers covered for him by sending him galley-proofs of their own news stories, which were rewritten by *Nationaltidende* colleagues under his by-line.

When the drive against Denmark's Jews began in October, Outze and his group became involved in organising the transport of refugees to Sweden, and *Informatión* played an essential part in ensuring that the operation ran smoothly.

A side benefit was that supplies of *Informatión* could now be sent to Sweden in the fishing vessels which carried the refugees across the Øresund.

Early in 1944, following a Gestapo raid on the *Nationaltidende* offices, Outze and his colleagues went underground and the preparation and distribution of *Información* became their full-time job. They often met in the Tivoli Gardens, in the centre of Copenhagen, where the pleasure-seeking crowds provided safe cover for the discussion of illegal business. However, the inevitable *stikker* was at work and on 27 May the Gestapo pounced. Outze had momentarily left the group to make a telephone call. He returned to see his comrades being hustled by armed Germans through an angry crowd. Somehow he managed to slip through the cordon surrounding the gardens and escape; but bereft of his key assistants he now had to seek help elsewhere and on the following day *Información* and *Nordisk Nyhedstjeneste*, who had long worked amicably together, were formally merged. The title *Información* was retained but it was agreed that Outze should no longer finance the work from his own pocket, supplemented by occasional donations. In future each recipient of the bulletins was expected every month to put two (later three) ten-kroner notes in an envelope marked on the outside with his code-number, thus providing for the first time a steady income for the service.

The value of *Información* to the Resistance movement was never better proved than in the general strike which began in Copenhagen on Monday 26 June 1944, following the imposition by the German plenipotentiary, Dr. Werner Best, of a curfew between the hours of 8 p.m. and 5 a.m. *Información* not only reported the subsequent events: it helped to create them. For example, on the first day a bulletin carried a story on the unrest at the giant shipyard of Burmeister & Wein. It stated:

The workers of Burmeister & Wein took the lead. They decided to go home early so as to make up for the loss of leisure in the evening. By two o'clock the city's biggest industrial plant had closed down. The workers resolved to issue a statement to Dr. Best which will go down in history as one of the most remarkable documents of the war. In short, the workers at one of the main centres of the German war effort in Denmark have informed the Reich plenipotentiary that while the curfew is in force they intend to take an occasional day off. This they regard not as a strike but as a need; for, as they cannot be guaranteed food as long as Germany is at war, they mean to cultivate their allotments. The crops of potatoes, tomatoes, and so forth, will be more important to them than the yield to Germany's war industry from B & W. ...'

The alleged resolution was indeed 'one of the most remarkable documents of the war', for it was written in its entirety by Børge Outze. The shipyard men saw it for the first time on the front pages of their illegal newspapers. Nevertheless, they took the hint and went home.

Throughout the strike Outze kept a team of fifteen reporters continuously engaged on gathering news for *Informatión*. The bulletins appeared not once but four times a day and on one day subscribers in Sweden received seven consecutive editions from Copenhagen. From Stockholm the news was transmitted to London, New York, and Moscow and the free world heard and read how the 'invincible' Germans were being defied successfully by the Danish capital's civilian population.

Regular consignments of *Informatión* were sent to Sweden from October 1943, by a variety of routes. They were taken by coasters and tramp steamers travelling legally across the Øresund and by the fishing vessels and power boats of the illegal refugee transport groups. Packages were suspended beneath the railway goods wagons ferried daily from Elsinore to Halsingborg and from Copenhagen to Malmø. Even the twice-daily commercial air service between the two countries was utilised, and *Informatión* was carried by plane, first in a hollowed-out wheel chock and later, in micro-photo copies, in a false sparking plug, from Kastrup to Malmø.

In Malmø the contents of the *Informatión* bulletins were telephoned promptly to the Danish Press Service in Stockholm, who at once sent short versions of the more important and urgent news stories to the semi-official Swedish Press Service for transmission to the Swedish radio, Niels Grunnet's Danish-language radio news service, and all Swedish newspapers. Fuller news bulletins were issued in Swedish translation twice daily to every newspaper in Stockholm and to the leading Swedish provincials.

An English-language bulletin was sent daily to the Reuter, Associated Press and United Press agencies and to the principal foreign correspondents in Stockholm. A bulletin in Russian went to Tass, the official news agency of the USSR.

Most of the news from Denmark was telegraphed round the clock to the BBC's Danish desk, headed by Robert Jørgensen— a service which at its peak provided London with up to three full newspaper columns a day. Daily telegrams also went to ABSIE, the American broadcasting service in Europe. During the later stages of the war the *Información*–Danish Press Service was so efficient that the BBC and Swedish radio constantly 'scooped' the illegal newspapers inside Denmark.

Información's existence was threatened on 14 October 1944 when the Gestapo arrested Børge Outze, and the group was temporarily disrupted. Outze was jailed but allowed to 'escape' on 24 November after persuading his captors that he was willing to spy for them in Moscow. He managed to get to Sweden and until the end of the occupation worked with the Danish Press Service in Stockholm. The Germans' hope that they had seen the last of *Información* was disappointed. Outze's work was taken over by Sigvald Kristensen, a crime reporter on *Social-Demokraten*, and Peter de Hemmer Gudme, foreign editor of *Nationaltidende*. Gudme took a particularly grave risk in accepting the job, for the Gestapo had been hunting him for a long time. He was arrested on 28 November and taken to Shellhus, where, to avoid betraying his comrades under torture, he committed suicide by throwing himself down a stair-well. Kristensen escaped to Sweden and the leadership of *Información* was assumed by Carl Næsh Hendriksen, a *Politiken* crime reporter, Kaj Johansen, Press relations officer of the Danish Agricultural Council, and Eigil Steinmetz, a sub-editor on *Nationaltidende*. Despite every effort to capture them, these three men succeeded in publishing *Información* every weekday until the liberation.

The arrests of Outze and Gudme had taught the trio a valuable lesson. From that time on the strictest security was maintained in every department of production. Editors, reporters, printers, packers and distributors were unknown to each other; the only link between the different sections was by cut-outs. Reports were sent to PO Box 188 at the Copenhagen general post office and to newspaper offices and collected by couriers, who delivered them to cut-outs in the street. They in turn delivered the reports to *Information*'s editorial office, where the edited copy was dictated to Melukka (Herta Jensen). At the end of each day's work the original reports were destroyed, leaving only the manuscript in Melukka's private shorthand, which could not be deciphered by outsiders. A typewriter and a stock of stencil plates were kept in a safe-house near the editorial office and there Melukka typed the day's output of copy, usually running to about ten foolscap pages. The completed stencils were then delivered through a cut-out to the duplicating office. For some time the duplicating was done in a room at the State Serum Institute at 80 Amager Boulevard, with a red light burning outside the door to indicate 'Dangerous experiments in progress'. The vital list of *Information*'s subscribers, for which the Gestapo would have given a king's ransom, was kept in the cholera room behind a row of skulls.

With the Germans constantly on their heels, the group could never remain long in one place. In November 1944, the duplicating office was moved nine times, the editorial office eleven times, and the addressing office five times; yet always *Information* reached subscribers on schedule. Since the production of each daily bulletin involved at least fifty punctually-arranged meetings between couriers and cut-outs in all districts of Copenhagen, this was a remarkable feat. It should be noted to the credit of the civil servants that during the final year of occupation the work was financed entirely by money channelled illegally from government funds. Recognition is due also to the legal newspaper proprietors who, in most cases, kept their reporters on full salary even after they had gone underground to work for *Information* and the other illegal publications.

During 1944 the two hundred and fifty-four illegal newspapers served by *Information* attained a combined circulation of eleven million copies. With greater amounts of cash at their disposal, largely derived from the parallel publication and sale of forbidden books, the bigger groups were able to improve their production methods and often found it possible to issue properly printed, multi-page editions, well illustrated with photographs and drawings and sometimes even with a front page in full colour.

February 1944, saw the establishment of *Frihedsraadets Bladudvalg* (the Freedom Council's Press Committee), on which members of the council met the editors of the leading illegal newspapers in Copenhagen to discuss changes in the political situation and to hammer out a common line on all essential questions. The meetings were beneficial to both sides. The council members were kept in closer touch with the general feeling among the population while the editors gained a fuller knowledge and understanding of the council's programme for Denmark's liberation and post-occupation future. A vital plank in that programme was a guarantee that the Resistance movement would be represented in Denmark's first free government.

The Freedom Council's policy, notably expounded in unsigned articles by politicians like the social democrat H. C. Hansen and the conservative Aksel Møller, was consistently supported by the illegal Press. To ensure the widest possible distribution of newspapers, the Zealand Organisation was formed. Particular attention was given to serving the rural population. Country-folk, though in general sympathetic to the Resistance movement, tended to play a less active part than the town-dwellers and now, with the frequent arms droppings in Jutland and Zealand and the spread of railway sabotage and other operations, their help was urgently needed. Several papers orientated specifically to the agricultural community were founded, among them *Plovfuren* (The Plough Furrow) and *Landboen* (The Country-man), and rural postmen acted as willing distributors.

In the period between 1 January and 5 May 1945, the circulation of illegal newspapers (by that time reduced to two hundred and forty-two, mainly by mergers) rose to 10,131,000 copies—almost as many as the total production during the whole of the preceding year.

Following the capitulation the illegal Press became the mouth-piece of the Allied armed forces, of the Freedom Council and of the local committees. It was largely owing to its influence that the restoration of peace and democracy in Denmark was achieved with quietness and dignity.

6: THE STUDENTS

When the Germans marched into Denmark Arne Sejr was a seventeen-year-old schoolboy living with his parents at Slagelse, in western Zealand. Throughout the first day of occupation he wandered around the town, watching the behaviour of the people in the streets. He was shocked by the friendly way in which many treated the invaders, talking to the soldiers and, even worse, listening to and applauding the German military band which was giving an open-air concert of Danish national music. The front page of the local newspaper carried across several columns an official German statement claiming that the soldiers came as friends and asking for the cooperation of the civil population. There was also a message from King Christian, telling the people to behave like good Danes. Sejr read the King's message several times.

'What is a good Dane?' he asked himself. 'How does a good Dane behave in a situation like this, when his country is occupied by an enemy?'

He tabulated his answers under the heading *Danskerens 10 bud* (Ten Commandments for the Danes) and typed out twenty-five copies:

1. You must not take work in Germany or Norway.
2. You must do worthless work for the Germans.
3. You must work slowly for the Germans.
4. You must destroy important machines and gear.
5. You must destroy everything useful to the Germans.
6. You must delay all transports.
7. You must boycott German and Italian newspapers and films.
8. You must not trade with Nazis.
9. You must deal with traitors as they deserve.
10. You must defend everyone persecuted by the Germans.

JOIN IN THE FIGHT FOR DENMARK'S FREEDOM

He made a list of Slagelse's most influential citizens—the mayor, the bankers, the doctors, the journalists, and the local politicians—and on the evening of 10 April he pushed copies of his commandments through their letter-boxes.

'I felt very illegal,' he said, 'ducking through the dark, deserted streets where the only sounds were made by the hobnailed boots of the German patrols.'

He played truant for a few days. When he returned to school he found no one inclined to work. The scholars were less concerned with their studies than with the exciting things happening outside the classroom; the teachers were bewildered and did not know quite what to do. Sejr quickly discovered that fellow-members of the conservative youth club shared his resentment of the German intrusion. They expressed their indignation by small nuisance actions like putting sugar into the petrol tanks of German cars and army vehicles. More effectively, they wrote propaganda leaflets which they duplicated and mailed to students in high schools throughout the country with the request that the material should be copied and sent still further afield.

At the beginning of 1941 the group got in touch with Nielson, the editor of the town's conservative newspaper, who gave them news items which he dared not print and supplied them with paper for their leaflets and for posters which they pasted after dark on walls and shop windows. When Fritz Clausen's Danish Nazi party held a congress in Slagelse, the group hoisted a skull-and-crossbones flag over the office of the Nazi leader and stuck posters on every available space, paying special attention to shop windows fitted with sun-blinds. When the shopkeepers rolled down their blinds, there were the anti-Nazi posters for all to see.

At the end of the year Sejr and many of his friends left Slagelse to become students at Copenhagen University. That was something for which they had planned. It was difficult to damage the German cause to any extent in a small town like Slagelse, but in the capital, the very heart of the country, they could expand their activities. The group, at first numbering about thirty, acquired a duplicator and began production of a

news-sheet, *Studenternes Efterretningstjeneste* (Students' Information Service). There were good reasons for that choice of
title. It was most important for the public to realise that the
paper was not being produced by a gang of irresponsible boys or
hooligans, and university students then had a very high standing in the community. It was also important to impress readers
with the fact that the news they were being given was accurate
and from reliable sources. The paper appeared irregularly—only
when there was real news—and at first in editions of only five
hundred copies. Production was financed by the students themselves. At that time five hundred sheets of duplicating paper
could be bought for six kroner, not an onerous expense when
shared between thirty people. Later the group were able to
collect money from their families and other older sympathisers,
and that helped considerably. Gradually a print of two thousand
copies was achieved.

The group's first duplicator, which they bought very cheaply,
was a primitive, manually-operated machine but it worked well
enough. On it, in the winter of 1942, Sejr and Ib Christensen
(Knud) printed the group's first book, John Steinbeck's *The
Moon Is Down*. The copy from which they worked was smuggled
from Sweden, with other proscribed books, by a fisherman and
the duplicating was done in the house of Knud's parents, Mr.
and Mrs. Ernst Christensen, on Rødkildevej, Copenhagen. The
first fifty copies were numbered and sold at one hundred kroner;
the remaining four hundred and fifty copies fetched ten kroner
each. The money raised by the sales enabled the group to buy
two new duplicators and to print the newspaper regularly every
fortnight. Other books were published, notably Kaj Munk's
poems and a White Book on the events of 9 April 1940, with
the relevant correspondence between Berlin and the Danish
foreign ministry. These papers were passed to the group secretly,
through channels, by John Christmas Møller, chairman of the
conservative party and a former government minister. Five
thousand copies of the White Book were stored in an underground arms repair depot which was raided by the Gestapo, and
were lost, but the group reprinted and sold a further five thousand copies. In all, during the years of occupation, the group

printed at least fourteen illegal books.

By the end of 1942 *Studenternes Efterretningstjeneste* contacts in Copenhagen had widened to include journalists, printers and booksellers, and technical facilities had improved accordingly. The group operated from 72 Østerbrogade, an apartment block which functioned as a students' hostel. On the night of 10 December 1942, three trunks full of illegal newspapers were in Sejr's apartment, ready for distribution. One was to be taken at once by a student to his lodgings not far away; Sejr had charge of the second, and another student was to take the third to his home next morning. Just before midnight the first man set out but almost immediately ran into a Danish police patrol. They asked him what he was carrying and he said: 'Just some clothes. I'm going on a trip with a friend and I'm on my way to meet him.'

One of the policemen hefted the weighty trunk. 'Clothes?' he repeated sceptically. 'What are you wearing, iron underpants? Get in there!' He backed the student into the entrance to the hostel and told him to open the trunk. As soon as he saw the papers he said: 'You're under arrest. Now where did you get this stuff?' The student stalled but finally admitted that he had got the trunk from the hostel. Leaving one man in charge of the prisoner, the other policemen started to search the building, looking for the duplicator.

When Sejr heard his door bell ring, he knew that trouble was coming. He went into the hall of the apartment and through the glass panes in the old-fashioned door he saw the blue light which the police always carried. He ran back into the sitting-room, grabbed the valise which he kept packed ready for emergencies, and went out of the back door and over the wall into the street. There he met the other student, who had succeeded in breaking away from his guard. They walked about the city for most of the night, seeking a place to hide, and finally found shelter in a house on the island of Amager. From that time onwards Sejr and his friends were always on the run from the police and from the Gestapo.

Now that they had been forced underground they could no longer attend the university and were free to devote all their time to organising printing and production centres and arranging cut-outs between the different sections. By the beginning of 1943 the circulation of the fortnightly newspaper had grown to fifty thousand copies in six-page editions, the country editions always containing about two pages of local news. By August *Studenternes Efterretningstjeneste* were carrying on four separate operations: illegal newspaper production; illegal book publication; a news-gathering service; and, with the help of a group of Danish army officers and non-commissioned officers, a military intelligence service. In addition, a stock of pistols and ammunition had been acquired by raiding military stores with the cooperation of the Danish guards. On one occasion the students got word that there was a large store of rifles, pistols, and revolvers on the top floor of the naval offices at Amager. They raided the building and cleared it, only to find that seventy-five of the weapons lacked firing-pins. To get over that difficulty they set up a repair shop in a rented room on the third floor of 10 Mikkelbryggersgade, with a man from the military technical headquarters at Amager as foreman. They then stole a supply of firing-pins, which were fitted into the unserviceable guns by the technical expert and his helpers.

One evening in September 1943, Sejr and Niels Larsen, a medical student, were returning from a meeting. It was past curfew time, they had neither identity papers nor passes and they were afraid that they might be picked up by the police before they could get back to the place where they were living. They decided to stop overnight in the repair shop on Mikkelbryggersgade. A typewriter and stencils were kept there and so they could spend the evening profitably. They went to the room, locked the door, blacked out the windows, switched on the lights and began typing news for the paper.

At eleven o'clock they heard footsteps on the stairs. They hid the typewriter and stencils, sat down at the table, and dealt out a couple of hands of cards. A few seconds later a knock came at the door. Sejr opened it. Two policemen stood outside. They told him that the black-out was faulty and light was shining into the street. He promised to attend to the matter and they went away. Sejr did not like it; he was sure there was nothing wrong with the black-out. However, neither he nor Larsen was greatly worried. They finished their typing and went to sleep.

Between one and two in the morning they were awakened by more footsteps and the sound of running motors. Larsen looked out of the window without switching on the light. He could see cars in the street and he could hear German voices. Obviously the Gestapo were about to pay a call. The two men barricaded the door with a chest of drawers and tried to get out of the window. Larsen went first and Sejr tried to push him up to the next floor, so that he could smash the window of the room above with the butt of his pistol and pull himself through, with Sejr following. But the Gestapo moved too quickly. Sejr had barely time to climb out of the window and flatten himself on the narrow ledge beside it before they burst into the room. They poured a volley of shots at the window and leaned out, peering into the darkness. They did not see Sejr but they heard Larsen's voice from above. They shouted 'Upstairs!' and Sejr heard them running towards the corridor.

He climbed back into the room, with his pistol in his left hand. He hoped to escape through the rear of the building, but when he opened the door into the corridor a Gestapoman was waiting. They fired together. Sejr was a poor marksman, especially with his left hand, and his gun was a huge Mauser 9mm machine-pistol, made around 1910, with a kick like a mule. His shot missed. Then his gun jammed and he could not fire again. With a bullet through his leg he slammed the door, crouched behind the table and tried to clear the breech of the Mauser. The other Gestapomen had heard the shooting. They rushed into the room and grabbed him. They twisted his arms in a double back-hammer, threw him to the floor and kicked away his pistol. Then they pulled him up, shoved him savagely against the wall and demanded: 'Where's your pal?'

They soon found out. Larsen was sitting on the roof, yelling and shooting every time a German stuck his head through the window. He had tried to escape by climbing over the roofs of the adjoining buildings but the slippery tiles had beaten him and he was trapped. He sat there firing until his ammunition ran out. Then he climbed down, gave himself up, and was taken to Dagmarhus.

Sejr's leg was bleeding profusely, making it impossible for the Gestapomen to judge how serious the wound really was. Sejr pretended to be in agony. He could not use his leg at all, he protested; they would have to carry him down to the street. A Danish police patrol arrived on the scene and a furious argument began. The Danes wanted Sejr handed over to them. The Gestapomen refused. Eventually the policemen accepted the situation. They asked Sejr if there were anything they could do for him. He replied: 'Just pass the word around police head-quarters that J.J. and Niels have been taken.' The students had many good friends among the police and he knew that his comrades would be warned. The group had an agreement that if a man were taken by the Gestapo, he would try to hold out under interrogation for at least twenty-four or, better still, thirty-six hours. If he could not stand the torture any longer, he was free to talk—but the others had up to thirty-six hours in which to get clear.

Sejr was taken to the German hospital on Nyelandsvej. The doctor who examined him said that the injury was merely a flesh wound but Sejr's pretence of unbearable suffering was so convincing that he changed his mind and decided that the bullet must have grazed the bone. He put a dressing on the wound and Sejr was ordered down to the coal cellar. A Gestapo-man tied his wrists with flex and, still moaning and groaning, he hopped across the yard towards the cellar. The Gestapoman accused him of shamming and ordered him to run. Sejr said he could not do it. He hopped on. The Gestapoman started to bash the injured leg with his rubber truncheon and Sejr fainted. After a while he began to regain consciousness. He could see the other man's face and he could see his mouth moving. As if from a long way off he could hear him yelling: 'Get up!' Sejr tried to stand and he was half-dragged, half-carried into the cellar, where, despite the intense cold, he was stripped naked. The Gestapoman unstrapped his wristwatch and gave it to another guard standing by the door.

Sejr lay where they had thrown him, trying to work out a

story to account for the presence of the guns and explosives in the workshop on Mikkelbryggersgade and for his own connection with them. He kept up the groaning because he could see that guards outside the door were watching him constantly, but it was no longer all pretence; he was running a high fever.

Early in the morning two Germans entered the cellar and told him that he was wanted for interrogation. They said he could be questioned where he was or upstairs. Sejr knew that he had no chance of escaping from the cellar, so he said that if the men would help him to walk he would go upstairs. They gave him his trousers, shoes, and a sweater and took him to an office where a Gestapo official was sitting with a stenographer and an interpreter. Although he spoke German fairly well he denied any knowledge of the language and every question had to be translated for him. That gave him more time in which to think out his answers and he gained further leeway by keeping up the pretence of suffering from his wound. He claimed that he was about to faint and begged for the window to be opened. He asked for a cigarette and wasted a few more seconds while he tried to light it with shaking hands. He stood up and sat down restlessly, acting like a man in extremities of fear and misery, but all the time he was sizing up the situation, trying to make out where the Danish section of the hospital was located, where the walls were, and what chance he would have if he jumped out of the window. He played his part so well that the Gestapomen concluded that he was too weak and too cowed to give any trouble. At the end of four hours' interrogation they got up and left the office and a doctor came in to dress the wound. He had with him as assistants two German soldiers who had been wounded or sick and were convalescing. Neither was armed. Only the doctor had a pistol and Sejr thought it improbable that he could use it. The doctor inspected the wound and applied fresh bandages. Then, as Sejr was pulling up his trousers, suddenly all three men turned their backs to him and busied themselves with the trolley which carried the dressings. That was his chance. He leapt through the open window, landing in the yard among a group of convalescent soldiers. Before they could recover from their surprise he was on his way to the

wall separating the Danish and German sections of the hospital.
He ran through the Danish wards unchallenged and out into
Nyelandsvej.

A few yards down the street he stopped a man on a bicycle
and asked for help but the man would not part with his machine.
Sejr limped on, taking side-turnings at random to shake off
possible pursuers.

'When I was certain nobody was following me,' he told me, 'I
ducked into the main entrance of an apartment block and
climbed the stairs to the third floor. The door of one of the
apartments was standing open. I slipped through and closed it
behind me. A woman was coming out of one of the rooms.
When she saw me she screamed. She probably had reason. I
didn't look very pretty. Two big men who were helping the
woman to move some furniture came out and told me to stop
scaring her. I explained the position and said I was leaving
right away. I warned them that if they tipped off the Germans
they would be shot. I went out of the back door of the apartment, down the stairs and into the cellar. From there some steps
took me into a courtyard at the rear of the building and to the
back door of a dairy. I went in and told the woman in the back
room of the shop that I had a heart attack. I said I dared not try
to get home alone and asked if I could sit down and rest for a
while and then phone a friend to fetch me. She gave me permission and I called Erik Bunch-Christensen, who was later to
be killed in an action. I told him not to stop his car outside the
dairy but to drive slowly past, covering the door with a Sten-
gun. While I was telephoning the woman saw the blood on the
chair where I had been sitting and knew that I was on the run.
She was very kind. She gave me a white jacket and bread and
milk to carry, as if I were a dairy roundsman. Erik's car arrived
and I got away safely. As we drove along we passed parties of
Germans who were hunting for me. I was taken to a safe-house
and put straight to bed, for I still had a high fever and my leg
was swollen like a tree-trunk. Later I was taken out of town to
a friend named Oliver Sandberg, a civil engineer who owned
an estate called Christinelund, south of Præstø and close to the
southern part of the Øresund. After a couple of days I was

moved to a big villa on the outskirts of a forest which belonged to him.'

At the beginning of October the villa became a reception centre for Jews who had been helped by the doctors' group to get away from their homes in Copenhagen. The students had organised two escape routes to Sweden—one from Møn, a very small island south of Zealand, and one from the villa in which Sejr was hiding. To get the refugees across the Øresund, Sandberg had bought a fishing-boat and this was manned by two local fishermen and the game-keeper on the estate. Sejr acted as host at the villa until his wound had healed.

On 7 October he returned to Copenhagen and resumed his work with *Studenternes Efterretningstjeneste*; but his luck was running out. Shortly after returning to the capital he was wounded again in a skirmish with a German patrol and on 6 December he was trapped by the Gestapo.

The group received a telephone call from a man who said he had a letter from a student with whom he had been in Horserød concentration camp. They were uneasy about the call but if there were really a letter they had to get it, since the man in the camp might be in a bad way and in need of help. After some discussion it was decided that Sejr and another of the group, Erik, should investigate. One would talk to the fellow who had telephoned while the other would remain in the car and cover him. A shake of the head would indicate that the man was untrustworthy and he would be shot immediately; a nod would indicate all was well. Sejr and Erik drove in a taxi to the appointed rendezvous, the busy Nørrebros Runddel cross-roads. A car was parked at the kerb. Erik went across and spoke to the man at the wheel. Apparently the reply was satisfactory because Erik brought the man back to the cab and followed him into the rear seat beside Sejr. But as the driver started his engine and began to pull away the stranger drew a pistol and ordered him to stop. Realising that they had picked up a Gestapoman Erik and Sejr jumped out of the cab and fled in opposite directions. As Erik ran down the street more Gestapomen sprang out of hiding and opened fire. Erik fell, wounded in both legs, and was captured. The Gestapoman in the taxi turned his fire on Sejr. Four or five bullets drilled Sejr's overcoat and suit and another hit him in the head, yet by a miracle he got away. Following that incident the group concluded that after three close shaves in as many months he was becoming too big a risk; so, on the night of 17 December, he crossed to Sweden and reported to Ebbe Munck in Stockholm.

Many students, including some of the key men, were arrested in April 1944, and Sejr returned briefly to Copenhagen to re-organise the group. He returned again in May to organise the transport of arms and ammunition from Sweden. This would assist the groups in Jutland and Zealand who were receiving weapons from the air because in one load a ship could bring in more guns than one aircraft could carry in ten trips. The *SE* transports were organised on the Danish side by Peter Fyhn, a student, and Ejler Haubirk, a ship's mate, and on the Swedish side by Sejr and Hjalmar Ravnbo. The group used six coasters, ranging in burden from seventy-five to one hundred and eighty tons, which carried cargo from Bornholm to Copenhagen and from Copenhagen to Aarhus and Aalborg. On every voyage the vessels had to pass very close to the Swedish coast, which made it possible for the group to go out in fishing craft, meet them in open water, and put on board the illicit consignments for Denmark. In these ships arms and ammunition could be taken direct into harbour in the centre of Copenhagen. The weapons, packed in crates labelled 'Smoked herrings', were loaded on to trucks. There was always a line of trucks loading up with legitimate cargo from the vessels. The students knew exactly where the guns were placed in the holds and they had only to slip their own vehicle into the line in such a way that it would arrive alongside the hold at the moment when the 'smoked herrings' were ready for discharging. The truck would then drive to a secret storehouse, from which other groups collected the weapons for distribution.

In the autumn of 1944, *SE* transport attempted to capture five customs boats which were lying in Vordingborg harbour, with a view to using them in their work. They succeeded in getting only one of them, *Ørnen*, to start. It was sailed to Sweden by two young seamen, Kim Malthe-Bruun and Knud Rasmussen.

They had better luck with two powerful speedboats, one belonging to Prince Axel and the other to A. C. Bang, the Copenhagen furrier, which they 'captured'—with the owners' blessings—shortly before Christmas and sailed in rough weather from Copenhagen to Malmø. These craft were used for raids from the Swedish coast, for direct runs to Amager and into the harbour on the northern side of Copenhagen, and for runs to Nivaa, high on the north coast of Zealand, where there is dangerous swampland. There, by secret paths through the quagmire, couriers could be landed and refugees taken out to Sweden.

It was with the speedboats that *SE* transport captured the Bornholm steamship, *Carl*, which had done magnificent service to the Resistance on her voyages between Bornholm and Copenhagen. There were always two Gestapomen aboard as controls and usually there were a few other Germans making business or social trips. Shortly before the capitulation the students were told that the captain and crew were to be arrested when they reached Copenhagen and the group were asked to go out in the speedboats and try to take the ship. They got aboard in the Falsterbo channel, under cover of darkness, overpowered the Gestapomen, and took the *Carl* into Malmø harbour.

The speedboats, with exhausts muffled, were also used to transport Danish leaders and officers of the Allied forces from Sweden to Amager for consultations with Resistance groups in Copenhagen. On the eve of the capitulation a party of international newspaper correspondents were taken from Malmø to Amager, so that they could write eyewitness stories of the liberation, and their reports were carried back to Sweden by the same route.

Just before the liberation twenty-five mobile hospital units were given to the Resistance movement by the Swedish ministry of health. Ten of these were transported to Denmark in good time by the students; the remaining fifteen arrived after 5 May.

The magnificent work of *Studenternes Efterretningstjeneste* was not achieved without great cost. At least five men were killed in action, ten were executed, and others were murdered in cold blood. Eleven died in German concentration camps and three others died shortly after release and repatriation.

The first casualties, in 1943, were Arne Sejr's eighteen-year-old brother, Jørgen; Jacob Thalmay, 39, a Polish-born optician; and Cato Bakman, 25, a medical student. Thalmay, arrested on 15 November, died in Melk-Donau concentration camp on 9 March 1945. Jørgen Sejr, taken on 11 December, survived imprisonment in Denmark and seven months in Neuengamme concentration camp, but, after repatriation by the Red Cross, died at Katrineholm in Sweden on 28 April 1945, of dysentery and tuberculosis. Cato Bakman was arrested in October, while helping to get a party of Jews to Sweden. He was taken to Dagmarhus but released after one night of interrogation. Shortly afterwards, during a skirmish between a German patrol and Resistance men, one of the latter was wounded and taken to the Rigshospital. It was known that the Gestapo were demanding that he should be handed over to them and Holger Larsen and Bakman were asked to get him to Bispebjerg Hospital, where he would be safer. Bakman went to Dr. Køster's apartment to make the necessary arrangements but found a party of Gestapo-men already in possession. Unluckily, among them were the men who had arrested him. They took off his shoes and began to question him. He tried to escape by jumping out of a window but was badly injured, partly by the fall and partly by the volley of pistol shots fired at him from the window. He died a few hours later in hospital.

On 6 March 1944, a meeting of the students' leaders was called at an apartment of Haveselskabetsvej. Among those ordered to attend were Erik Bunch-Christensen, a theological student, and Troels Bredkjær, a medical undergraduate. When Bunch-Christensen arrived he found the apartment full of Germans and Bredkjær under arrest. He slammed the door of the apartment and escaped on a bicycle which he found in the street. He knew that many papers of vital importance to the organisation were hidden in an apartment on Tagensvej. He went there and got them but was taken by a German patrol as he was pedalling away from the building. The student's situation was desperate. He was surrounded by five armed men, but somehow he had to get away. If the papers he was carrying fell into the hands of the Gestapo, it would mean mass arrests throughout the whole of the Resistance movement. He threw himself against his captors, broke free and bolted. The Germans drew their pistols and fired. One bullet hit him in the lung and another in the shoulder but he ran on. At last he found a safe-house and gave the papers to the occupier, who immediately burned them. Bunch-Christensen collapsed and shortly afterwards he was found by the Gestapomen. He underwent an operation at the German hospital on Nyelandsvej, where he lay without further attention until on 12 March he died from his wounds and resultant pneumonia. Bredkjær was deported to Germany and died in Porta concentration camp on 19 February 1945.

Christian Fries, leader of the students' military group, was arrested on 2 April 1944, and Ebbe Holmboe, an art student, eleven days later. Both died in German concentration camps before the year was out. In June Elkan Bierberg, a publisher, Arne Jørgensen and Birge Mouritsen, clerks, and Kjeld Frederiksen, a law student, were taken. They, too, died in concentration camps a few months after deportation.

Romeo Jacobsen, a furrier, was arrested on 7 July and died in Neuengamme six months later. On 11 September August Sponholtz was murdered by a gang of German terrorists in his barber shop in Copenhagen. Svend Rasch, a shipping clerk, was shot down by another murder gang outside his home on 29 October. Niels Laub, a student, arrested in the same month, died in Hamburg concentration camp on 28 March 1945.

On 20 October Ejler Haubirk, organiser in Copenhagen of the arms-smuggling operation, went to the Odin Restaurant in the Trianglen district to meet another *SE* leader. There he was recognised by the notorious *stikker*, Bothildsen-Nielsen, who immediately gave the alarm. Haubirk tried to escape but was shot down and killed outside the restaurant.

Hakon Hygom, a student of architecture, was arrested in November and died in Dessauer Ufer concentration camp five months later.

Between 5 and 19 December, in a determined drive against the group, the Gestapo captured Kim Malthe-Bruun, Jørgen Winther, a head clerk, and the students Erik Crone, Axel Christensen, and Peter Fyhn. Erik Crone was shot on 27

February 1945, at Ryvangen, a stretch of parkland on the outskirts of Copenhagen which was the official place of execution.
Kim Malthe-Bruun, Peter Fyhn, and Jørgen Winther died there
together on 6 April 1945. Count Ludvig Reventlow, also an
outstanding member of *SE* transport group, was executed with
them. Axel Christensen survived Dachau and Neuengamme but
died in a Copenhagen hospital on 28 May 1945.

Knud Rasmussen, a merchant seaman, was arrested on
22 February 1945. As a result of brutal treatment in Vestre
Fængsel he contracted tuberculosis and died in hospital on
4 July the same year.

Helge Mogensen, a solicitor's clerk, was shot down by the
Gestapo in Copenhagen's free port on 2 May and Erik Andersen,
a law student, died on the day of liberation. On 5 May he was
driving in his van, with three other Resistance men, along the
highway from Roskilde to Sorø. At Albertikrydset crossing they
ran into a roadblock manned by members of the newly-mobilised
underground army. The latter, nervous and inexperienced, mistook them for Hipos and opened fire. Andersen and two of his
companions were killed outright. The fourth man died a few
hours later in hospital.

It is a tragic and fearful record. Today some Danes ask
themselves to what real purpose these brave men sacrificed
their lives. Their answer lies in a letter which Kim Malthe-Bruun,
21 years old, wrote to his mother on the day before he was
executed:

I wandered along the path which I have never regretted. I
have never gone back on anything my heart told me to do,
and now I think I can see the connection. I am not very old
and I ought not to die, and yet it seems so natural and simple
to me. At first the abruptness of it makes one a little apprehensive. Time is so short and there is so much to think about.
It is hard to explain but I feel so absolutely calm. I so much
wanted to have been a Socrates—but I had no audience. I feel
the same calmness that he did and I do want you to understand that fully.

I want you to realise that there is nothing that wrings my

heart. I am possessed of something which lives and burns in me, a love, an inspiration—name it as you wish—but something which I was never able to express. Now, as I am going to die, I wonder if I have been able to ignite a small flame in someone, a flame which will outlive me, and yet I am calm in the knowledge that nature is rich—no one notices if a few shoots are trampled underfoot and die as a result. Why should I despair, when I realise there is so much richness, which still lives in spite of everything.

Finally—the children: they have been so near to me in my thoughts recently and I had so much looked forward to seeing them and to living together with them a little again. My heart has beaten with pleasure at the thought of them and my hope is that they grow up as men that see more than just the road in front of them. My hope is that their minds thrive—and never under narrow-minded or prejudiced influence. Give my love to both of them, my godson and his brother.

I can see what way it is going in our country, but remember —and I want you all to remember—that you must not dream yourselves back to the times before the war, but the dream for you all, young and old, must be to create an ideal of human decency, and not a narrow-minded and prejudiced one. That is the great gift our country hungers for, something every little peasant boy can look forward to, and with pleasure feel he is a part of—something he can work and fight for.

Finally there is she, who is mine. Make her see that the stars still twinkle and that I was only a milestone. Help her to go on. She *can* be very happy!

7: EXODUS

If the Danish government's original policy of cooperation with the German authorities had no other virtue, it had at least protected the Jews in Denmark from the miseries suffered by their co-religionists in other occupied territories. The Danish ministers would never agree to any form of 'special' anti-Jewish legislation and as long as the Germans wanted their cooperation a Jewish persecution was unthinkable; but with the rejection of the Berlin ultimatum of 28 August 1943, and the resignation of the government, that protection was lost. Though Dr. Werner Best, the German plenipotentiary, repeatedly denied that action against the Jews was contemplated, two Gestapo raids within fourteen days on the Copenhagen synagogue's archives hardly inspired confidence in his protestations, and anxiety mounted steadily.

Curiously, since he had never evinced marked anti-semitic tendencies, it was Best who, on 8 September, triggered the explosion with a telegram to Ribbentrop, asking for a decision on the Jewish question in Denmark and emphasising that action against the Jews would create a host of constitutional and political problems for the occupying power. It is difficult to understand what he hoped to achieve by this message and he appears to have had second thoughts about it almost immediately. He expressed his doubts to G. F. Duckwitz, the shipping expert at the German legation, who made no secret of his dislike for the Nazi ideology. Duckwitz protested violently that the telegram should never have been sent and, with Best's agreement, went to Berlin to try to intercept it. He was too late. The telegram had already reached Hitler and on 18 September the order for the deportation of the Jews was issued.

It was received with something less than enthusiasm by many of the German officials in Denmark, among them Dr. Rudolf Mildner, the newly-appointed security police chief in Copenhagen, who had no desire to begin his activities with an action against the Jews. Unprepared for such a big operation and lacking the staff to carry it through, he appealed to the Gestapo supremo, Himmler, to have the order rescinded. His plea failed but his 'weakness' was noted. A few months later he was replaced by the ruthless Otto Bovensiepen.

Duckwitz went to Stockholm to warn the Swedish government of the impending tragedy and to seek their aid, but his mission had little practical effect and by 28 September he had to admit that he could do no more. As by that time he knew the date when the round-up of the Jews was to begin, he passed on this information to two Danish social democrat politicians, Hans Hedtoft and H. C. Hansen. They in turn gave the news to the head of the Jewish community, the high court advocate C. B. Henriques, so that he could warn his people. On 29 September, the eve of the Jewish new year, the congregations at the early morning services were told of the danger facing them, and urged to seek refuge at once with Christian friends. So, thanks to the selfless humanitarianism of the German official Duckwitz and the speed with which his warning was transmitted, the Gestapo found only a few Jews at home when, on the evening of 1 October, the first raids took place. Some were caught because they would not leave their homes. They just would not believe that harm could come to them in Denmark. The King would not permit it.

On 2 October the following official German announcement was carried by all Danish newspapers:

After the Jews, who, with their anti-German agitation and their moral and material support of acts of terrorism and sabotage, which to a high degree have caused a deterioration of the situation in Denmark, have been segregated from public life and have been prevented by German measures from further poisoning the atmosphere, then—fulfilling a wish which is felt by a widening circle of the Danish population— in the next few days the interned Danish soldiers will be set free as quickly as is technically possible.

This was a blatant attempt at a deal. There had been strong rumours that the Danish forces interned on 29 August were to be sent to prison camps in Germany. The Nazis hoped that by releasing the soldiers they would create goodwill among the Danes, so that there would be no real opposition to the internment and deportation of the Jews. As so often before and afterwards, they miscalculated hopelessly. The drive against the Jews brought home to the Danish people more forcibly than any amount of printed or verbal propaganda what they could expect if the Germans won the war; and further, it precipitated the unification of the growing Resistance movement. Until that time the military intelligence service, the parachutists, the arms reception committees, the saboteurs and the illegal Press groups had worked more or less independently. Now the necessity of getting some seven thousand men, women, and children out of the country in the shortest possible time meant that their efforts must be co-ordinated and systematised; and now, as never before, they could rely on the active backing of a thoroughly aroused population.

Overnight, spontaneously, a gigantic rescue organisation was created. It had no chief. Nobody was subordinate. Each man worked independently on his own problems. Everybody worked under responsibility towards his friends. If one man fell, another took his place and the organisation remained intact. Everybody helped: schools, hospitals, doctors, nurses, priests, industrial firms, port authorities, public transport concerns, shipowners and charterers, captains and chief officers, coastal police, fishermen, and harbour workers. They helped by housing, hiding, and transporting single fugitives and large parties; by putting men and materials at the disposal of the Resistance groups, and by finding fishing boats, coasters and embarkation points for the fleeing Jews. Institutions, firms, and private citizens provided cash, oil, petrol, paraffin, gas-generator wood fuel, cigarettes, and beer. Private homes were turned into safe-houses which became refuges for Jews and helpers when the Gestapo hunt was up. It was a great fellowship, inspired by a common rage against the brutal treatment of a helpless minority—and in justice it must be recorded that not a few Germans who disapproved of Gestapo terrorism helped if and when they could, if only by a certain 'blindness' at the right moment.

Throughout October and into November thousands of Jews were carried to safety in Sweden from Copenhagen and from many places along the Danish coast. Since fishing vessels were the most usual means of transport, most of the traffic was based on small fishing hamlets but fugitives also escaped, hidden in the holds of coasters, from the harbours of the larger towns. The work was always difficult and dangerous. Sometimes it ended in tragedy. On 2 November *Studenternes Efterretningstjeneste* reported:

A young Dane has lost his life in attempting to help Jews to get out of the country. The man in question is a twenty-year-old engineering student, Claus Heilesen, who on 9 October helped to ferry Jews out of Taabæk harbour. Heilesen was aboard a fishing-boat which was just about to sail when a German patrol boat suddenly appeared. The fishing-boat was fired at. The Germans continued to shoot even after the fishing-boat's engine had been damaged and it was attempting to return to the pier, and Heilesen was hit in the temple by two bullets. The fishermen and the Jews were arrested.

Numerous unpleasant minor incidents are occurring in these hectic days in harbour towns all along the coast. In Gilleleje, for instance, 163 Jews and their helpers sought refuge in the parish hall and in the church loft to escape the German patrols. The Gestapo arrived, however, guided by three Danish informers. For a long time the fugitives refused to let the Germans in, but when a number of the Jews present could no longer stand the nervous strain they gave in to these people after several hours and opened the doors. The helpers were taken into custody but are now free again after several days' detention in Vestre Fængsel.

On Sunday morning a trolley bus collided with a German lorry packed with Jews. An elderly Jewish woman was badly injured. Her daughter begged to go with her to the hospital but she was not allowed to do so.

Early on the morning of 13 October, 170 Jews who had been interned in Horserød were taken to Elsinore and from there sent by train to Germany via Gedser.

Of the incident at Gilleleje, a small coastal town in North Zealand, the rector, Pastor Kjeldgaard Jensen, recorded in the parish register: 'October 5 was a terrible day for the whole town of Gilleleje. On that day the occupying power carried out a raid here in the town to capture Jews. Further raids were made in the days which followed and many Jews, known and un-known (at least 1,200–1,300), were gathered here in the town in private homes and, unfortunately, also in the church loft and in the parish hall. These premises were just those raided by the Gestapo, the German police. Before this, the undersigned rector had repeatedly been up to the loft to comfort and give assistance in this desperate situation. I suppose 100 Jews were taken to Horserød internment camp, from which they have since been taken away—to what destination? Happily, however, the great majority of the total mentioned above succeeded in reaching Swedish harbours. The people of Gilleleje behaved admirably in this affair and showed their Danish spirit. It should be noted that the raids only succeeded at all with the aid of informers. May God have mercy on His old and stubborn people and keep them from harm.'

On some of the first trips the Danish fishing vessels sailed right across the Øresund and landed their passengers on the Swedish shore, but later, when things were better organised, they were met in Swedish waters by Swedish ships or small boats which could row the fugitives the last part of the way. Once safely ashore the Jews were taken to reception centres where they were provided with clothing and everyday necessities and either assigned at once to work for which they were qualified or taken to a camp where they could adapt themselves to their new circumstances. The Swedish government and private com-mittees helped to ensure that none of the refugees suffered want.

Typical of the Resistance men engaged in the great escape operation was Christian Algreen-Petersen (cover-name Christian), the teenage son of a Copenhagen doctor. Christian was doing his national service when the Germans rounded up and disarmed the Danish army in August 1943. After internment at Nyborg and Kerteminde, on Funen, he was released on 13 October and

Above: Arne Sejr and Ib Mogens Bech Christensen (Knud), leader of the 1944 Group

Pastor Harald Sandbæk, photographed after his escape from Gestapo headquarters in Aarhus University following the R.A.F. raid, 31 October, 1944

G. F. Duckwitz, the German legation official who warned the Danes of the impending 'Purge' of the Jews

Below: A party of Jews escape across the Øresund to Sweden in a little rowing boat

Tuborg Harbourmaster Johannes Johannesen standing beside the Resistance Memorial which marks the spot in the harbour from which thousands
of Danes escaped to Sweden

Kim Malthe-Bruun

Poul Erik Krogshøj Hansen (Dahlin)

Knud Petersen (Ole)

The Elsinore Boys: All executed at Ryvangen, 12 April, 1945. At the last Bopa meeting they attended before their arrest, Lasse said: 'God grant that we shall soon be living like normal people and not like hunted animals.'

Jørgen Erik Skov Larsen (Lasse)

Henning Wieland (William)

allowed to go home. Immediately he joined his parents in the work of the doctors' group.

'Father and mother worked with a team of young students, among them Peter and Ole Fyhn and my cousin Karl Møller,' he said. 'My job at first was to deliver messages. The big rush was over. In the beginning the Jews had been cramming our apartment, where my mother took their names and asked how much money they had. That was important. Some of the Jews were rich but many had only a few hundred kroner and some had no money at all. At that time we had to pay the fishermen one thousand kroner (about £55) a head for passengers and we could manage only by getting the richer fugitives to pay for the poorer. The high charges were largely the Jews' own fault. In the first panic frantic people had rushed to the fishermen and offered them huge sums for an illegal passage. And to be fair, the fishermen had to save money to buy new boats if their old ones were confiscated by the Gestapo.

'Gradually we got system into the business. Money poured in. We had only to contact the Medical Association and say how much we needed. It was always there. We usually shipped ten Jews per boat at ten thousand kroner a time. When several boats sailed simultaneously it cost us plenty. Our cars cost money, too. Black market petrol was expensive and taxis were almost impossible to get. We had to be very careful about the cars and kept a list of safe drivers.

'One evening Peter came home and told us: "We put a man on ice today." He'd been out with Jews all day, keeping the same taxi because he couldn't be sure of getting another. While he was at Bispebjerg Hospital fetching a new load, another cab driver had told him his driver was a Danish Nazi. Peter got some of the hospital staff to help. They dragged the Nazi into the hospital refrigerator and left him there for twenty-four hours with the corpses. Then they detained him for a further day to see his health had not suffered. When they finally let him go, he swore he would never contact the Germans again. He had had enough!'

While the doctors and students did the outside work, Christian's mother sat at home by the telephone.

'That was tricky, too,' Christian recalled. 'She never knew whether a patient or a fugitive was ringing. Sometimes the caller said a man had to go to hospital. Was it a genuine patient or a Jew who had to be helped to Sweden? Words like "Jew" or "saboteur" were never used over the phone. We said "a box of fruit", "a bad box of fruit", "a crate of herrings", "cigarettes", or something like that. It was easy enough when the regulars rang but there were difficulties if new people rang before they had got used to our code. In the beginning so many Jews turned up at the house that we had long waiting lists. The telephone and the door bell rang all the time.'

By mid-October only one or two boats a day were necessary. When a new party was ready somebody went to a little café on Gammel Strand and asked for Slette-Hans, one of the fishermen. Price, time, and place of departure were then agreed. Amazingly, the canals in the heart of Copenhagen were regular embarking points, even in broad daylight, but later Islands Brygge and Fiskerihavnen, in the south-west of the city, were used almost exclusively. At first there were sailings all day; but as the traffic slowed, dusk became the favoured time.

'We had to promise the fishermen that there would be no saboteurs among our passengers,' Christian said. 'When we had to get a saboteur to safety we impressed on him that he would be a Jew or half-Jew. One day a Negro turned up. He had been in Horserød camp and had escaped. We decided that he'd have to be a quarter-Jew and stressed that he must stick to that story. He should have been got away under cover of darkness but the only available ship was to sail in the afternoon. He would have to take his chances.

'The Negro went to the rendezvous, but instead of getting into the waiting car he stood in the middle of the road where every passer-by could see him. And black men at that time were as scarce in Denmark as roses in December! We hustled him into the car and drove off towards Fiskerihavnen. On Vesterbrogade, Copenhagen's main street, we met a column of German soldiers. When the Negro saw them he rolled down the window, pushed out his black face, and yelled: "There they go, the swine!" We hauled him out of sight just in time.

'Slette-Hans had never met a Negro. When he saw this one he asked, horrified: "What sort of creature is this?"

' "He's a quarter-Jew, married to a Jewess," I said. "And he's got to get to Sweden in a hurry." I don't know whether Slette-Hans believed me but he took him aboard and got him away with the rest of the load.'

The Nordisk Bookshop on the fashionable Kongens Nytorv was a main collecting point for Jews. It was also the headquarters of the major sabotage group, Holger Danske, then led by the brothers Jørgen and Mogens Staffeldt and Jens Lillelund. Jørgen Staffeldt applied to the doctors' group for a passage for a woman saboteur named Klinting. This woman had worked so well for her German employers that she soon won promotion; but when she put a match to the plans of some new Luftwaffe aircraft she was thrown into Vestre Fængsel. She feigned serious illness. The Germans took no notice. So then she shammed madness—shrieking, biting, and scratching the faces of the guards. That was too much. She was transferred to hospital. The Resistance got her out of there the day before she was to be shipped to Germany.

'Now we had to get her away, together with her fiancé, who was also a saboteur,' said Christian. 'In the same party we had Mrs. Ørum, the wife of a Danish officer who had gone to Sweden a few days earlier. I contacted Slette-Hans and told him we had to ship sixteen passengers that afternoon but that we could pay only five hundred kroner per person. I said I knew another fisherman who would do the job at that price. Slette-Hans retorted: "Let him!"

'I hung around the café until I found a fisherman who would cooperate and who could be trusted. I asked him to have his boat at the Islands Brygge rowing club at exactly 5 p.m. Our first car would be there on the dot, then three more at two-minute intervals. We were all there on time but there was no sign of the boat. In order not to create suspicion I sent all but my own car away. The minutes crawled by. Still no boat arrived. And the Gestapo might come down on us at any second.'

The party were in a dangerous situation. Christian had to act quickly. He went into the rowing club and bluntly explained the situation to the members. To his relief they agreed to hide the fugitives in the boathouse. One of the oarsmen, a young policeman, took his stand in the road and halted and checked all traffic until the party was under cover.

At 6 o'clock Christian decided to go back to the café and try to find another fisherman or, in the last event, get hold of Slette-Hans and pay him his seven hundred kroner. The car was waiting up the road. He got in and drove back to the café. Slette-Hans would not back down on his price. He would do the job for seven hundred kroner a head but first he would have to empty his boat of fish, and that would take an hour. With that Christian had to be content. He went back to the boathouse.

'Suddenly a car stopped outside,' he said. 'A form loomed out of the darkness. We feared the worst. But it was only Slette-Hans. He said he dared not sail over to us; instead, he had arranged with the Swedish guard to take the party on board the Malmø ferry. At 4 a.m. he would run his fishing boat alongside and trans-ship the fugitives.

'Once more we packed our passengers into cars which Ole Fyhn got from the city. Most of the party went direct to the Swedish ferry but we found a safe-house in Carl Langsvej for the saboteurs and Mrs. Ørum. We arranged to pick them up at half past three.'

Now Christian and his father had to find beds for themselves. They had not been able to use their own home for some time. The Gestapo kept a constant watch on the house. The Missions Hotel in Colbjørnsensgade, off Vesterbrogade, had vacant rooms. The two men told the manageress, Mrs. Jørgensen, that they were uncle and nephew and asked to be called at 3 a.m.

'She didn't believe our story,' said Christian, 'but she was a good Dane and knew we needed help. She gave us a room without asking questions. We used the Missions Hotel on many occasions after that, even when the Gestapo had taken over one of the floors. It is often safest to sleep in the lion's den. Mrs. Jørgensen called us that morning dead on time. We fetched our three VIPs from Carl Langsvej and drove to the Malmø ferry.

'Slette-Hans kept his word. His fishing-boat drew along-side on the stroke of 4, picked up our party, and in due course landed them in Sweden.'

One of the most colourful pioneers of the escape routes was Johannes Johannesen, the harbour master at the Tuborg Brewery in Hellerup, Copenhagen. Short, round-paunched, with thinning brown hair and grey eyes which twinkled behind shell-rimmed spectacles, he looked like Mr. Pickwick in mari-time uniform. But looks can be deceptive. Despite his jovial, easy-going manner the former deep-sea skipper could be very tough indeed.

On the morning of 9 April 1940, Johannesen was about his normal business when a military car, embellished with Nazi markings, swept on to the quayside. Three men stepped out of the vehicle, two German officers and an NCO who carried a camera. The senior officer asked Johannesen: 'Have you stabling here for horses?'

'I don't know,' the harbour master replied. 'My business is with ships.'

'Very well,' said the officer. 'But at least you know where the beer is kept. Bring some.'

'I'll send for some. It needs an order from the stores.'

Bottles were brought and opened by a scowling storeman. The officer handed a glass of beer to Johannesen and another to the customs officer, who had also been summoned. 'Now you will line up with us and raise your glasses,' he said. 'We shall take a picture showing how gladly you Danes welcome your German protectors.'

'Like hell!' Johannesen said. 'We choose our own drinking company.'

The German kept his temper. The high command had laid down that the Danish population were to be treated correctly. He said quietly: 'It is an order. And it is better to drink than to be shot.'

'All right, take your picture,' the harbour master said. 'But don't expect us to smile.'

The camera clicked. The Germans got into their car and drove away. Johannes Johannesen resumed his interrupted round thoughtfully. The officer's civility did not fool him. Sooner or later the mailed fist would show, and against that day it would be well to be prepared. Johannesen began pondering how people could be smuggled quickly out of Denmark when the need arose. The Germans had posted two soldiers as harbour guards. His first move was to follow them unobtrusively on their patrols, making an exact time-table of their movements.

Under the new administration Tuborg Harbour proved to be on the border between two German military districts and the authorities never made up their minds exactly who was supposed to look after the area; hence inspections were never as thorough as they might have been. The ships using the harbour were coasters, mostly motor-vessels of 100–150 tons, taking coke from the gasworks behind the brewery to Jutland and returning with cargoes of empty beer bottles. Carefully, over many beers, Johannesen sounded out their skippers, listening to their views on the new German 'masters', estimating their courage and their ability to keep a shut mouth. Gradually he built a team of good, loyal seamen who would be prepared to co-operate in running an escape operation.

Next, the routes had to be plotted. Ships carrying fugitives could not sail direct from Tuborg Harbour to neutral Sweden. Every ship on that run was already being searched thoroughly by German patrols. The logical procedure would be to set course ostensibly for Jutland and then divert to the Swedish island of Hven in the middle of the Øresund or to some other place off the Swedish western or southern coast. For more than two years Johannesen worked on his plans, discussing them with nobody but the chosen skippers. And at last the emergency he had so long anticipated came.

One evening early in October 1943, Johannesen received a visit from a director of the brewery. Was it possible to contact a skipper who might ship a party of people to Sweden, with no questions asked?

'I don't know,' said the harbour master cautiously. 'I'll see what I can do. Have your people ready, just in case....'

Next day, in broad daylight, the Jews arrived by taxi and private car. With them was a Danish student wanted by the

Gestapo for sabotage. They were hurried to Johannesen's office on the quay and hidden there for half an hour; then, one by one, while the German guards were out of sight, they were taken aboard a coaster and stowed in the after-peak.

Among the Jews were an elderly, stateless couple who for years had roamed Europe before finding sanctuary in Denmark. Now once again they were fugitives, and the grey-haired woman's loud wailing threatened to bring the sentries down on the party. But it was the saboteur who gave Johannesen his worst moment. No sooner was he safely below than he produced a letter which he wanted mailed to his girl friend. Johannesen opened it. It not only gave details of the sailing; it even gave the name of the vessel. The harbour master's comments on the youngster's stupidity almost blistered the paintwork.

The coaster sailed—officially on its normal run to Jutland. Johannesen freely confesses that for him and for his wife the two days which followed were the most worrying time of their lives; but when after forty-eight hours no gun-butts hammered on their front door they concluded that the party had got to Sweden safely.

A week passed. Then another Tuborg executive came down to the office on the quay. Another party of Jews was ready for shipment. For the first time Johannesen realised that his activities were no longer a secret and that the brewery staff were behind him to a man. Within the following two months some sixty Jewish families had been sent from Tuborg Harbour across the Øresund. Among those who reached Sweden by the Tuborg route was the wife of Frode Jakobsen, founder of the important *Ringen* organisation and a member of the Freedom Council.

Thanks to the efforts of the illegal transport groups—chief among them *Dansk-svensk Flygtningetjeneste*, *Speditøren*, *Dansk hjælpetjeneste*, *Studenternes Efterretningstjeneste* and *Lise*—by the end of 1943 almost the whole of Denmark's Jewish population had found refuge in Sweden. The luckless 474 who had been captured by the Gestapo were deported to Theresienstadt in Czechoslovakia, a dismal town in which only a few houses had piped water. The original population had been evacuated in 1942, when the place was designated as an assembly centre for Jews. In the spring of 1943 more than sixty thousand Jews were crammed into houses which had previously been occupied by five thousand people, but a typhoid epidemic rapidly thinned their ranks, so that by October, when the Danish Jews arrived, there were only forty-three thousand inhabitants. The town, surrounded with barbed-wire barricades and guarded by Czech police, was administered internally by a German-appointed 'Jewish elder' and a council of twenty to thirty elders. The few Nazi SS-men had contact only with the Jewish leaders. There was a constabulary of about two hundred Jews aged from forty-five to fifty-five, the so-called 'Ghetto Watch'. Curfew was in force between 8 p.m. and 6 a.m. (later between 9 p.m. and 5.30 a.m.) and smoking was strictly forbidden. It was also forbidden to possess jewellery, precious metals, and money, but this was a meaningless regulation since the Jews had been stripped of all they owned before their arrival in the town.

In Theresienstadt the Danes were forced to wear the Star of David on their clothing, and Chief Rabbi M. Friediger has recorded: 'The first time I fastened that yellow patch to my chest it burned through my clothes, burned deep into my heart, and I felt a stinging pain as if my heart would break. It was the evil purpose expressed by the yellow patch which caused the pain. This was how it had been in the Middles Ages also—the Jews were to be disgraced, ostracised, segregated from their surroundings and regarded as carriers of disease, pariahs to be avoided. That was why they had to wear pointed hats or the yellow patch on their clothes. This was also the reason for the yellow patch we now had to put on.'

From the summer of 1944 many thousands of Jews were transported from Theresienstadt to the extermination camp at Auschwitz but the Danes were spared this fate. They were, indeed, better treated than the Jews of other nationalities and from March 1944, they received Red Cross parcels from Denmark which not only supplemented their diet but enabled them to buy certain privileges from their guards. Nevertheless, fifty-three died from their privations before, in April 1945, the Danish Jews were repatriated by the Red Cross to Sweden.

8: THE TRANSPORTERS

It was inevitable that Henrik Kraft, advertising manager of the Tuborg Brewery, should be drawn into illegal activities since his wide circle of friends in Copenhagen included Børge Outze, Kaj Johansen, Svend Truelsen, Arne Sejr, Leif B. Hendil, the editor of *Ekstrabladet*, and others deeply involved in Resistance work. He was particularly friendly with Outze, Johansen and Truelsen, with whom he met regularly to exchange news of what was happening around the country. Since the beginning of the occupation he had been preparing uncensored news reports for his chairman, Herbert Jerichow, and the Tuborg board, and these gradually gained a wider, clandestine circulation. After *Die Frie Danske, Studenternes Efterretningstjeneste* and the other illegal newspapers got into their stride, the Tuborg advertising department often helped with fresh supplies when duplicators and stocks of paper had been seized by the Germans.

On the evening of 29 August 1943, Kraft heard from one of his newspaper contacts that the Germans intended immediately to arrest several hundred well-known Danes. He telephoned Einar Dessau, a Tuborg director whose name had been mentioned, to warn him not to stay at home but Dessau refused to believe that he was in danger. He was taken that night.

Next morning he pointed out to his captors that Danes were used to starting their day with a glass of beer and asked permission to get some for the prisoners. Surprisingly, the Germans agreed. They said that if he promised to speak in German he could telephone from their office. Dessau rang a colleague at the brewery. 'I've been arrested,' he said. 'A number of us are being held at the Algades School. I'd like you and Henrik Kraft to bring ten cases of beer here as soon as possible.'

The two men took the beer to the school. Their taxi was allowed only as far as the main entrance, where some of the prisoners were ordered to unload the crates and carry them into the building. Suddenly a paper was pushed into Kraft's hand. It was from Einar Dessau and it contained a list of all those who had been arrested. It was an impressive roster—leading politicians and ex-ministers, stars of the Royal Theatre, youth leaders, and others, all popular and well known. As soon as he could get away from the school Kraft went straight to the foreign ministry. 'Do you know where these people are?' he asked. Until he produced his list the officials had not known exactly how many had been taken or where they were being held. Kraft and his wife spent the rest of the day telephoning the families of the prisoners, assuring them that the men were being well treated, and letting them know that they could take such necessities as pyjamas and toilet articles to the school. Through this incident he made new friends who were to prove valuable later on.

When, in October, the Germans began their abortive purge, some of Kraft's Jewish friends appealed to him for help. He knew of skipper Johannesen's activities at Tuborg Harbour but for security reasons he was reluctant to seek assistance in that quarter. However, he had heard that Leif Hendil was also running an escape route. He went to see him at the *Ekstrabladet* office and asked: 'Could you help me to get some people out of the country?'

'With pleasure,' the editor replied. 'Send them along.'

Hendil's transport operations had started on 29 August when he organised the escape of his wife's hairdresser and her husband, the communist Mogens Klitgaard, together with a Jewish merchant, Jørgen Polack, and a Danish army officer. The party was taken by rowing-boat from Snekkersten to the island of Hven and thence trans-shipped to the Swedish mainland. After that there had been sailings every night.

Kraft's friends got away safely and a few days later he asked Hendil whether he could help with another party of four or five people. The editor shook his head doubtfully. 'It will be pretty rough tonight,' he said. 'I have enough refugees at Snekkersten to fill five fishing-boats and I shall be working there single-handed. It's going to be very difficult.'

'Well, if it will help, I can come with you,' Kraft said. 'I've been warned not to go home tonight. Arne Sejr has been arrested and his friends are very much afraid that he may have my name in his notebook. We had an appointment for tomorrow.'

That evening he met Hendil at Snekkersten, a fishing village on the coast between Copenhagen and Elsinore. A local policeman helped to keep the road clear while the parties of refugees were being made up and taken to the fishing-boats in which they would cross the Øresund. After a couple of parties had been got away the two friends were sitting in the old inn, relaxing over a beer, when the door opened and the policeman came in.

'Hendil and Kraft, out!' he ordered. 'Disappear immediately. The Gestapo are coming. Get your papers and gear out of here. I'll take care of the refugees.'

They hurried out and started walking down the Strandvej, Hendil pushing a bicycle. He had a summer house at Espergærde, near Elsinore, where he stayed while engaged in illegal work, but he told Kraft: 'I don't think it would be wise for you to sleep at my house. Do you know any people around here with whom you could stay?'

Kraft knew that one of his Tuborg colleagues had a summer house in the district. He gave Hendil the address and said: 'This is where I shall be. Tell the policeman, so that he can get in touch with me in the morning and let me know where the refugees are.'

He had only a nodding acquaintance with his colleague but he knocked at his door and asked: 'May I sleep here tonight?'

'Naturally,' said the Tuborg man. 'You're very welcome. Come in and meet my wife and our friends. We've been playing cards and we're just about to have some smørrebrød. Join us.'

It was 11 o'clock at night. Kraft had never visited the house before. Yet neither his host and hostess nor any of their friends asked why he had suddenly appeared out of the darkness uninvited.

Early next morning the policeman called. 'I can tell you where some of the refugees are,' he said. 'I know nothing about the others, but I can tell you that the Gestapo got none of them. The worrying thing is that the Germans know Hendil's name. I've told him that he will have to vanish.'

On the following day there was a meeting between Hendil, Kraft, and some of the coastal police chiefs, who advised the editor to leave Denmark. 'The Germans know too much about you,' they said. 'We can't protect you any longer. You're too well known and too easy to find.'

'All right, I'll go,' he agreed. 'But the work must continue.'

The problem was to find somebody to take over the leadership on the Danish side. Hendil thought he knew the right man. Robert Jensen and Werner Gyberg, partners in the Copenhagen radio firm of Gyberg and Jensen, had worked with some of the first parachutists and had helped Captain Kaj Oxlund and the brothers Sigfred and Thorbjørn Christoffersen in their attempt to cross the frozen Øresund in the winter of 1942. Following that incident Gyberg had to go to Sweden but Robert Jensen (cover-name Tom) had remained in Copenhagen, importing and distributing British and American propaganda material. Since September 1943, he had also been getting Jews out of Copenhagen in one of the large Danish merchant ships sailing to Gothenborg and Oslo. Hendil and Kraft went to his office on Vesterbrogade and asked him whether he would take over the work of operating the transports. He agreed, provided Kraft would continue to help.

The three met again before Hendil left for Sweden. They had learned that the Germans knew through informers the points along the Swedish coast where the Jews were being landed and were watching the boats suspected of carrying them. It was decided that Hendil should try to arrange for Swedish vessels to meet the fishing-boats at sea and take the refugees ashore. In that way nobody could know which Danish boats had been used as transports.

In Stockholm, through the good offices of Ebbe Munck, Hendil got in touch with an organisation of Swedish Jews who owned a fishing-boat called the *Julius*. This had been lent to a young German Jew, Erik Marx, who had escaped from Bornholm, to enable him to earn a living. He had as crew Ole Helweg, a Danish architect who spoke good Swedish, and Erik Stærmose, a Danish naval officer. All three carried papers as Swedish fishermen. They agreed enthusiastically to cooperate and Hendil took over the *Julius*, together with a smaller fishing-vessel manned by two Danish naval officers, Sigurd Barfoed and Nygaard Christensen. The trans-shipment difficulty was solved.

On the Danish side Tom and Kraft had two, three, and later four fishing-boats as transports. In the largest they could pack up to fifty or sixty persons and the thirty-ton stone-fisher *Rømø*, used for dredging material from the seabed for road-making, was equipped with a secret hold for sixteen to seventeen people. The refugees assembled at several places, most of them south of Copenhagen. The main base of operations was the big inn at Rødvig, owned by Werner Christiansen, proprietor of the Coq d'Or restaurant in Copenhagen, while at Gjorslev, further up the coast, Edward Tesdorph and his family provided shelter and active help.

As the organisation improved the *Julius* and other Swedish vessels often sailed direct to the Danish shore to deliver mail and pick up passengers. Later a power-boat, one of two which Hendil had acquired, made the run from time to time but because the sound of its motor was liable to attract German patrols it could be used only at night and on special missions. It could take only two or three passengers and it was impossible to use it in bad weather. On one occasion in 1944 when Helweg and Barfoed had taken the boat over to Stevns, near Gjorslev, a heavy storm blew up and they were unable to take off again for Sweden. They hauled down the Swedish flag, ran up the Danish ensign and left the boat in the harbour all night. They went to Gjorslev and from Edward Tesdorph's home rang the Danish police to ask them to tell the Germans that the power-boat was a Danish police patrol vessel. When they finally set course for Sweden the engine failed and they were left drifting in the middle of the Øresund. They hoisted their shirts as a distress signal and eventually were found by a fishing-boat which towed them into Malmø.

As long as operations were concerned solely with the evacuation of the Jews the Germans were surprisingly quiescent. Many

of the German army and navy officers and harbour officials disapproved of the purge and made little more than token
opposition to the transports. The really dangerous people were
the Gestapo, the Danish traitors, and the paid informers who
infested the Swedish harbours. That situation changed completely after the Jews had been taken to safety. By that time
sabotage had begun in earnest, the illegal Press was daily growing in strength, and ordinary citizens who hitherto had been
passive were sheltering and aiding Resistance men on the run
and Allied airmen who had been shot down over Denmark.
The authorities knew that the people the transports were getting out of (and into) the country were working directly against
the German military machine and action against the illegal
routes intensified. The work became more and more difficult
and many men were lost. The casualties might have been even
higher but for the cooperation of the chief of the Danish coastal
police and some of his officers, who warned the transporters
about the places where the Germans had posts and controls and
indicated safer locations from which to operate.

Apart from the Hendil-Tom combination *Dansk-svensk
Flygtningetjeneste* (Danish-Swedish Refugee Service), other
groups had now started transport operations. They included
Speditøren (the Forwarding Agent), who later took over Johannesen's Tuborg Harbour group, *Studenternes Efterretningstjeneste, Dansk Hjælpetjeneste* (Danish Aid Service), *Liseruten* (the
Lise route), and a military group who operated from a base on
the south coast of Zealand. Difficulties arose when it transpired
that two or more groups were planning to ship parties from the
same harbour at the same time, obviously a very dangerous
procedure. Consequently, a meeting was held between delegates
from all the groups to get things better organised.

The biggest menace with which the transporters had to con-
tend was the informers who wormed their way into the parties
of genuine refugees. To counteract their efforts it became
necessary to tighten up the investigation of people who wanted
to cross the Øresund. Young men from one or other of the
groups daily visited the places where would-be escapers, after
having passed through several 'links', were assembled for ship-

ment. There they collected photographs, names, ages, and pro-
fessions of the escapers, who also had to give reasons why they
should be got out of the country. Six or seven group members
met daily at a secret headquarters to decide who should be
shipped to Sweden, who should be assisted in other ways, and
who should be rejected. Before an escaper was accepted his background was checked with the Danish police headquarters and,
if possible, with the Resistance group with whom he claimed to
have been working. This thorough investigation meant that the
departure of a ship might be delayed for a couple of days but it
also decreased the risk that a *stikker* would wreck the operation.

The importance of this security-check was demonstrated by
the case of an informer who, having betrayed one transport
to the Gestapo, tried again. He submitted his photograph and
personal particulars to the investigators and gave an apparently
reasonable explanation for his anxiety to leave Denmark. As
references he gave the names of several Resistance men who,
after the first debâcle, had been taken to Horserød, the German
concentration camp in North Zealand. The photograph was
smuggled into Horserød and the prisoners recognised the man
as the *stikker* who had betrayed them. Confronted with their
statements he confessed and was handed over to a Holger Danske
squad for liquidation.

Sometimes a group was put in jeopardy almost by accident.
The building which housed *Speditøren*'s first headquarters was
destroyed by a German terrorist gang in a reprisal action a
month after it was taken into use and all papers and the safe
containing the group's funds had to be salvaged from the
blazing apartment in the middle of the night.

'Getting refugees down to the coast from Copenhagen was
always a tricky operation,' Henrik Kraft said. 'We had no cars.
We had to use taxis driven by loyal Danes or send people by
train. Those we sent by train were told to get out at different
points on the route, so as not to have about twenty-five arriving
simultaneously at some small station and so arousing suspicion
immediately. They would be picked up by local taxis and driven
to the place where they could be hidden until the boat arrived.
During the Jewish evacuation some of the dangers were created

by the Jews themselves. Many of them came down to the boats with too much luggage. We used to tell them: "Look here, this isn't a pleasure cruise. It's very serious." They appeared to find great difficulty in understanding that. However, all went well for a long time, though I remember getting a great fright after taking one party down to Stevns. We had our passengers hidden in a fishing hut on the fringe of the woods which came down almost to the sea. I was walking along the beach, listening for the arrival of the *Julius*. It was a moonless, overcast night and I could see nothing beyond the white line of foam washing the sand. Suddenly, almost at my shoulder, I heard a voice: "Is that you, Kraft?" It was Stærmose, who had come silently ashore in a rowing-boat. I was never more shocked in my life.'

In the autumn of 1943 the *Julius* was nearing the Danish coast to pick up a party in the care of Christian Algreen-Petersen when she was intercepted by German patrol vessels. Marx, Stærmose and Helweg were taken so completely by surprise that they had no time to throw overboard the sack of mail they were carrying. They even forgot to throw out their hand-grenades. The ship was stopped and escorted into Rødvig harbour. Luckily, Werner Christiansen saw the arrival of the convoy and called Tom.

At 5 o'clock that morning Kraft's telephone rang. He lifted the receiver to hear Tom say: 'About that picnic we were supposed to have today, I don't think it's a good idea. The weather is terrible. I'll come and talk to you about organising something else.'

Twenty minutes later Tom arrived at the house and Mrs. Kraft brewed the last of the family's coffee ration to make the men a drink. Tom explained what had happened. He said that some Danish fishermen had seen the sack of mail from the *Julius* being taken ashore with the prisoners. After discussion it was decided that Tom should go at once to Rødvig, find the refugees, and see about organising another transport for them. It took a day or two but finally he got them over to Sweden from a point north of Copenhagen. Meanwhile Kraft visited the people whom he thought might be in danger if there were letters in the sack for them. Some heeded his warning to disappear for a time. Others would not listen and were arrested by the Gestapo. Kraft himself moved with his family into an apartment owned by friends who had already gone to Sweden.

Marx, Stærmose and Helweg were taken by the Gestapo to Dagmarhus for interrogation. They maintained that they were innocent Swedish fishermen with no interest in Danish affairs. They said a man had come down to Malmø harbour and asked them to give the sack of mail to a Danish fishing-boat and tell the skipper to deposit it in the left-luggage office at Copenhagen central railway station. He had given them fifty kroner for their trouble. As for the hand-grenades, a Danish refugee had asked them to dispose of those at sea and they had forgotten.

Marx and Helweg, who was married to a Swedish girl, spoke fluent Swedish. Stærmose, who did not know the language, had been ordered to say nothing at all and to act as if he were half-witted. All three claimed (Stærmose by shaking his head and grinning vacuously) that they had never heard of Hendil, Tom, or any other Resistance men. They played their parts so well that finally the Germans were convinced.

During the course of the interrogation the Gestapomen had become very interested in Marx, who was an intelligent young man, and they now invited him, on his return to Sweden, to help them find 'that damned Jew, Erik Marx'. He agreed willingly, and they gave him money, a Luger pistol, and a paper asking all German patrol vessels to give him every assistance in hunting himself.

Off the three went and, to the surprise of the harbour loungers at Malmø, the *Julius* returned to port manned by her original crew. Sadly, the illegal Press got wind of the story and published it before Marx could make contact with the German agent in Malmø, a meeting which might have had interesting consequences.

Despite their protests Hendil refused to make any further use of Marx and his shipmates.

'Next time you might be arrested and shot,' he said, 'and I shouldn't like to have that on my conscience.'

There was further trouble to come. One of the men taken by the Gestapo after the seizure of the mail sack had held out under interrogation for a week but finally had given Kraft's name. Kraft heard from his parents-in-law, who lived near, that the Germans had been twice to his house. With his cover blown he had no option but to go to Sweden. He knew too much about the organisation of the transport groups to risk capture. It was arranged that he should cross the Øresund from Elsinore with his wife and their three children, a girl, nine, a boy, six, and another girl only about a year old. Two days before Christmas they travelled by taxi to the home of Knud Parkov, a director of the Wilbroes Brewery, Elsinore, who was an active member of Hendil's group. After darkness had fallen the baby was given a sleeping powder and the family boarded the *Rømø*, which, when not stone-fishing, carried beer from the brewery to Copenhagen and returned to Elsinore with consignments of empty bottles. The vessel had been adapted to transport refugees in a small compartment made by putting walls between the fore and after holds.

The family were not making the trip alone. Others were also bound for Sweden. They went aboard in twos and threes. As they were trying to make themselves comfortable in the bitterly cold compartment, Mrs. Kraft asked suddenly: 'Where is our son?'

'I've left him with the skipper,' her husband replied. 'You know what boys are like. I thought he would be happy up there on the bridge.'

Kraft knew that if the boat were sunk, those huddled below decks were doomed, while on the bridge the boy would stand a chance of survival. It was the skipper who had given him the idea. 'Let the boy stay with me,' he had suggested. 'If the Germans stop us, I will say he is my son.'

Kraft could not explain this to his wife but fortunately he did not have to endure her anger for long. After only fifteen minutes at sea the boat was met by a Swedish warship and the passengers were transferred. The stone-fisher continued her trip and the refugees were taken to Halsingborg.

Tom remained in hiding until Christmas Eve, when he learned that the man he had feared might give his name, a doctor, had been released by the Gestapo. He was able to return

home and enjoy the *Julefest* with his family. Those who had
been taken by the Germans had been kept in prison for some
time but they had no real difficulties. Most of them had not
known Tom and had no way of finding out about him. Those
who did know had succeeded in keeping silent, so all was well.

After landing at Halsingborg the Krafts went to Stockholm to
spend Christmas with relatives. Later, friends got rooms for
them in a boarding-house in the city. With the family settled,
Kraft was able to meet Ebbe Munck, Torp-Pedersen and Hendil
to discuss the future of *Dansk-svensk Flygtningetjeneste*. It was
becoming more difficult to raise funds in Denmark to keep the
transports going and it was decided to ask rich Jews in Sweden
whether they would be prepared to help.

The friends spoke to Carl Otto Henriques, a banker of world
repute and one of the most respected men in the Danish Jewish
community. He listened sympathetically but said: 'First you
must get the consent of the Danish ambassador to your proposals. Many of my friends would refuse to sign a paper or take
any other action without his specific approval.'

The ambassador, when approached, asked for time to think
about the plan but, after consulting Torp-Pedersen, accepted it.
With this major obstacle overcome, Hendil and Kraft were able
to proceed. Kaj Simonsen, a Danish lawyer, who knew most of
the wealthy Danish Jews, persuaded them to sign papers in
which they promised to pay to *Dansk-svensk Flygtningetjeneste*
an agreed sum of money when they returned to Denmark after
the war—on condition, naturally, that their fortunes had not
been stolen by the Germans. These documents were collected
by Simonsen and Kraft and placed in sealed envelopes which
were then deposited in the strongroom at the Danish legation.
Nobody but Simonsen and Kraft knew the identity of the
signatories.

It was arranged with the Tuborg chairman, Herbert Jerichow,
and Niels Andersen, a barrister of the supreme court, that if a
man whom they knew came to them from Sweden and said, for
example, 'Three hundred and fifty', they could draw up to
350,000 Danish kroner from a bank or some other financial house
in Copenhagen for the use of *Dansk-svensk Flygtningetjeneste*.

Usually the courier had no idea of the meaning of the message
he carried. The figure he gave always represented the maximum
which Simonsen and Kraft had managed to raise. The first
collection amounted to 500,000 Danish kroner and the second,
about nine months later, to 250,000, making a total of 750,000
Danish kroner (about £42,000). The initial contribution had
been a gift from Swedish Jews and friends of Denmark in
Sweden of 210,000 kroner which had helped Hendil to begin his
work when he arrived in Malmø.

The donors knew only vaguely the purposes for which their
money was to be used. They understood only that it would be
employed in helping people out of Denmark and 'for other
things'. Jerichow and Andersen, who drew large sums from the
bank in Copenhagen on the strength of a courier's spoken
message, never knew who had backed the papers said to be held
in the strongroom of the Danish legation; nor for that matter,
did the legation, who also contributed to the fund. All relied
completely on the word of Simonsen and Kraft that they held
trustworthy signatures for the amounts involved. And every
krone was paid after the war by the people who had signed.

The money did not go exclusively to *Dansk-svensk Flygtningetjeneste*. In all, that service used 375,000 kroner, while
180,000 kroner went to other transport routes. People in difficulties in Denmark were helped to the extent of 120,000 kroner;
aid to the illegal Press accounted for another 56,000; the Freedom
Council received 47,000; and a further 47,000 was spent on
'special jobs'. All the accounts were controlled by a Danish
state-authorised accountant-auditor, himself a refugee in Sweden.

Once the financial situation had been stabilised Kraft was
free to spend most of his time in Malmø, working with Hendil
and Jørgen Polack on the practical operation of the route. With
more funds at their disposal they could extend their activities.

'At different times we had up to four fishing-boats,' Kraft said.
'Two of them had been bought in Sweden. One could hold
about ten people; the other could take up to forty-five. Later,
some of the fishermen who had been working with Tom in
Denmark had to leave when the Germans got suspicious of
them. They came over in their boats and those, when the

registration numbers had been changed, could also be used in the service. We met in international waters the ships bringing refugees from Danish harbours.

'There was a schooner going once a week from Copenhagen to the island of Samsø and to Frederikshavn in Jutland. She was loaded at Nyhavn and Tom could put up to thirty people in her. They went aboard one at a time at intervals of two to three minutes. Since the ship was trading only between Danish ports, the German inspection was not very thorough. She left Copenhagen at dusk, went up the coast and just after passing Elsinore veered off-course a little to the east, closer to the coast. We were waiting at Kullen and the passengers were transferred. We always took them straight to Malmø. The Germans could find out through informers where people landed, and if parties came ashore regularly at the same place they naturally would be able to tie that up with the fact that a certain ship always seemed to be at that place at the same time. But they would not connect people landing at Malmø with a ship bound for North Jutland.

'Tom also used the stone-fisher which went from Copenhagen to Elsinore with empty beer bottles. She sailed late in the afternoon and when she came up the Øresund from Copenhagen she diverged around the wrong side of Hven, where we were waiting with the Swedish boat.

'During the last six months of the war we had another special route. The two brothers Knudsen and a cousin, Zimling, who worked as fishermen on the island of Saltholm, off Copenhagen, had a boat with an under-water exhaust, which ran very quietly. The men learned they were on the Gestapo's list of suspects and joined us in Malmø. With their silent vessel they could make the run across the Øresund to Amager, where there was a huge rubbish dump extending down to the shore, not more than three hundred metres from a Danish fort which was occupied by the Germans. The boat sailed in there several times a week, taking two or three people into Copenhagen and getting as many out. This route, which was never detected by the Germans, was often used by the intelligence service. It was the quickest way of getting from Sweden to Copenhagen.

'Early in 1945 Ebbe Munck asked us to take over an official from the British ministry of agriculture. This man was to meet Danish agricultural officials to discuss post-occupation plans and our job was to get him into Copenhagen and out again. The Englishman went by train from Stockholm to Malmø and that night he was taken over to Amager, where two bodyguards from Ib Christensen's *1944* group met him and escorted him to a private apartment in the capital. There, for two days, he held his meetings; then he was taken back to Sweden. Looking back, it seems incredible that this man could be taken by illegal transport to Copenhagen, conduct his business and return to Stockholm in less time than it would have taken him during the six months *after* the war ended.'

The transport of passengers was not the group's only concern. One day they received a message from Tom, asking: 'Could you send over two hundred small watches? They are needed for making time-bombs.' They filled the order through a Danish refugee who was working in a Swedish watch factory. On another occasion they were asked to supply explosives for saboteurs who were planning to blow up the German cruiser *Nürnberg*, which was lying at Copenhagen. The ship was not blown up but the saboteurs effectively put her out of action. Other little chores undertaken by the group included importing text-books for the schools for Danish children in Sweden and sending technical literature and scientific papers to the doctors in Denmark, so that they could keep up with developments in the free world. 'It was a very mixed business,' Kraft said. 'We were a sort of Marks and Spencers of the Resistance.'

Between October 1943, and April 1945, *Dansk-svensk Flygtningetjeneste* transported to Sweden 1,888 people—military, police, politicians, seamen, fishermen, and three priests. The passengers included 150 foreigners—Britons, Americans, Norwegians, Dutch, Poles, French, Belgians, and others. Among them were at least 40 Allied airmen who had been shot down or had made forced landings in Denmark. Some of the Frenchmen were Alsatians who had been forced to serve in the German army and who had deserted at the first opportunity. Kraft particularly remembers ten Americans who were shot down over Stevns. He said: 'A good friend, a taxi driver who also owned some trucks, went out to the forest where the airmen were hiding and brought them into the little town of Præsto. From there they were taken to Tom in Copenhagen in a truck loaded with hay. Tom hid them in an apartment in the city for two days and then they came over to Sweden in a fishing-boat. Ten was a pretty risky load but they were all very happy. They even had a conducted tour of Copenhagen before going down to the boat.'

Things did not always go so smoothly. The search of coasters and deep-sea vessels using the port of Copenhagen became daily more rigorous. A coaster which had been working with Tom's group and others took in three saboteurs. Just before the boat was due to sail the German control went on board and searched for two hours. They found nothing but they refused to let the boat leave. They said they knew that five people had boarded, yet only two were visible. Where were the other three? The skipper said that the only two men aboard were himself and his mate but the Germans would not believe him. After four hours they brought in police dogs and the three saboteurs were found hiding below.

'We got the story very quickly,' said Kraft. 'We went to a firm making medical supplies in Sweden and asked what could be done to prevent another such accident. Their scientists got to work and made a mixture of dried rabbits' blood and cocaine. We sent a supply of the powder in small glass phials to all the transport groups operating in Denmark. Every skipper kept a phial in his pocket and when he saw the control coming, he shook a little of the powder on to his handkerchief. As soon as the dogs came on board he would shake the handkerchief. The dogs would sniff and in a few moments their noses had become numb and they could smell nothing. We knew the scheme would work because we had carried out trials with Swedish police dogs. The powder was very powerful. You could put down a bone with plenty of meat on it and the dogs would pass by without noticing it. The best part was that you could see nothing wrong with the dog. It was apparently quite normal. The Germans never tumbled to the trick.'

More dangerous than the German harbour patrols was the stupendous folly of many of the refugees who had reached Sweden safely. Danes love to talk, it is one of their more endearing traits, but in Sweden, in wartime, gossip could lead to tragedy. Kraft was in Halsingborg when one of the big Danish ships running between Copenhagen, Gothenborg and Oslo was stopped by a German gunboat. It was a ship which had taken many passengers to Sweden for the groups. The stopping had been seen from the Swedish coast and had caused great excitement. Kraft met some Jewish refugees, who told him: 'That was the ship in which we came over.'

'What are you talking about?' he said angrily. 'You've forgotten how you got here.'

'No, we came...'

He said: 'You were warned never to talk about how you came over or whom you contacted. This ship has been stopped, but nobody says the Germans have found anything. You don't know anything about it, so keep your mouths shut.'

The ship was searched. Nobody was found in her and she continued her voyage. But there could have been disaster.

It was impossible to make the refugees understand that even in Sweden informers were listening to every scrap of gossip. Many people in Denmark were betrayed unwittingly by refugees having spoken out of turn or by letters carelessly written. The peril became so great that early in 1944 the leaders of *Speditøren* had to send the following urgent message:

Distress signal to our assistants in Sweden

The situation of the routes has deteriorated during the past two months. Many experienced and good men have been killed, wounded, imprisoned, or have had to escape. The rest are in daily danger. The informers have succeeded to an incredible extent. Both route people and others have been endangered because of the fantastic recklessness with which mail has been carried from Sweden to Denmark. During the past few weeks several large mail consignments have been taken by the Germans because inexperienced and thoughtless people have handed them over to other inexperienced route

people and in open boats. The major point about mail consignments is *where* and *how* it is landed in this country and
not how it is got rid of in Halsingborg or Malmø district. Get
rid of the reckless people *mercilessly and at once.* If you do
not act at once it amounts to treason towards the few who are
left here. Furthermore, get the mail properly censored. The
last mail consignments handled so recklessly have contained
several letters containing sketch-maps and descriptions of
buried arms arsenals, etc., addressed to good Danes with their
names and addresses. To protect us against this, we have in cooperation with the Freedom Council issued a warning which
will be included in all mail to Sweden, asking senders in
Sweden to limit all ordinary letter writing for illegal transport,
and preferably not to write at all.

The accompanying warning read:

It is at the moment very difficult to send illegal mail and, as
some consignments have lately been seized by the Germans,
we plead with you not to write unless it is absolutely necessary.
A letter should, if possible, have a false name for both
addressee and sender. If you have no previous arrangements
for this, the letter should not contain surnames, place descriptions, or details which might make it clear whether you are
mother, sister, father, or fiancée of the addressee, as this may
lead the Germans to you if the mail consignment is confiscated. Write only short letters. If you choose to send a letter
via the legal channels, you must realise that the Germans keep
a very strict control over those who write to each other in
Denmark and Sweden, and we therefore warn you once again:
Please do not write in the short time left of the war. But if
it is really necessary, remember that by being careful you
may keep yourself out of danger, but we who help the mail
through are in daily danger of losing the freedom we are
fighting for.

This warning was enclosed in every letter sent from Denmark
to Sweden and was published in the Swedish newspapers. It was

also included in broadcasts by the BBC Danish Service. It had its effect and very soon the refugee mail shrank from hundreds of letters to only a few.

There were, however, other grave dangers.

On 7 February 1944, Tom wrote to Hendil from Copenhagen: 'Dear S4—This has been a week of so much tragedy which could have been avoided. On Thursday evening at half past five I was sitting here, talking with Møller and Christian. A quarter of an hour later the one was killed and the other seriously wounded. Our eight passengers were all safe. A baby of six months got a bullet through the cot but was not hurt. I have written to you before, and I repeat it, this is really a bloody serious business. We do not want any longer to send over children who would be completely safe here in Denmark. We don't want to send over servants or fiancées. We must keep the route open for those who really need it and who are in real danger— and for nobody else. Sundby, one of the fishermen, had an engine breakdown and was drifting on the sea. He only got back this morning. Stensen has been lying here in port with passengers for three days because of very strong currents. He has been forced to return three times. This morning he started for the fourth time. I hope he will succeed. All in all, a very sad week.'

The tragedy to which the letter refers had occurred four days earlier. It was engineered by the *stikker* Berthelsen, who paid for his treachery with his life.

On 2 February, Frits Blichfeldt Møller visited Tom at his office on Vesterbrogade. He said that on the following evening a transport was sailing for Sweden from Asiatisk Plads in Copenhagen's Inner Harbour. There was room in the ship for a few more passengers. Tom was delighted. He had a number of refugees, including a woman with a baby, hidden in the Kongens Nytorv area, waiting for just such an opportunity. It was arranged that Christian Algreen-Petersen, with Søren and Ole, two other members of the group, should collect the party and take them to the corner of Strandgade and Torvegade. There they would meet a man called Leif (the policeman Hans Christiansen), who would accompany them down Strandgade and through the gate to Asiatisk Plads, where the ship lay.

On the evening of 3 February Algreen-Petersen and Søren drove to Kongens Nytorv. They had been able to get only one taxi, and this was reserved for the women. The other refugees were told to travel with Ole in a street-car. The baby, heavily dosed with sleeping medicine, was lying in a cot improvised from a wooden box fitted with handles. Søren and Algreen-Petersen picked up the cot and sat in the taxi with the women. The driver was told to pull up at the first street-car stop after the Knippelsbro bridge and there the party got out.

Leaving Søren in charge of the baby, Algreen-Petersen went ahead to the corner of Strandgade, where Møller and Leif were standing. As they waited for the refugees to join them, Algreen-Petersen saw that Søren appeared to be having difficulty in carrying the baby and went back to help him. He took one handle of the cot and the pair followed Møller at a distance of about ten to fifteen metres. The baby's mother was very frightened but Algreen-Petersen said soothingly: 'Don't worry; nothing will happen to your child.'

The words had hardly left his mouth when there came a deafening burst of machine-gun and pistol shots. As Møller and Leif had turned in through the gate of Asiatisk Plads a gang of Danes and Gestapomen, led by the notorious collaborator Nedermark-Hansen, had opened fire from a cellarway. Møller was killed and Leif was so badly wounded that he died a few hours later in Vestre Fængsel. Søren and Algreen-Petersen turned and ran back up Strandgade, the cot swinging between them. They had not gone far when Algreen-Petersen felt a shattering pain in his back and dropped with a scream. The cot clattered to the sidewalk and he heard Søren running away. He lay there, helpless, desperately trying to breathe. A Gestapo bullet had gone through his back, pierced the left lung and lodged between the gullet and the aorta, the body's main artery.

A man came out of a building and asked if he could help. Algreen-Petersen gasped: 'In coat pocket ... Wallet and papers ... send to Søndermarksvej 2 ... See to baby ...'

He felt the man fumbling at his pocket and heard him promise to do what he could.

There had been a break in the firing but now another volley came and a Gestapoman yelled: 'Anybody still on the street in three minutes will be shot!'

A couple of pedestrians came down Strandgade and bent over the wounded man. He was past speech but he made them understand by signs that they should disappear as quickly as they could. Somehow he, too, had to get away. He had no illusions about the fate awaiting him if the Gestapo got their hands on him.

The night was pitch-dark. The sky was wholly overcast and a cold drizzle was falling. He dragged himself painfully along the sidewalk, the rough stones cutting into his hands and face. At last, lifting his head with great difficulty, he saw a flight of area steps leading down to the entrance of an antique shop. Somehow he got down the steps and tried the door. It was unlocked. He dragged himself through and hauled himself up on to a divan.

The owner of the shop came out of a back room and switched on the light. He stared, frightened and angry, at the scarecrow figure sprawled on the divan. 'What do you want here?' he demanded. 'You're ruining my furniture. You're filthy.'

'I'm wounded,' Algreen-Petersen said faintly. 'Call an ambulance.'

The old dealer looked at him, bewildered. 'Ambulance?' he repeated. 'I . . .'

His son emerged from the back room. 'What the hell's going on?' he asked. 'Why have you put the light on? D'you want the bloody Gestapo shooting through the window?'

The dealer pointed wordlessly to the figure on the divan, and the younger man said: 'Good God! What happened to you?'

Algreen-Petersen pleaded: 'Get an ambulance. I think I'm dying.' Despite the fire that was eating his lungs, he managed to get out his name and address. A few seconds later he heard the son telephoning; then he relapsed into semi-consciousness.

When he revived, two armed Danish policemen were standing beside the divan. One of them asked his name. He tried to give it but succeeded only in coughing up a stream of blood. Eventually an ambulance arrived and he was taken to Sundby Hospital, where an emergency operation was performed. Afterwards he was transferred to the Øresundshospital, which possessed the best equipment for lung surgery, but there the doctors decided against another operation. In a few days word came that the Gestapo probably knew of Algreen-Petersen's presence in the hospital and he was removed for safety to a private clinic for treatment under Professor E. Husfeldt, a famous lung surgeon and a member of the Freedom Council. After a month in bed, followed by a month's convalescence in Jutland, he returned to Copenhagen to continue work with the transports.

The menace of the *stikkers* grew ever more serious. On 4 June 1944, *Speditøren*'s helpers in Sweden reported: 'The informer and Gestapoman Ole Bjørn Bendtsen, calling himself Ole Skevsbo and working partly for Dr. Wäsche in Reventlowsgade, Copenhagen, and partly at Dagmarhus, is hiding with his fiancée, the mannequin Else Thulin, at Frederiksberg Bredegade No 5, first floor, tel. Fasan 1211. People arriving here claim he is so dangerous that he is in need of a perforation. Please issue warning on Poul Dierlich, salesman. Has been employed by *Wehrmacht* in Lemvig. Is working solely for the Gestapo. Is now a travelling salesman in tobacco and pipes, which he "distributes" to relatives of imprisoned patriots, at the same time questioning them. Very dangerous informer, about thirty years old.'

The motives of these and other traitors differed. Some—the more understandable, if no less culpable—were of German descent or had German family connections. Some had been members of the Danish Nazi party long before the occupation, while others were convinced that Germany would win the war and hoped by treachery to secure their own futures. Most, however, were activated solely by greed and were prepared to sell anybody for a handful of kroner.

Some cases were more complex. Henrik Kraft remembers a young photographer. 'I knew him very well,' he said. 'At the beginning of the occupation he took a lot of interesting pictures which he gave to the illegal newspapers or kept for use after the war. Suddenly, one day, he denounced a Resistance man to the Germans. The man was shot. The photographer was arrested after the liberation and confessed the betrayal. He had a sister who was engaged to a German and I believe he just wanted to impress the fellow with his inside knowledge of the Resistance. It was a very strange business. He could have denounced me. I was badly wanted by the Gestapo at that time and he knew about my activities, but he said nothing. He was in contact with many other people known to be on the German black-list but he didn't denounce them. Why, then, betray that one man?'

What prompted the young man known as Søren to turn traitor is equally puzzling. Though he was said by some to be a spendthrift, it is doubtful whether he worked for the Gestapo merely for money; indeed, so far as is known, his financial rewards were comparatively small. Some claim that he wanted to be recognised as a Resistance hero and went bad only because he felt he was not being trusted by other members of his group. Even allowing for his weak character, that seems an unlikely explanation. Christian Algreen-Petersen, who knew him better than most people, certainly does not accept it.

He said: 'Søren came from Jutland, where he was wanted by the Gestapo after railway sabotage. He was sent to *Dansk-svensk Flygtningetjeneste* by *Nordisk Boghandel*, another very well-known Resistance centre, for us to ship him to Sweden. This we did, but after some months he suddenly reappeared in Copenhagen. He explained that he hadn't been able to settle down in Sweden, knowing there were jobs to be done in Denmark. Reports about him being satisfactory, we used him to begin with for small jobs, but he had no knowledge of and no access to our headquarters on Vesterbrogade or Forchhammersvej until after the Asiatisk Plads affair, when I was wounded and out of action. At that time Tom took him into close co-operation. One night, when I was arranging for some people to be shipped to Sweden, one of the refugees came up to me and, nodding towards Søren, asked whether I knew him. He said they'd shared a cell in a Gestapo prison and that Søren had un-accountably been released after very few days. I had no idea of this and mentioned it to Tom that same night. We decided to ask Søren if it were true. He admitted it, explaining that he hadn't told us because he was afraid we wouldn't have dared take him into the group. His explanation was plausible but we didn't like the situation. We considered sending him back to Sweden but Tom was against that because, as he very rightly said, it would be extremely easy for him to make trouble there as well.

'My opinion is that Søren had been arrested by the Germans for railway sabotage. During his interrogation he had received the same offer as several other prisoners (including Marx and myself) to join the Gestapo. He took the chance, thinking that he could fool them, but little by little he found that he was really caught in their net and had to do something to satisfy them.

'Just after the liberation I was confronted with Ib Birkedal-Hansen. He was a notorious and feared collaborator and he'd participated in the Gestapo action against Forchhammersvej 7. He told me that Søren had reported direct to the Gestapo chief, Kriminalrat Bunke, that Forchhammersvej would be an interesting place to visit and Bunke immediately arranged for a squad of ten or twelve men to make the raid.'

Following the capture of the *Julius* and the loss of the group's mail sack, Tom had shifted his headquarters from Vesterbrogade 30 to a ground-floor apartment at Forchhammersvej 7, in the Frederiksberg district of Copenhagen. There, on the afternoon of 24 July 1944, he was to meet Christian Algreen-Petersen, Werner Christiansen, Ole Geisler, the SOE parachutist, and Svend Tronbjerg (cover-name Thorkild).

Before keeping the appointment Algreen-Petersen lunched with his parents and then went to Vesterbrogade to meet Tom's son, Erik Jensen. Erik walked with him to Forchhammersvej but left him at the door of the apartment.

'It was four o'clock when I rang the bell and Tom opened the door.' Algreen-Petersen said. 'Thorkild, Ole Geisler and Werner Christiansen were already in the apartment but Christiansen left shortly afterwards. I was looking through the latest copy of *Informatión* when the doorbell rang. I got up to open the door but Tom said: "I'll go". I sat down and picked up the paper again but I had hardly read a couple of sentences when there came a violent hammering and the crash of breaking glass. There was a shout: *"Deutsche sicherheitspolizei!"* followed by a burst of shooting. Tom rushed back into the room. "They're here!" he shouted. He grabbed his briefcase and ran out into the kitchen to try to escape through the back garden. Thorkild followed him. We had our revolvers, but they weren't much use against Gestapo machine-pistols and hand-grenades.

I ran blindly after the other two, but the shooting was even fiercer in the garden. I knew the three of us would never get out that way, so I turned back into the sitting-room. It was sheer hell in there. Bullets were coming in through all the windows and every now and then a hand-grenade burst. The house was completely surrounded and there was a barrage from all sides of the building. It was clear that I shouldn't last long where I was but it seemed equally likely that I should be killed if I tried to bolt through the garden.

'A lull came in the firing. I crouched and ran to the only unbroken window overlooking Forchhammersvej. Tom had smashed the other with the telephone to warn us. I pushed up the sash and looked out. All was quiet. It was my big chance. I swung myself through the window and down into the street. There was still no movement anywhere. I started to run, but I'd gone only a few strides when a Gestapoman sprang from behind a corner of the house where he'd been hiding. He turned his machine-pistol on me and fired a burst. I threw myself to the ground. I hadn't been hit but I knew that only a miracle could now save me from capture. As I lay there, the Gestapoman turned and fired into the garden. I suppose it was stupid of me to try to escape when he was less than three metres away but I jumped up and began running again. The Gestapoman whipped round and let go with another burst. That time he didn't miss and I fell to the sidewalk. He kept firing at my legs and I was hit again and again. Then he came up and said, grinning: "Now bloody well try to run. Next time I'll aim for your belly."

'A grenade exploded close by and I rolled into the gutter to try to get a bit of cover. My skin crawled when I saw the Gestapoman's finger tighten on the trigger but he held his fire. He could see that I was helpless.

'Little by little the shooting died down and the Germans signalled their cars—three in all—from their position on the corner of the street. At the same time the Danish police arrived. One of them approached me and I tried to give him my name but a yell warned him to keep away. I could have cried with rage.

'Another Gestapoman came out of the garden and looked down at me. "Why didn't you finish him off?" he asked his mate sourly. They went through my pockets and took everything I had, even my cigarettes; then they threw me into an Opel car. A Gestapoman sat on each side of me and in the front seats there were two more, all with cocked pistols. They said they were taking me to the German field hospital. Well, that was better than Shellhus, I thought. I looked down at myself. my trousers hung in shreds and blood was dripping through the material on to the car floor. I was in shirt-sleeves. My jacket was still hanging in the sitting-room at the house. That worried me because it held my false identity papers and several keys, one to the place where our weapons were stored. I asked for a cigarette. A Gestapoman put one of my own in my mouth. It was soaked with blood.

'At the field hospital I was taken to the operating theatre and dumped on a table. An orderly took my clothes off and I lay there stark naked. I had lost so much blood that I was barely conscious. A Gestapoman roused me by grabbing my hair and banging my head against the operating table. "Where is Flammen?" he demanded.

' "I don't know him," I said.

' "Where is Søren?"

' "I don't know."

'He said: "You're lying, but we'll soon get the truth out of you." He pounded my head again. "Now, where's Søren?"

'I fainted, came round to more brutal treatment, and fainted again. I don't know how long the nightmare lasted but at last I revived to see a doctor standing beside the table.

'The Gestapoman said with relish: "Your right leg will have to come off. It's smashed. Isn't that so, doctor?"

'The doctor examined my leg. "Yes," he agreed. "It will have to be sawn off about here." He indicated a point above the knee. I looked down. The whole of my leg was a gory pulp. I said without hope: "But couldn't you save it? You Germans are known to have good surgeons."

' "For ourselves," he said coldly. "Not for you."

'The door of the operating theatre opened and two stretchers were carried in. On one lay Thorkild and on the other Tom. Tom looked as if he were sleeping.

' "Do you know them?" the Gestapoman asked.

'I nodded. "Are they dead?"

' "Yes. Be glad it isn't you lying there."

'I didn't answer. I saw the Gestapoman unstrap the wristwatch I had given Tom as a present and put it into his own pocket. I was too weak to protest.'

That was the end of the road for Algreen-Petersen. He was sent to Vestre Fængsel and from there, six months later, to Frøslev concentration camp in South Jutland, where he remained until the liberation.

Ole Geisler was more fortunate. He had tried to leave the apartment just as the Gestapo began their attack. Four or five of them grabbed him but he fought his way free, jumped over a high fence and escaped under a hail of fire.

The raid on Forchhammersvej 7 was a major disaster for *Dansk-svensk Flygtningetjeneste*. Left leaderless by Tom's death and with vital documents in Gestapo hands, the group in Copenhagen were in desperate trouble. Many, like Herbert Jerichow of Tuborg, had to get out of the country in a hurry. Once any citizen's name went into the Gestapo's files, flight was the only option. Among those who went to Sweden were Søren and Tom's son, Erik.

'They came to see Hendil,' said Henrik Kraft. 'They wanted to continue the work in Denmark on their own but Hendil refused to consider it. Erik was far too young for the job and Hendil didn't trust Søren at all. Nevertheless we had to do something. The old group were scattered and we had to get back into operation with new people. Eventually Svend Aage Munck, of *Berlingske Tidende*, put us in touch with one of his colleagues, Erik Lagergreen. He was ready to help us and set up a new office on Nytorv. Søren and Erik Jensen went back to Copenhagen to join him. Three weeks later he was denounced and arrested by the Gestapo. That was the raid in which Lotte was taken. Only one man—Søren—could have done the denouncing. He was picked up, interrogated for many hours, and finally admitted his guilt. He was disposed of by a Holger Danske liquidation squad.'

Erik Lagergreen's arrest and the unmasking of Søren led to a general overhaul of security measures throughout the transport organisation. The antecedents of would-be recruits to the individual groups were checked and cross-checked; the credentials of intending refugees were examined minutely; and men wanting to leave Sweden for Denmark had to satisfy both the transport agents and the Swedish police of their integrity before being granted passage. Contact between the different groups could be made only through Selmer Jørgensen, a director of Wibroes Brewery, and Erik Reitzel, manager of the King's Brewhouse (a Tuborg brewery), in Elsinore. These two men were the sole liaison between *Dansk-svensk Flygtningetjeneste*, the *1944, Lysglimt*, Fritz Drescher, *Caprani* and military intelligence groups, and several lone-working fishermen. In that way the risk of total catastrophe was reduced considerably.

It was most important that Hendil should be able to inform Copenhagen about men who had to be got into Denmark, often at very short notice. In this work, as long as regular commercial flights between Denmark and Sweden continued, the air crews and ground staff of the Danish airline (today incorporated in the Scandinavian Airlines System) gave invaluable service. Later, a second line of communication was established through officials of the Danish metal company, Paul Bergsøe and Son, which had an office in Landskrona. They would call the firm's Copenhagen office with such innocuous queries as: 'Will two hundred tons of iron do for you?' The man who took the call rang a special telephone number and repeated the inquiry word for word. Then the group leader knew the exact time and place at which he had to meet the incoming passengers. When telephoning became more difficult an operator equipped with a portable transmitter sent similar messages from a high point in the coastal town of Skodsborg to another operator on Hven; but because German police vessels constantly patrolled the Øresund this method of communication became too dangerous and had to be abandoned.

For a fortnight after Børge Outze's arrest in October 1944, no copies of *Information* reached Sweden. At last Kaj Johansen made contact with *Dansk-svensk Flygtningetjeneste* in Copenhagen and the daily service was resumed in the group's own

boats and by rail and air. Alfred Wickmann, a Danish air
mechanic in Malmø, who devised ingenious hiding-places in the
aircraft for micro-filmed copies of the news bulletins, was a key
figure in the operation. He is today on the staff of the Scandinavian Airlines System in Copenhagen.

The round-up of the Danish police, including the coastal
detachments, on 19 September 1944, and the Gestapo's intensified
activity against the transports made it necessary for all the
groups to use provincial ports and harbours to a greater extent.
Operations spread to Køge, Elsinore, Frederikssund, Kalund-
borg, and Korsør in Zealand, to Odense in Funen and to Vejle,
Fredericia and Aalborg in Jutland. That meant longer journeys
for passengers and forwarders but the embarkations were usually
less dangerous since the Germans in the provinces were less
alert than those in the Copenhagen area. For a short time the
Gestapo tried putting control officers in ships leaving Copenhagen. The control did not arrive until the ship was being
searched before departure. One morning a schooner often used
by *Speditøren* was sailing for Bornholm. The control went on
board, and since the skipper had no chance of putting ashore
the four escapers he had taken in during the night he had to sail
with them. A storm blew up and when the control went below
to shelter, the skipper saw to it that the stove heating the cabin
was well stoked. Then he produced bottles of akvavit and strong
lager and invited the German to drink. After the party had
been going for a couple of hours he stopped the engine, so that
the schooner was tossed about in the heavy seas like a walnut
shell. Naturally, the control officer was violently sick. When he
became so ill that he was forced to retire to his bunk, the
skipper started the engine again and the escapers were put over
the ship's side into a Swedish naval vessel.

October 1944 was a black month for the Resistance movement.
There were many arrests and the newspaper and transport
groups in particular suffered heavily. On the evening of
14 October *Speditøren*'s headquarters in Gammel Mønt, Copenhagen, were raided and a large part of the group's records,
together with stamps for false papers and other compromising
material, fell into the hands of the Gestapo. This raid led

indirectly to the death of the great freedom fighter Citronen.

By the end of the month the situation had become so critical that *Speditøren* were driven to desperate measures. They knew that a large speed-boat was moored in the German naval harbour in Copenhagen, a place so tightly guarded that nobody would think of it as the possible starting-point for an escape route. They got a trusted boat-builder to refit the craft and even made trial runs, with a Danish policeman as engineer, in plain sight of the German naval units. The escapers were being led to the harbour when a Gestapo raid began in the area and the party had to disperse hurriedly. Next evening twelve people were taken aboard the speed-boat under cover of darkness; the engineer started the motor and the boat left its berth with all lights blazing, as if it were on a legitimate cruise. Unluckily the motor failed half-way across the Øresund and the boat had to cough its way into Swedish territorial waters on two cylinders.

With shipments from Copenhagen growing more hazardous, the group opened another route from a point on Sjællands Odde, the narrow peninsula which forms the north-western tip of Zealand. This route could take eighteen escapers at a time but the journey from Copenhagen was long and arduous and it was not easy to drop eighteen refugees and two forwarders at a small country station without arousing dangerous curiosity. However, the local organisation managed to enlist the aid of sympathetic taxi-owners and after that small parties could be put down at intermediate stations, where cars were waiting to collect them. Embarkation took place sometimes from the beach and sometimes from the little harbour. Each method had its advantages and drawbacks. From the beach passengers had to be ferried out to the transport vessel by rowing boat. That took a long time but there was only a remote chance of interference from *stikkers*. From the harbour the escapers could go straight on board but they had to evade strong German patrols in order to reach the fishing-boat. Often the weather deteriorated after the escapers had left Copenhagen and an embarkation had to be cancelled. Then shelter had to be found for twenty people in the vicarage, the home of the local doctor, and a few trusted farms.

The Sjællands Odde route, which was used with few interruptions until the end of the occupation, was especially suitable for the transport of women and children because there was no search before the boat left and the refugees could sit or recline in a cabin throughout the crossing. Several priests were among the passengers and every time, shortly after a cleric had been landed in Sweden, *Speditøren* would be asked to send a fresh collar over to him. Now a Danish priest's collar is not like the Anglican variety; it is, in fact, a large white, stiffly starched ruff of the type worn in Shakespeare's day. To get such a bulky and crushable article across the Øresund in good condition was not simple, so the group made it a rule that any priest desiring passage must take a clean collar with him.

In December 1944, *Speditøren* achieved one of their greatest coups when, in collaboration with another transport group, they successfully shipped from Copenhagen harbour a party of no less than fifty-four people, among them a 'shadow' cabinet minister, two of the most wanted saboteurs, two well-known communists, and other personalities high on the Gestapo's 'wanted' list. The ship, a large merchantman, should have sailed at noon but was delayed by a more than usually thorough search. Nothing was found and she was allowed to proceed. Two hours later the group were shocked to receive a message that a couple of E-boats had gone after the ship and had ordered her back to Langelinie for a second search. Miraculously, all the Germans found were a few innocent letters which one of the seamen had promised to take to Sweden, and the vessel was again sent on her way with the escapers safe in their hiding places.

The new year brought a German order that all ships sailing from Langelinie must go to Nordre Tolbod (the northern customs office) or to a control point at the lock in the South Harbour for search. That was a severe blow to *Speditøren*, especially as it was clear that the searches would be rigorous. The Swedes had by this time forbidden traffic within their three-mile limit, so that ships could not pass through the Falsterbo channel, and the boats on the Swedish west coast could not be used because of the double control which the Germans had imposed after the escape of the fifty-four refugees. Only the smallest fishing-craft were left and the January storms, snow, and frozen harbours put even those out of action. *Speditøren* reported to Sweden: 'We are very downhearted, these days. We are considering giving up the work and letting other, better people have a go, since we apparently have come to a dead end. One arrangement after another falls through.'

Members of the group travelled to all parts of Zealand in search of possible embarkation points. They sat for hours in ice-cold trains (no trains were heated in Denmark during the occupation) and still they got nowhere. The boat-owners would not, could not or dared not go out for them. Finally they found a fisherman in Copenhagen who was prepared to co-operate. Seven times they tried to get refugees into his boat; seven times they failed because the Germans were everywhere. On the last occasion they had to retire hastily with the Gestapo hard on their heels. They sent another message to Sweden: 'The big catastrophe was nearly upon us, for the harbour from which we were to have embarked at six o'clock this morning had been taken over by the Germans during the night. Another boat has been taken, but we don't know yet whether it had mail or passengers on board. We managed to withdraw all our people. Unfortunately it means that we must let the place have a rest for some time. Sorry you had to wait in vain, but the position is very difficult at the moment.' At the eighth attempt the transport succeeded.

On 15 February the Germans closed all the harbours in Zealand and forbade all traffic near and on the ships by people who did not work there. Merely to board a ship without authority became a criminal offence. *Speditøren* discussed the situation and decided that they would have to take their passengers out to ships one by one, dressed as seamen or dockers, and put them aboard in broad daylight. The new German order meant that a few skippers retired, but *Speditøren* no longer had to work after dark; further, their passengers did not have to spend a whole night huddled in a cold and dirty hold.

Towards the end of the month the group learned that one of their ships was on her way through the *Store-bælt* (Great Belt) and that she could put into Korsør for two hours without suspicion. Korsør was an unknown harbour to *Speditøren* and it was forbidden to go near any ship, but the chance was too good to miss. Sweden received a message: '*P1* should leave from Korsør harbour with ten men on board. Sounds easy, doesn't it? This is what happened. On Saturday afternoon we got ten men together in Copenhagen. That took us all afternoon, as the escapers and refugees weren't to be found in their homes. On Monday morning at five o'clock they left with two forwarders. When they got to Korsør they found that the ship hadn't arrived. Back to Copenhagen by the last train of the day. To Korsør again Tuesday morning. No boat yet. Waited all day. Just as they were going to return to Copenhagen, two men were missing. One of the forwarders stayed behind. The three of them got to the station just in time to see the last train leave. No accommodation to be found. They found an empty summer-house, smashed a window and climbed in. No blankets, no mattresses, no heat. That was a cold night. They took the first train to Copenhagen. The same day the ten left Copenhagen again, and this time the ship was there.' A footnote reported: 'Ten men sent off.'

Eight days later another fifteen men got away in *P1*, this time, direct from Copenhagen. Four were wounded saboteurs, one of whom had a wooden block in place of his foot. He had to be taken down to the harbour by bicycle, while the other three walked. The ship was lying between the Bohnstedt-Petersen works and the North Harbour shipyards, which were full of Germans. A German naval vessel was berthed at the same end of the dock. In the course of an hour fourteen men were put in *P1* and there remained only the problem of the crippled saboteur. An invalid with a wooden block for a foot and riding on the crossbar of a bicycle is a fairly uncommon sight in a dock area and his attempt to board a ship would require considerable explanation. The arrival of a Gestapo patrol of sixteen men made it necessary for the forwarder to cycle around with him for a while but eventually he was carried safely on to the ship.

On the night of 4 January fifteen thugs led by the notorious Henning Brøndum and Bothildsen-Nielsen forced their way into the Tuborg Brewery at Hellerup and blew up the brewhouse, the power station and the fuel storage installation in the harbour. Eight of *Speditøren*'s escapers were hiding in a wooden hut only fifty metres away from the huge petrol tanks; but thanks to prompt action by harbour master Johannesen the fire brigade managed to prevent the blaze from spreading to the hut. Since the whole area was swarming with soldiers and Gestapomen, the escapers had to stay put until the next morning.

Between September 1943, and May 1945, more than one thousand refugees were sent from Tuborg Harbour to Malmø by *Speditøren*, working in conjunction with other groups, and instructors, couriers, and SOE officers were brought in from Sweden by the same route. The traffic also included quantities of arms, ammunition, and explosives, mainly transported by the students, and a cargo of medical supplies to the value of DK 100,000 brought in by *Speditøren*.

In March 1945, *Speditøren* were faced with the job of evacuating a party of French, Dutch and American airmen and decided on an evening embarkation from Havnegade, in Copenhagen's Inner Harbour. As a forwarder and two of the American pilots were walking through St. Kongensgade, they were stopped by a German patrol. The forwarder was ordered to stand facing a wall with his hands up while the other two were searched. The Germans spoke to the Americans in very poor Danish, but the airmen, not understanding a word, merely grinned broadly and repeated: '*Ja, ja, ja.*' The patrol moved off and the forwarder, breathing a great sigh of relief, rejoined his charges. There were times, he reflected, when a lack of linguistic skill had distinct advantages.

Probably the first of all the escape routes was *Dansk Hjælpetjeneste* (Danish Aid Service), established in January 1943 by Tom's business partner Werner Gyberg and the merchant A. Gylding-Sabroe. The group, who operated between Gothenborg and Frederikshavn in North Jutland, were certainly one of the first to engage in arms transport and to build their own specially-equipped boats for the purpose. With Arne Elstrøm in control at Frederikshavn they got many refugees out of Jutland and sent much-needed consignments of weapons and explosives to Denmark. It was a very dangerous route because there were many German patrols in the Kattegat but the ships got through without too many losses and casualties.

In October 1943, a group led by Lieutenant Erling Kiær started a route between Elsinore and Halsingborg, using a fast motorboat. After Kiær's arrest in May 1944, *Dansk-svensk Flygtningetjeneste* provided funds to enable Police-Inspector Ejnar Andersen to reorganise the group under the name *Øresundstjeneste*.

One of the most important links in the transport chain was *Liseruten* (the Lise route), originated by Svend Aage Munck, business manager of *Berlingske Tidende*. The heroine of this operation was the East Bornholm Steamship Company's passenger liner *Carl*, which sailed several times a week between Bornholm and Copenhagen. On her way she had to pass through the Falsterbo Channel in South Sweden and during this stage of her voyage the Swedes insisted that all foreigners, including Germans, had to be kept below deck, with all portholes clamped, so that they could see nothing as the ship passed along the coast. At a certain point escapers and other illegal passengers were taken up to the bridge, and when the pilot went aboard they were transferred to the pilot boat and taken to Sweden. Naturally this efficient 'switch' had to be arranged with the Swedish military authorities, police and secret service. After the Jews had been evacuated the route was closed to ordinary escapers and was used strictly to transport very important passengers, such as wounded saboteurs, Allied airmen, members of the Freedom Council, and politicians who had official business in Sweden. It was so secure that, though Gestapo controls were carried on every trip, the Germans discovered nothing about the *Carl*'s illegal activities until the final month of the occupation. Even then, thanks to the students, she was kept out of their hands.

It is worthy of record that though the captain, his officers and the crew knew all about their illegal passengers, not one of them spoke a word—and none of them ever accepted a krone for his services.

10: KNUD

At twenty, Ib Mogens Bech Christensen, student of painting at Copenhagen's Royal Academy of Fine Arts, was an idealist. 'One of his most outstanding traits,' a friend has said, 'was a deep-felt hatred for every form of injustice, encroachment on personal liberty, and oppression. He was a convinced pacifist and a conscientious objector.'

The German invasion swiftly and decisively changed his thinking. Under the cover-name Knud the peace-loving art student was to become one of the ablest and most daring leaders in the fight for freedom.

His first brush with the Danish police, for the comparatively mild offence of painting anti-German slogans on walls, led to imprisonment in Vestre Fængsel from November 1941, to February 1942. On his release he joined *Studenternes Efterretningstjeneste* and in cooperation with Arne Sejr edited the newspaper and published several illegal books, including Steinbeck's *The Moon Is Down*, from his father's home. Unhappily, the two men could not work together. Sejr, a conservative, was suspicious of Knud's political opinions. Friction developed and at the end of June 1943, the partnership broke up. Knud transferred his allegiance to *Frit Danmark* and, following the German drive against the Jews, worked also with the transport groups.

During the latter six months of 1943 he distinguished himself in many fields. He was a prolific, forceful contributor to *Frit Danmark*; he seized supplies of paper, ink, stencils and duplicating machines for the illegal Press from Danish firms working with the Germans; he took an active part in the shipment to and from Sweden of mail, newspapers, passengers, weapons, and explosives and he raided fuel stores to get petrol and benzole for the boats. When he heard that the Germans were going to commandeer the weapons and ammunition which the citizens of Copenhagen had been forced to surrender and which were stored at the Blegdamsvej police station, he and three friends, all wearing police uniform, drove to the station, collected two hundred and forty-eight pistols, rifles, and shotguns and took them to his father's house on Rødkildevej for distribution to unarmed Resistance groups.

Shortly afterwards, while working with the transports at Stevns, Knud was told that the arms of an infantry company were hidden in a summer house at Boserup, near Lake Bure, having been transferred there from the barracks at Holbæk. He and his frend Jens Martens (Jakob), a saboteur of the Bopa group, went to Boserup and verified the information. On the following night, with ten comrades, they collected one hundred and fifty rifles, ten light machine-guns, two hundred hand-grenades, and many cases of ammuntion. The load was taken by lorry to Rødkildevej and distributed as before.

Early in November Knud and Jakob went to Sweden to buy books and other literature suitable for publication by *Frit Danmark*, but having completed their business they found to their anger and bewilderment that the Danish police in Malmø would not permit them to return to Denmark. Since no explanation for their detention was forthcoming, they decided to get out of the country without going through either Danish or Swedish police channels. Two attempts failed, but at six o'clock on the evening of 20 November they took a dinghy from a harbour just north of Halsingborg and set out for Zealand. About midnight, after six hours of battling against gale-force winds, heavy seas, and strong currents, they dragged themselves ashore near Hellebæk. From there they hired a taxi to Copenhagen, only to learn that Knud's parents had gone to Malmø that same evening and that their homes were under Gestapo observation.

'While Jens and my son were in Malmø, a conservative student denounced them to the Germans,' Ernst Christensen said. 'The Gestapo called on Jens's mother and told her: "We'll find them. We know where they are." *Frit Danmark* asked the police in Sweden to hold the boys and sent my wife and me over to warn them not to return to Denmark. I suppose we should have had to go in any case. We had two hundred and forty pistols and a hundred and forty-five rifles in the house, together with some sub-machine guns, and at that time the Gestapo were making many raids and many arrests. It could have been our turn next. We went to Malmø by fishing-boat on the night of 20 November only a few hours before Ib and Jens started out in their dinghy. We stayed in Sweden until 2 May 1945. We were to see our son again only three times.'

Unable to return to their homes, Knud and Jakob went underground. Jakob rejoined Bopa to continue his work as a saboteur. He was arrested on 23 December 1943, and sent to Vestre Fængsel. From there he was sent to Horserød concentration camp, where he remained for eight months. When new evidence piled up against him he was taken back to Vestre Fængsel and from there to Shellhus. On 9 August 1944, he and ten other men of Bopa and Holger Danske were murdered during transport along Roskildevej, ostensibly while trying to escape. The murders led to a 24-hour protest strike in Copenhagen and a number of provincial towns.

Towards the end of December 1943, Knud broke with *Frit Danmark*, saying that he was not prepared to take orders from the Comintern, and started his own group. On 1 January helped only by his future wife, Helle Gertrud Termansen, he published the first issue of *1944*, a journal which eventually was to attain a monthly print of seventy thousand copies.

During January 1944, Knud and Helle were fully occupied in obtaining ink and paper, preparing and printing the second issue, and maintaining contact with Sweden, where, during his stay in November, Knud had met a Norwegian-Swedish couple who were to assist him greatly until the end. (After the liberation both were awarded the Norwegian and Danish Freedom medals.)

As the group grew, the field of activities was extended to include sabotage, the 'organisation' of tank-lorries for the collection and storage of petrol for the boats to Sweden and for the cars of group members, contact with the illegal Press in Norway for contributions to *1944*, and towards the end of the year, the collection of documents from German archives for legal proceedings after the war against Danish collaborators and informers.

On 2 February armed squads took three thousand litres of petrol from a German depot on Frederikssundvej and five hundred litres of benzole from the Valby gasworks. Two months later, on 5 April, the group staged an even more daring raid on the UFA Film headquarters in Strøget, Copenhagen's celebrated complex of shopping streets open only to pedestrian traffic.

One who took part said: 'The evening before Maundy Thursday Knud told me to go to the chap we knew as "the Architect" to get instructions for a bit of monkey-business. He asked me jokingly if I could run fast, because I'd have to do so. That was all I could get out of him and I was somewhat apprehensive when I got to the Architect's place. I was the first one there, so I sat down and waited for something to happen. A little later a small, thickset man arrived. He wore a reefer jacket and a cap with a shiny peak. He looked like a fisherman. He asked me if I knew what was in the wind but I told him I was as ignorant as he and we found something else to talk about. We'd been waiting for about half an hour when Knud showed up. He brought a map, which we studied closely while he explained what we had to do. The target was the UFA Film building on Nygade.

'The plan was beautifully simple. One of the UFA projectionists had some overtime work in another cinema that evening. When he had finished that and was going home he was to be kidnapped and the UFA keys taken from him. Then two of our men were to go home with him and guard him until after the action. Another two men were to go to Nygade with the keys and meet us there between 11.15 and 11.30 p.m., when the fun would start.

'About five or six of us were now at the Architect's place. Knud had gone to meet the chaps who were to waylay the projectionist. The rest of us just hung on until the telephone rang to tell us that the keys had been taken and we could go to Nygade. I went with Tom. We each had two hand-grenades and a pistol. We kept our eyes skinned while we were walking through Strøget, where as a rule there were plenty of "light green" patrols. When we got to the rendezvous the lads with the keys hadn't arrived, so we dispersed and went to different street-car stops, not to look too suspicious. One *Feltpolizei* patrol after another passed by, but they didn't bother us. Finally one of our people went across to the building in Nygade and opened the door, so that we could go up the back stairs to the UFA offices on the fifth floor.

'A little later Tom and I strolled into the courtyard. When we had all gathered there Knud, I, and two others went upstairs. We had a lot of trouble finding the right key to the offices but finally managed to open the door. I found the room where I was supposed to work and began emptying one box of film after another on to the floor. They made quite a heap and I was blissfully unaware that they were non-inflammable newsreels. I dragged coils of film out into the corridor and stapled them to films which had been pulled out of other rooms. When I'd finished Knud told me to start carrying typewriters down to the courtyard. That was quite a job. I could only carry one at a time and it was a hell of a long way down the stairs. My legs felt like lead and my arms felt as if they were coming out of their sockets. As I came down for the last time a night watch-man arrived, to be promptly held up by one of our sentries. He was shaking with fright but when we told him we weren't using explosives he calmed down. I dumped the last typewriter and went upstairs again. Great festoons of film had been dragged from all the rooms and from all the boxes in the corridor. Knud pulled about ten coils out on to the back stairs and stapled them together with two copies of *Berlingske Tidende* to delay the ignition. We had to have time to get down the stairs before the fire got too much of a hold. Knud poured some paraffin over the papers and said that everything was ready. We were to signal him when we were safely in the courtyard. We loaded the type-writers into a car and then signalled to Knud, who came run-ning down the stairs. Knud and a couple of men drove off with the typewriters and the rest of us dispersed.

'It was a bit of an effort to walk away; the temptation to break into a run was almost irresistible. Just as I reached the police station on Nytorv I heard a hollow crash. The big sky-lights in the UFA building couldn't stand up to the heat and had fallen in. I stood for a little while and discussed what could have caused the bang with the policemen on duty at the station. They were sure it was sabotage but it didn't seem to occur to them that I might have had something to do with it.

'By the time I reached the fire station the pumps were on their way, but I knew they could do no more than prevent the blaze spreading to other buildings in the street. I strolled into the fire station and sat in the central administration office, following the attempts to control the fire. One report after another came in and I read them as they arrived, so that I could give Knud full information next day. I slept the night in the fire station, where I knew all the chaps.

'That little joke cost UFA Film more than 250,000 kroner and the destruction of their files caused so much confusion that the compulsory showing of German films in the cinemas was delayed for quite a time.'

On 19 June ten men of the *1944* group joined forces with Citronen, Flammen, and five other members of Holger Danske to settle accounts with the hated *Schalburgkorps*. At half past eight in the evening eight men in two cars and nine in a coal lorry drove up to the *Schalburgkorps* headquarters, the Free-masons' Hall on Blegdamsvej in the Østerbro district of Copenhagen. One squad drove slowly past the hall, shooting down the four sentries, and brought their car to a halt across the lines to block the No 3 street-car going towards the Triangle junction. The coal lorry reversed up to the hall's main entrance, with sub-machine guns trained on the doors, while the second car stopped short of the building to block the route of street-cars coming from the Triangle. Two men jumped out of the car and threw hand-grenades through the window of the guardroom while the gunners in the lorry blasted open the main doors. Most of the Schalburgmen kept under cover but two came running round the side of the building and one showed himself at a window on the first floor, all firing at the lorry with machine-pistols. They were cut down and there was no further shooting from the hall. The attackers continued to pour shots through the doors and windows but the action had gone on too long and the signal was given to withdraw. The job of blowing up the hall had to be abandoned, but that proved to be a blessing in disguise for, unknown to the Resistance men, inside were two or three hundred *Wehrmacht* troopers, attending a party as guests of K. B. Martinsen and Krenchel, the *Schalburgkorps* leaders.

H. P. Kristensen, of the *1944* group, was killed in the fighting and two others were wounded. The *Schalburgkorps* losses were twenty-one killed and wounded. During the action the steering-wheel of the car in which Citronen and Flammen were sitting was shot away, and Citronen had to make a more than usually hazardous escape, using only the steering column to control the vehicle.

When the general strike in Copenhagen was called on 26 June, some of the city's transport staff refused to cooperate. On 3 July Knud boarded a street-car at the corner of Hillerødgade and Godthaabsvej and asked the driver why he was still at work. The driver, an elderly man, said he had no option; if he refused to do his job he might lose his pension. The only other passenger sprang so hotly to his defence that Knud concluded he was a German collaborator and decided to get off at the next stop. Unluckily, this was at the corner of Borups Allé, opposite the old waterworks, which were occupied by the *Wehrmacht*.

As Knud prepared to jump, the collaborator grabbed him in a bear-hug and yelled for help from the sentry outside the water-works. The soldier cocked his rifle and ran towards the street-car. Knud tore himself free, pulled out his pistol, and fired. The soldier dropped. Knud turned on the collaborator and pressed the trigger again, but the gun jammed. The man snatched at Knud's hair, ripping out a large tuft, but he ran down the car to the rear platform and threw himself backwards through the glass pane of the door. The collaborator caught one of his feet but he freed himself by hammering the man's hands on to the jagged glass in the door frame. He dropped to the ground and, under heavy fire from the Germans at the waterworks, ran to a chemist's shop. An assistant helped him to get out through the back premises and, having tried vainly to get first-aid at a near-by school, he finally reached the group's doctor, who treated his injured scalp and the extensive cuts he had sustained in diving through the street-car window.

This was a bad time for the group. On the previous day Knud and Helle had run off a broadsheet, *Fortsæt (Carry On)*, on a duplicating machine. One of the distributors was arrested and in his possession was found a diary containing the telephone number of Helle's parents. Sixteen Gestapomen in four cars went immediately to the Termansen home. As Knud was not there, they took Helle and her father to Shellhus and thence to Vestre Fængsel, where the girl was detained for six weeks and her father for eight days. Both were released after convincing the Germans that they knew nothing of Knud's whereabouts.

On 22 July Knud sailed for Sweden to arrange liaison between the *1944* group and *Dansk-svensk Flygtningetjeneste*. Two days later came the news of the disaster at Forchhammersvej 7. Knud went to see Hendil and Kraft, who were looking for somebody to reorganise the Copenhagen end of the operation, and they agreed that he was the right man for the job. He returned to Denmark and cooperated with the Knudsen brothers in establishing the highly-efficient route between Malmø and the rubbish dump on Amager. In particular the *1944* group assumed sole responsibility for finding safe-houses for the refugees and providing bodyguards for important passengers travelling from Malmø to Copenhagen. For the help given to American pilots in difficulties Knud was posthumously decorated by the United States government.

Throughout the autumn and winter of 1944 the group continued to plague the German overlords. With the help of an expert in the Copenhagen telephone exchange they established a listening post on the line to the *Schalburgkorps* headquarters at the Freemasons' Hall. This provided information on *stikkers'* reports, on the split in the Danish Nazi party, and on those who rang officials at the hall. On the basis of this intelligence the group visited, among other collaborators, Leif Ørnberg, one of the principal dancers of the Royal Theatre Ballet, and took away his pistols and *Waffenschein* (firearms permit). After the round-up of the Danish police on 19 September they removed several private cars from the garage at Politigaarden, the police headquarters, and others belonging to Germans and collaborators from the parking lot outside the German offices at Vesterport.

On 12 December the mail for Dagmarhus, Shellhus and Vesterport was seized in a raid on the general post office on Tietgensgade. The group occupied the sorting office, where the staff enthusiastically extracted all mail destined for the Germans, which was then taken in a post office van to Utterslev Mose on the northern outskirts of the city. This action yielded valuable information on the collaboration between Germans and bad Danes. There were letters from suppliers of foodstuffs and war materials to the Germans and from others offering supplies of materials vital to Denmark; there were reports to the German central office at Vesterport on public opinion in different parts of the country; and there were many letters from informers. Because these came into the hands of the Resistance, dozens of lives were saved.

At the opening of the room dedicated to Knud's memory at the Freedom College in Copenhagen, Professor Carsten Heøgh said: 'It is thanks to Ib that I am here today, for had he not intercepted that informer's letter to the Gestapo, I should certainly have been executed immediately.'

On 21 December, to meet the group's need for petrol, Knud planned a raid on the German fuel depot at Hillerød. Parties in two tankers and three private cars drove to the town by different routes and met at the depot. While the *Wehrmacht* sentries were held under guard in the lavatories, the staff were ordered to fill the two tankers and another which the group found parked on the premises. The tankers were then driven, again by different routes, back to Copenhagen. One, escorted by a Ford car driven by Leif Schiønnemann, took the Kongevej route but at Sandbjergvej, in the Forest of Rude, the vehicles were stopped by a German road block. There were five men in the car: Schiønnemann and another member of the *1944* group in the front seats and three policemen, armed with Sten-guns, in the back. Their orders were that in a situation like this they were to put the car into second gear, slow down and then, just before reaching the barricade, give the engine full throttle. Simultaneously the three Sten-gunners were to open fire on the sentries, driving them to cover. But things did not work out that way. The car was not in second gear, and in third gear it did not accelerate quickly enough. There was no time to push the gun barrels through the windows before the Germans began shooting. One of the policemen, Gunnar Alsvold, was fatally wounded and as he collapsed he pulled the trigger of his Sten, killing Leif Schiønnemann. William, sitting next to Schiønnemann, grabbed the steering-wheel and managed to get his foot on to the accelerator. Under cover of a patrol car which was standing near the barricade, the party escaped with the loss of two dead and one wounded.

In January 1945, the group again raided the sorting office on Tietgensgade and removed the German official mail; and by way of celebrating the new year, a prototype U-boat engine was blown up at the Titan engineering works. On 19 February six hundred posters of a map of Europe in two phases were put up in Nørrebro, depicting the Germans at Stalingrad in 1942 and the Allied forces on the threshold of Germany in 1945. On 4 March the German mail was taken from Tietgensgade for the third time. Two days later the group raided the offices of Friedrich and Company, who rented pro-German 16mm newsreels, documentaries and feature films, and removed everything in the place, including correspondence and lists of customers.

On 16 March Knud and Helle crossed to Sweden to be married in Malmø by the Swedish priest Hagbart Isberg. It was the last time that Knud, his parents and his bride were to be together.

Hans-Henrik Gottschalch, 23-year-old son of two well-known Danish theatre personalities and one of the most courageous members of the 1944 group, was killed on 17 March. While carrying the Swedish mail from Amager, he and a companion ran into an ambush on Øster Allé, near the Triangle. Gottschalch was mortally wounded and died in the German field hospital on Nyelandsvej.

Knud returned to Denmark at the end of the month and on 5 April, the anniversary of the first action, led another raid on the UFA Film headquarters, this time to clear out the correspondence files. Shortly afterwards the group seized a large consignment of children's clothing, ordered from Danish firms for export to Germany. The captured garments were handed over to a Copenhagen orphanage. On 9 April, the fifth anniversary of the German occupation, two cameramen of the *1944* group, located at the top of Copenhagen's city hall tower and on the roof of the Richshus, shot the dramatic scenes as the crowd gathered in the square for the two minutes' silence at noon. The films were sent to Sweden for distribution throughout the countries of the free world.

The group's crowning exploit came on 17 April, when Knud led a raid on the German Chamber of Commerce. For more than three hours seventeen men loaded into two pantechnicons, christened Adolf and Slagelse, more than half a million letters, maps, card indexes and office equipment, stripping the rooms down to the bare walls and floors. The job was done so thoroughly that on 21 April the management had to inform the executive committee that the chamber could no longer function and that the staff had been dismissed. To cover the action three men with Sten-guns hidden under their overcoats were posted outside the building, one man with a rifle with telescopic sights was placed at a window on the landing of the first floor, and two more were stationed with light machine-guns in the back of Adolf—all with their weapons trained on the German-held Købmandskole (commercial college) on the opposite side of the street. Despite its lengthy duration, the raid was carried out without incident.

After the liberation the enormous amount of captured material was examined and positive proof was found that the chamber had been nothing but a camouflaged spy-nest, whose officials under cover of fostering commercial relations between German and Danish firms had worked systematically on 'Aryanisation' of the whole of the Danish business world. The president of the chamber, a German citizen, was a spy. Letters were found from the secretary-general in Germany to the party managements in Copenhagen and Berlin, dated from 9 April 1940, in which he informed them that from the foundation of the chamber in 1936 he had never granted agencies for German products to Jewish firms and that, qualifications being equal, he had recommended first German citizens, then German nationals and, in the last instance, Danish firms who were members of the chamber. He favoured Danes who informed on Jewish and anti-German firms and individuals.

There was a card index (*Warnkartei*) which had certainly been used against the Jews and their helpers during September and October 1943, and which equally certainly would have been used against anti-German Danes if Hitler had won the war. It was also evident that the chamber had systematically given information to Berlin on Denmark's capacity in industry, farming and fisheries for use in Germany's demands for supplies.

The books, files and correspondence removed from the chamber established conclusively that at least five thousand firms in Denmark had distinguished themselves unfavourably and, in certain cases, criminally. The records showed that almost all German citizens and nationals resident in Denmark, and many Danes, had been ready to provide Berlin with information on internal Danish affairs of interest to the German government and on the attitudes of firms and individuals to the Third Reich, even when this information could have proved fatal to the people concerned. There was also clear proof that some Danish businessmen had informed on Jews and anti-German competitors in order to take over the agencies they held. There were applications from Danish firms to be appointed suppliers to Germany and to the *Wehrmacht* in Denmark, and unprincipled young Danes had written to ask for underpaid work in Germany and German-occupied countries to 'improve efficiency in the German language and culture for the new, post-war Europe under Germany's leadership'.

All the documents, together with the letters taken by the *1944* group in their raids on the sorting office in Tietgensgade, were passed to the reorganised Danish police after the liberation for use in prosecuting the collaborators. The whole of the correspondence, including that of the five thousand compromised firms, is now deposited in the Danish official archives, where it has been placed on the 'secret list' for fifty years because of its dangerous—and too numerous—disclosures of un-Danish activities during the occupation. Copies of typical letters can be seen in the Clandestine Research collection at the Freedom Museum in Churchillsparken, Copenhagen.

On Sunday, 22 April 1945, the *1944* group met to plan the final shooting practice in Hareskoven, a forest to the north of Copenhagen. As the meeting broke up, one young man said: 'How I long to see the end of this business and live a normal life!' Knud answered: 'You're right. I'll write about that in the next issue.' But his article was never written.

On the following day the entire group, numbering some fifty men, made their way out to Hareskoven. Knud and two friends led the way in a small Morris car, followed by a covered lorry packed with men and weapons. After them came the rest on bicycles.

As they were approaching Skovbrynet, Knud, who was driving, saw by the level crossing at the foot of the hill a German road block manned by soldiers in armoured cars and on motorcycle combinations equipped with machine-guns. He turned the car round to go back and warn the others, but the Germans had spotted him and an armoured car and two motorcycles set off in pursuit. Realising that his little Morris could not out-distance them, Knud drove it across the sidewalk and into a hedge. His two companions jumped out and made off towards the woods. Knud, chased by two Germans in a motorcycle and sidecar, bolted in the opposite direction, firing as he ran. A bullet from his Colt automatic wounded one of the soldiers before the other, in the sidecar, cut loose with the machine-gun. Three bullets slammed into Knud's head and body, killing him instantly.

'News reached me in Malmö that my son had been arrested and was gravely wounded,' Ernst Christensen said. 'I came back to Denmark on 2 May and went around all the hospitals in Copenhagen, trying to find him, but nobody had any information to give me. I went back to Sweden and on 8 May, four days after the liberation, I returned with my wife and Helle. We searched everywhere for our son but not until 23 June did we hear that his body had been found in a field at Ryvangen, where the Germans had buried him.'

Knud was not left in that shabby grave. Today he lies in Mindelunden, Copenhagen's Garden of Remembrance, between his friends Jens Martens and Hans-Henrik Gottschalch.

During the first two years of the occupation sabotage played a very small part in the activities of the Resistance movement. A few individualists expressed their feelings by putting sugar in the petrol tanks or slashing the tyres of German military vehicles, there were minor arson attempts, and occasionally sand or emery powder was slipped into a factory machine, but apart from the high-spirited exploits of the schoolboy Churchill Club in Aalborg there was no attempt at systematic disruption. That situation changed at the end of June 1942, and during July and August the German and Danish authorities were shaken by a wave of communist-inspired sabotage in Copenhagen, Silkeborg, Aarhus, Aalborg, and other provincial towns.

The first and most active organised saboteurs were the group later to become known as Bopa. They were essentially a Copenhagen organisation and, although a few actions were carried out elsewhere in Zealand, almost all their activities took place within the boundaries of the capital. Their operations were aimed mainly at industrial targets and only to a limited extent at railways and other transport systems, which were harried efficiently by the Jutland saboteurs under Anton J. Toldstrup. Bopa squads certainly arranged some derailments (among them the first railway sabotage action in Denmark), raided trains in transit, and engaged in other transport sabotage, but their primary objective was the disruption of factories working for the German war machine. In this field the group were responsible for 80–90% of all major actions within the boundaries of Copenhagen, where most of the industrial sabotage in Denmark occurred.

The administrative preparations for the foundation of Bopa began during the winter of 1941–2, following the banning of the Danish communist party. Børge Houmann, formerly commercial manager of the communist daily *Arbejderbladet* and later a member of the Freedom Council, and Thorkild Holst, a top communist party functionary, were the prime instigators, though neither man was ever an active saboteur.

Most of the original members of the group were International Brigade veterans of the Spanish civil war. They were seasoned fighters but few of them had practical experience as saboteurs; their operations, therefore, were hampered as much by the paucity of technical and tactical knowledge as by an almost total lack of explosives, arms, and other equipment. During the first actions the only weapon available was one pistol—'to be shared'—and later this was found not to be in working order. There was a crippling shortage of funds and men on the run from the Gestapo and Danish police had great difficulty in finding safe-houses, for at that period most of the Danish population, in common with prime minister Vilhelm Buhl and his government, completely rejected the idea of sabotage. Much as they disliked the Germans, they could not bring themselves to sanction or take part in an active fight against the occupying forces which might also damage Danish property or endanger Danish lives. Consequently, few were prepared to give shelter to hunted 'terrorists'.

Bopa's first action, probably the first organised sabotage attempt in Denmark, took place on 9 April 1942, the second anniversary of the occupation. The intention was to set fire to some German railway trucks containing hay and straw which were standing in a siding at the Østerport station. It was a fiasco. The saboteurs were unable to ignite the soggy bales of fodder. Subsequent actions, for the most part arson and vandalism, were more successful. Explosives were used rarely, for the group's stock consisted only of very small quantities of gunpowder. The desperate need for supplies of more powerful agents led to an attempt to make aerolite in the kitchen of a private apartment. It was only by sheer luck that the experimenters did not blow themselves sky-high.

To obviate similar catastrophes and to deal with the many problems troubling members of the group, *Kogebog for Sabotører* (The Saboteurs' Cookbook), was produced. This unique publication ran to about one hundred typed pages, lavishly

illustrated with hand-drawn, stencilled diagrams. Five copies
were made, of which, to the best of my knowledge, only two
still exist. The author was Eigil Larsen, one of the first Bopa
leaders, with Johannes Glavind as technical consultant. The
book, a *vade mecum* for the apprentice saboteur, gave comprehensive instruction not only in the home-manufacture of explosives, bombs and incendiary devices but on the organisation
and conduct of sabotage groups, together with helpful sections
on railway regulations and similar matters. It would be unwise
to quote in detail the ingenious methods laid down for the
making of infernal machines from the most commonplace and,
even in wartime, easily obtainable materials, but an extract from
the chapter on group organisation may be not without interest:

Sections must not associate with each other and only in
an emergency may two sections of ten men work together.
The practical method is this: The group leader and the
leader of a ten-man team meet—at that meeting assigning the
jobs to be done. At the same time instructions are given so
that the work to be carried out can preferably be done on
the same day and at the same time by all the sections. The
more that happens at one time, the greater the effect.

Every section must help in procuring and *forwarding* information about suitable targets—and why they are suitable!

All sections must keep an eye on and report where suitable
materials for our purposes can be found. A section may use
such materials, however, only after specific orders.

No section may begin a job without specific orders; otherwise there is a risk of the same work being done on the same
objective by several sections. Because a section have sent in a
report about a suitable target, that does *not* mean they have
an exclusive right to it.

A section shall carry out their given task *before* they tackle
a new one. They must not busy themselves with anything else,
no matter how interesting it may be.

*There must be absolute secrecy on the part of all members
about all their section's affairs.* In no circumstances must there
be idle chatter or a 'knowing' smile or a wink to indicate that

one 'knows something'. Anyone who talks must be excluded immediately from further participation. It would be unwise —and false comradeship—to believe that 'everything will be all right'.

If by bad luck and despite all precautions a man is arrested, he must deny everything and not let himself be duped by 'your pal has confessed' or whatever else the police can find to say. It is never a comrade's statement which matters, it is always one's own; otherwise they would not go to such lengths to make the prisoner talk. Should it happen that a man, despite all instructions and pledges, fails to hold out, the police will naturally use his confession against others. In such an event, a man must continue to deny everything and take things coolly and calmly, even though he is confronted with the other accused party while he repeats his statement.

In the event of arrest—give only your name, address, and possible alibi, nothing else at all! No matter what happens! You may be promised the earth, but despite all such temptations you cannot escape by talking—but perhaps you can by maintaining absolute silence.

Most of those rules remained in force until the end of the occupation but some had to be modified in the light of experience. That as many as ten men were needed on every job and that as many actions as possible had to be carried out on the same day and at the same time were consequences of the way in which the work was done during the first months. The group was small and the operations were limited, so that it simply was not necessary (even had the numbers been available) to mobilise forty, fifty, or a hundred men for a single action. Equally, the aim of the early operations was to a great extent to encourage passive Danes to join in the work of hampering the German war production; therefore, 'as much as possible on the same day at the same time'. The instructions on behaviour under arrest lost much of their force when the Gestapo took over the handling and interrogation of captured saboteurs. The bravest and most steadfast are liable to break under torture. In that there is no disgrace.

Bopa's first big supply of explosives was procured by raiding the stores of the Faxe Quarry, about eighty kilometres south of Copenhagen. On the return journey some of the participants were arrested by the Danish police, so that the total haul amounted to only some ten or fifteen kilogrammes of aerolite; but even this was a triumph. Such raids were not much more than nuisances to the Germans but they aroused considerable public excitement and on 2 September 1942, prime minister Buhl found it necessary to make a radio broadcast condemning the saboteurs. Danish guards were hired to protect factories engaged in war production and the police redoubled their efforts to break the group. Almost all the most active members were traced and arrested by Danish policemen. Many, despite promises to the contrary, were handed over to the Germans and sent to German prisons. Aage Julius Nielsen, one of the International Brigade veterans, died in Vestre Fængsel on 18 October 1943, from injuries received during interrogation. A few months earlier, on 6 June, Harry Svend Plambech, wounded during an action, had killed himself to ensure that his comrades escaped. Svend Eduard Rasmussen was executed at Ryvangen on 22 November. Arne Egon Hansen was shot in the back 'while trying to escape' on 4 December. Victor Imanuel Larsen, Martin Villiam Andersen and Knud Enver Nielsen were killed on 26 December. Others, like Henry Jacobsen, Jonny and Harald Nielsen and Hans Petersen, were deported to convict prisons and concentration camps in Germany.

Successors were recruited, but the character of the organisation changed. The new saboteurs were younger, most of them between seventeen and twenty years old, and without the firm communist background of the pioneers. The name Bopa in fact resulted from the older members' slight dissatisfaction with this development, which coincided with efforts to establish a non-party political cooperation within the Resistance as a whole. One of the veterans said in a moment of irritation that eventually *Borgerlige Partisaner* (Bourgeois Partisans), not *Kommunistiske Partisaner*, would be the correct description of the group, and the name stuck in its condensed form.

The group had to be reorganised several times and from

the spring of 1944 until the liberation the practical management was in the hands of Børge Thing (Børge Brandt), a plumber in his middle twenties. Bopa members were a mixed crowd. Most were young labourers, artisans, clerical workers, apprentices and factory operatives but there was a leavening of engineers, teachers, doctors, and other professional men. There were no demands, requirements, or questions concerning political allegiances, and the widely-held concept of Bopa as a 'red' group stems merely from the fact that some (though by no means all) of the leaders were communists or communist sympathisers.

In accordance with classic 'underground' principles Bopa comprised a number of sections, normally of three to six people, each of whom had only one connecting link with the remainder of the group. That, at least, was the theory; in practice it was necessary to bend this rule because, among other considerations, many actions required the participation of more than one section. The number of sections varied but the combined forces of Bopa probably never at any one time exceeded two hundred men. It was the conscious aim to keep the *apparat* of the organisation so simple and flexible that it could be adjusted with the least possible difficulty to meet the ever-changing conditions during the occupation. From the formation of the Freedom Council Børge Thing was in close contact through intermediaries with the council and their commando committee, from whom Bopa received general directives on sabotage activities and were informed of specific targets. Through the SOE representative on the Freedom Council Bopa had a direct communication line to the Allied military command and several of the major actions carried out by the group followed direct requests from SHAEF. The tactical planning of each individual action was the responsibility of Bopa, who also determined many of the targets.

Kai Merved saw long service with the group. He was one of the 'Elsinore boys', who first got in touch with Bopa through one of the leaders, Kaj Beckmann (Bruhn). They had planned to blow up the Elsinore shipyard but the action was forbidden by the Freedom Council. Merved said: 'During 1942 Bopa carried out about twenty very small actions, using mainly home-made equipment. They could do very little damage at that time because they had only the things they could make for themselves. They were only about twenty strong but the famous KK (Jørgen Jespersen) was already one of the leaders. In the spring of 1943 the group did a lot of sabotage. They established contact with SOE agents and got a small share of the arms and explosives dropped into Denmark by the RAF. Luckily we were never solely dependent on that source of supply. Throughout the war we had great difficulty in getting explosives and arms and I know that Holger Danske had similar problems. The weapons dropped by the British didn't reach us. Some people seemed to be scared to put guns into our hands because we were thought to be communists, so we had to steal rifles and pistols from German soldiers or from guards in factories. We got some English stuff, but not much. We raided the magazines of the Danish navy and Danish contractors' stores for supplies of explosives and some of the lads got pistols and sub-machine guns in other actions. But many had nothing better than toy pistols, converted to take a single round of ball ammunition, in the early days.

'By August, 1943, Bopa had grown to between fifty and a hundred men and were doing a great deal of sabotage in factories in and around Copenhagen. On one night they carried out five actions against factories in Hillerød. At eight o'clock on the evening of 29 August that year a bomb was thrown through the window of a steel-hardening plant in Nørrebro, just to show the group was still alive. That action was planned by Poul Petersen (HH) and led by Victor Behring Mehl (Jens), later shot by the Germans. On 23 November, in another action planned by HH, a team led by KK attacked and destroyed the transformer station which supplied electricity to four hundred factories and all the houses and apartments in Nørrebro. It was the group's first daylight raid and hundreds of men and women stood on the platform of the railway station, high above the plant, and watched them. The people were with the saboteurs by that time. That's why they could work in comparative security. It's impossible to operate a Resistance movement unless the people are with you.

'I don't know how many actions Bopa staged altogether. I

know KK personally took part in a hundred and twenty-five at least. I suppose the total must have been around five hundred.

'In December 1943, the group destroyed the power station in the shipyard of Burmeister and Wain. The RAF had bombed the yard in January, twelve months before. They didn't do much damage to the plant but about twenty civilians were killed. Nobody was killed during the Bopa action, which showed that sabotage was less costly than bombing for the Danes.'

Five men, led by Jørgen Jespersen, took part in the attack. Two were apprentices at the shipyard and it was their job to get the explosives past the guards.

'We were going to use seventy-five kilos, partly of trotyl which we'd taken from a Danish army depot and partly of English plastic,' Jespersen said. 'It was smuggled through in a briefcase in lots of eight kilos each day. One of the apprentices carried the briefcase into the yard in the morning and hid the explosive in the cloakroom. But things didn't go according to plan. On the evening set for the attack a team were posted opposite the power station, on the other side of the canal, to cover the action-squad. The idea was that if the saboteurs got into difficulties, the cover-team would have a boat ready to ferry them across the canal. I don't know how it happened, but just as the action-squad were going into the shipyard two of the men on the boat fell into the water. The rumpus alerted the guards and I had to call off the raid.

'A few days later we tried again. We all wore workmen's overalls and got into the yard through a little-used door. Once inside, three of us hid under a machine near the power station while the other two went off to fetch the explosives. We saw that getting into the power station was going to be quite a problem. The building had double doors and it was fitted with internal and external alarm systems. According to the plan, one of the windows should have been left open but, to our dismay, they were all tightly closed. To add to our troubles, the night shift of the nearby gasworks began to arrive. We had to hold up seventeen or eighteen of them while we figured what to do next. Our situation was really unhealthy. At any minute the heavily-armed guards might come on the scene and we had only a sub-machine gun and a few pistols with which to defend ourselves. As we stood there, sweating, a man came out of the power house, propped a ladder against the wall, opened a window and went back inside. We could have cheered. Leaving one of the team in charge of the gasmen, three of the others nipped up the ladder and in through the window. The fifth went around to the main doors with the explosives. The power station staff had a hell of a shock when we burst in. The foreman was so upset that he couldn't utter a word. The thought of his beautiful diesel engines going up in smoke was too much for him. I could swear there were tears in his eyes.

'While one of the team held up the staff, the others got busy placing the charges around the four giant diesels. That took about twelve minutes. We could see the shift in an adjoining workshop watching us through the windows but they didn't interfere; they thought we were electricians doing a repair job. As soon as the three-minute fuses were lit we told the staff to get out and warn their mates; then we rushed out, slamming the doors behind us, and bolted through the shipyard with the workers, yelling into every workshop that the place was going up. Everybody got away safely but the power station was completely wrecked.'

Bopa's success was due, apart from the outstanding courage and skill of the saboteurs, largely to two factors: First, since young workers formed such a strong part of the group, it was usually possible to find or plant one or two 'Trojan horses' in the target establishments to supply detailed information and often to help in other ways; and secondly, there was an extraordinary flexibility. Bopa operations ranged from minor actions by individuals to massive organised assaults. Indeed, the destruction of the Globus works in the Copenhagen suburb of Glostrup came almost into the category of a full-scale commando raid.

Globus, one of the Germans' most vital factories in Denmark, made aircraft components and parts for the V2 rockets. It had long been one of Bopa's most coveted targets but it appeared to be almost impregnable. There were so many Nazis and collaborators on the staff that it was practically impossible to obtain any useful information about the guard system and the weapons with which the guards were armed. Every attempt to infiltrate group members as workmen failed. The management were too cautious. The group had general drawings of the factory lay-out, obtained from the building authorities, and they knew that the guards were recruited from the notorious *Sommerkorps*, formed by the Nazi Captain Sommer, and were all Eastern Front veterans. That was the extent of the information on which they had to build.

Men were sent out singly and in pairs to reconnoitre. They had to find out how many guards there were in the works and how they were armed; how many German guard posts there were in the neighbourhood, what weapons they held, and what alarm systems they had; the points from which reinforcements for the factory guards could be sent, how big a force could be raised and how quickly they could get to the scene of action. Transport of the Bopa men to the factory could be arranged, but how were they to get away again with their own and captured weapons? Gathering all this information took many weeks and entailed terrifying risks, but gradually a plan was brought to completion.

On 6 June 1944, cover-squads blockaded the whole district surrounding the Globus works, occupying all roads leading into the area, including the main artery, Roskildevej, between Vestvolden and Copenhagen to the east and Glostrup and Roskilde to the west. The German guards posted at Vestvolden were to be kept under observation and shot down if they made a move. At Avedøre a squad were posted to hold up any attempt at reinforcing the factory guards. The road was mined and parties armed with automatic rifles and sub-machine guns were hidden at all junctions.

One hundred men took part in the action against the factory. The attack was planned to begin at seven o'clock, but as it was still light at that time of the evening the approach had to be made with the utmost caution. The first squad set out early in the afternoon on bicycles. They were dressed as Boy Scouts but their rucksacks contained sub-machine guns and grenades and they carried pistols in the pockets of their shorts for use against any inquisitive German patrols. A second contingent made their way to Glostrup by rail, travelling in small parties by different trains during the course of the afternoon. The main body of the force, carrying the explosives, embarked in a fleet of seven trucks and cars 'requisitioned' at the last moment from the military, police and private owners.

At six o'clock the attackers closed in on the factory from all sides. Those in the south were protected by a railway embankment thickly grown with trees and bushes. To the north, where the factory faced towards Roskildevej, houses provided cover. In the east and west villas were occupied—with the owners' willing consent—and marksmen were placed in windows which gave a clear field of fire over the factory area. By seven o'clock everybody was in position. The plan laid down that the attack should open from the north. A hand-grenade thrown against the factory's top storey, where an armed German engineer was stationed, would be the signal for a general assault. However, if before the agreed time a Bopa man were seen by one of the guards, he should shoot and so signal the attack.

In a report typical of many, Børge Brandt relates: 'I lay on the south side with Knud. We had a whole lot of new people with us but they didn't seem to be nervous. With our sub-machine guns ready, we sneaked right up to the barbed-wire fence which separated us from the factory area. Under cover of the bushes we got so close to the guard that we were at most ten metres from him. He was marching up and down in front of a pillbox (there were concrete bunkers in every corner of the factory area). It was a couple of minutes to seven and it can't be denied that the waiting time seemed long to us. The minutes crawled by. Knud and I lay there, following the guard back and forth with our guns. The other men lay behind us, flat in the tall grass.

'Seven o'clock came and nothing happened. One minute passed, then two. A movement by Knud alerted the guard and he swung round, pointing his sub-machine gun in our direction and shouting: "*Hvem der?*" Just as he was about to shoot, Knud's gun went into action. I joined in and there was answering fire from all sides. In between the chatter of the sub-machine

guns sounded the slightly slower cadence of automatic rifles and
the dull boom of the hand-grenades. We saw our guard fall and
heard a scream somewhere else as we stormed over a fence into
a garden which lay near the factory. Every time we had to leave
shelter our comrades behind covered us with steady bursts from
their weapons. All around us we could hear shouts and screams.
We forced our way into the building in front of us, blowing
open the door with a hand-grenade. Just in case guards had
hidden themselves in any of the workshops we ran around,
chucking hand-grenades through the windows. In this way we
finally reached the guard house.'

After a stubborn resistance all the Sommerkorpsmen were
forced back into the guard house, which was raked with heavy
fire and bombarded with grenades. When the fight had gone on
for about twenty-five minutes, a despairing cry came from
within the building: 'Naade! Naade!' ('Mercy! Mercy!'). The
order was given to cease fire and the guards were commanded to
walk out and stand against the wall. After search they were
allowed to collect their dead and wounded and thereafter
herded together out of harm's way. Then the truck carrying the
explosive, one hundred and seventy-five kilos of trotyl, was
driven in and the charges laid. The fuses were set with a three-
minutes delay to give everybody time to get into the trucks and
cars. Meanwhile a runner had been sent out to order the cover-
squads to assemble in Roskildevej to meet the returning vehicles.
Hundreds of people gathered along Roskildevej to greet the
triumphant saboteurs. They cheered themselves hoarse and the
Bopa men sang and waved to them with their sub-machine guns
as they drove off towards Copenhagen.

The rearguard found that the petrol tank of their car had
been shot to pieces, so they commandeered a motor bus to get
them home. On the road to the city they picked up the group's
doctor, 35-year-old Erik Hagens. His car, also, had been disabled
by a shot in the petrol tank. He took over the steering-wheel of
the bus and the journey continued. Near the Carltorp engineering works (later blown up by Bopa) the party encountered a
Sommerkorps patrol who were heading for Globus. As the bus
passed, the Nazis opened fire. Dr. Hagens was hit in the back of

the head by a dum-dum bullet and killed instantly. Steeled as they were to losing comrades, his death deeply affected the group, who had regarded him affectionately as an elder brother.

It took from two to six months to plan some of the major actions. The group was helped by its good connections with the Danish police, the building authorities, and some of the insurance companies. All the latter had detailed plans of the buildings they covered and these were often made available to the saboteurs. There were also good friends among the railway officials. At daily meetings they kept Bopa informed of all traffic movements in and out of Copenhagen, which enabled them to deal with trains carrying ammunition and war materials. Most of the group's operations were 'quiet' actions, in which the object was achieved without a shot being fired, thanks to courage, cunning, ingenuity and thorough planning. The raid on Denmark's biggest arms factory, *Riffelsyndikatet* (Rifle Syndicate), was a good example.

That operation, which laid the syndicate's central workshops in ruins and stopped production for the duration of the war, was carried out on 22 June 1944. It was a masterpiece of planning and organisation. Following the assault on the Globus works and similar actions, security on all war production plants had been tightened considerably. The syndicate's sprawling territory in the Free Port was surrounded by a tall fence in which live wires were connected to alarm bells in the guard house. There were sixty to seventy Danish guards on the premises, all armed with sub-machine guns and trained so rigorously that the Germans regarded them as a model anti-sabotage corps. They worked in three shifts, with sentries posted along the works boundaries and the remainder of the squad in the centrally-situated guard house. At the main entrance to the works and along the perimeter there were concrete bunkers with direct telephone lines for calling up German reinforcements in case of attack. The fact that the works lay in the Free Port area, which could be sealed off easily, presented an additional problem for saboteurs.

'At about the time of the Globus raid a man from the army arsenal put us in touch with one of the syndicate guards,' said one who took part in the action. 'This chap was secretly a member of a military group, so we could trust him. He told us that his group had thought about raiding the factory to get arms but they hadn't the resources. Their leaders met ours and it was agreed that they should cooperate with us and have a share in the weapons we hoped to get but that they should leave the actual attack and blasting to us. By another stroke of luck, two more of the syndicate guards were willing to work with us. They pinched civil defence posters from the factory which gave us detailed drawings of the buildings and the whole lay-out.

'About twenty of us, not counting the military, were detailed for the raid and we had to work fast. We had exactly a week to get everything ready because we had been tipped off that the entire guard system was to be changed. We cleared the action with the Freedom Council and collected the necessary explosives; then we got down to the hard planning. On a job of this scale it was vital for every man to know exactly where he had to go and what he had to do, minute by minute. One small slip could put us all in the soup. Our usual rendezvous wasn't available, so we had to hold our instruction meetings in a hall normally used for dances and parties. We gathered round the tables with our sketch-maps spread out in plain sight, and with the waiters walking to and fro all the time it was a bit nerve-racking, but we managed.

'Timing of the raid was all-important. Knocking-off time for the syndicate workers was five o'clock and we had to let them get out of the place before we could begin. There were hundreds of them and we couldn't possibly keep an eye on them all. By six o'clock there would be only a hundred men in the works besides the guards, and we felt we could cope with that number. But we had to complete our job by half past seven at latest because the guards changed shift at eight o'clock.

'We had two motor lorries, which we had borrowed from the civil defence, and the military group had their own truck. Late in the afternoon of 22 June they were driven down to the Free Port and parked in a narrow alley opposite the customs post. Shortly before six o'clock eight men walked through the customs gate and strolled on past the syndicate fence as if they were going to an inn further along the harbour. Like the rest of us, they were dressed as workmen and carried pistols in their pockets. Two of the syndicate guards who were on our side were with that party; the third kept watch outside the bunker by the factory's main entrance, where there were three men with a direct telephone line to the Germans.

'On the stroke of six our two lorries pulled up at a side-gate to the factory and the drivers talked the gatekeeper into opening it. As soon as he did so, he was grabbed and taken into custody. Meanwhile two of "our" guards seized the sentry at the nearest post on the perimeter and brought him down to the gate while the third went into the bunker by the main entrance and held up the three men who were sitting by the telephone. A few minutes later, without noise and without fuss, every guard in the factory had been overpowered.

'The lorries were then driven in and for the next hour we were busy loading them. We took thirty or forty automatic rifles, two 20mm cannons, about thirty thousand rounds for the rifles, and two thousand rounds for the cannons. For good measure we relieved the guards of sixty sub-machine guns and a large quantity of ammunition. The lorries were so jam-packed with stuff that one of the cannons had its barrel sticking out over the tailboard.

'While all this was going on, the demolition squad were laying their charges. In the main building, which housed the rifling machinery, a fifty-kilo charge was placed against each of the four pillars to make sure the whole structure would collapse; two charges of twenty-five kilos were laid in the hardening department; and in the machine-hall there were six charges of twenty-five kilos each. The total of four hundred kilos was the largest quantity used in any known sabotage action in Denmark. All the charges were connected in series, so that the four in the rifling department exploded simultaneously, followed by the two in the hardening department, and then the six in the machine-hall.

'The job was done so efficiently and so quietly that few of the workers realised what was happening. Those who blundered into the area where the saboteurs were working were herded down to the main entrance, where the guards were being held. There was one awkward moment when a man who claimed to be a photographer for one of the illegal papers suddenly appeared. He was probably what he said he was but we couldn't take chances and he was sent down to the gate with the others. When all the charges were laid and the fuses lit, the factory's air-raid siren was switched on, the lorries drove out, the workers and guards took cover and we departed hurriedly.

'The two lorries and the military truck got away safely but the driver of the lorry which had the cannon sticking out at the back didn't dare to go to the depot until darkness had fallen. He parked the lorry in a courtyard and there it stood, unattended, for several hours with its load of some ten thousand kroners' worth of arms and ammunition. When it finally reached the depot, it had to be unloaded in the street and quite a few passers-by stopped to watch. We heard afterwards that they thought the cannon was some kind of spraying apparatus. Well—it was, in a way. Six months later it "sprayed" with deadly effect in an attack on a factory in the South Harbour, completely destroying the German bunkers and guardroom. That was the only time a cannon was used in a sabotage job in Copenhagen.'

Following the Rifle Syndicate action and an equally successful raid on another factory which netted twelve hundred Sten-gun barrels, Bopa decided to go into arms manufacture on their own account. Their plans were not ambitious; the aim was merely to make an efficient sub-machine gun patterned on the Sten. Peter Emil Vilhelm Haslund, a skilled mechanic, was put in charge of the work, with a German deserter as helper. Later two other assistants were recruited. The section worked in complete isolation from the other Bopa members. Only one saboteur knew the location of the workshop and had contact with Haslund.

Production began in a small cycle factory on Køge Landevej, in the suburb of Valby, but after a close friend of the owner had been arrested by the Gestapo the section moved to Holte and established a workshop above a garage on Kongevej. They

had none of the gunsmith's specialised equipment. All the work
had to be done on drilling machines and lathes of the types to
be found in any little repair shop. A Sten-gun has about forty-
five component parts, excluding the barrel, and every single
one of these had to be hand-cut with metal-shears or similar
tools. Obtaining oxygen and acetylene gas for welding was also
a problem. There was a very great shortage of both and only
authorised master-smiths could get supplies—and then only if
they were regular customers. At last the section found a pro-
ducer willing to cooperate, once he knew the uses to which his
wares would be put. To protect him, the gas cylinders were
ordered on legitimate forms through a motor works on Kongevej and were collected by the section on a specially adapted
tricycle. Further to protect the supplier and his staff there were
carefully written accounts and receipts for every delivery.
Under similar safeguards another friendly manufacturer supplied the section with some hundreds of metres of tubing and
the rest of the materials needed was acquired in raids on factories working for the Germans. Sten-gun barrels, the only components the section could not make, were 'requisitioned' from
the military arsenal on Amager and from the stores of the Rifle
Syndicate.

Throughout the winter of 1944 and the spring of 1945 the
four-man section carried on in their secret workshop, undis-
turbed by German or Hipo patrols. They not only copied the
Sten-gun successfully; they even improved upon it. The original
Sten, with its long metal skeleton butt, was difficult to conceal
under a coat. The Bopa-gun was given a wooden pistol butt
and, as the barrel was only fifty centimetres long, the weapon
took up surprisingly little room. Because of their limited equipment and the difficulties in getting materials, the section could
turn out only about ten guns in a week, but every one was
thoroughly tested before it was issued for service. When a batch
was ready, two men from the section went in the middle of the
night to the Rude Forest, and while one kept watch the other
put up a dimly-lit target and blazed away until he had tried all
the guns or the target was wrecked. From these and other test-
shootings it was established that the bullets from a Bopa-gun

fired at ten metres range could penetrate a three-millimetre steel
plate or a ten-inch slab of pine.

The finished weapons were taken to Copenhagen from Holte
by S-train (the fast suburban passenger service). Packed in
corrugated paper, they were slung up into the luggage rack like
any ordinary parcel. Bopa had many arms depots in the capital
but the men who brought the guns from Holte knew of only
one. If they were taken by the Gestapo while making a delivery,
the group would lose only that depot. Similarly, part of the
stock of gun-making materials was spread around depots in the
city; so, if the workshop had been raided, the group would still
have had enough stuff to start production again.

On one occasion a cannon which Bopa had taken from a
German aircraft was being transported to the workshop by
S-train. As two of the workshop section stepped out on to the
platform at Virum with the bulky package on their shoulders,
three or four of the German station guards walked purposefully
towards them. Said one of the pair: 'Our blood ran cold. We
thought that we had carried the joke too far and we expected
the worst. But they only wanted a smoke. They hadn't had a
smoke all day, and now they saw a chance to sneak a whiff by
walking behind us under cover of our load.'

Though they preferred to stick to making and repairing Bopa-
guns and similar weapons, the section gradually became experts
in all types of firearms from revolvers to anti-tank guns and
bazookas. One of their productions was an effective hand-grenade.
A two-inch water pipe was cut into pieces about seventy centimetres long, each piece being provided with a welded base.
Trotyl was used as the charge and the cover was fitted with a
detonator similar to that used in army hand-grenades. This
weapon proved somewhat dangerous to make and to use, so,
since grenades could be procured elsewhere, production was
switched to Parabellum cartridges for the Bopa-guns.

An even more ingenious device was developed in the spring
of 1945. It was a miniature torpedo, one metre long and carrying
thirty kilos of explosive, for use against German shipping in
harbour. The forward compartment of the hull held the charge,
to be exploded by an electric detonator when two leads were

short-circuited on contact with the ship's side; amidships was a six-volt car battery to supply the power; and aft was a self-starter motor from a car, connected with the propeller. The motor was started by pulling a contact up through a vertical, eight-inch-long tube welded to the top of the hull. When filled, the torpedo floated submerged just beneath the surface of the water. A fishing-line was attached to the rudder, so that the torpedo could be steered from the shore. The weapon had a range of one hundred to two hundred metres and a speed on test-runs of about ten kilometres an hour. Its effectiveness was never proved because the capitulation came before it could be used.

The extent and diversity of Bopa's operations during the three and a half years of the group's existence are remarkable. In 1942 they carried out thirty-one sabotage actions; in 1943 three hundred and fifty-four; in 1944 two hundred and sixty-four; and in 1945 one hundred and twenty-eight. Of these, three hundred and thirty-eight actions were against factories; forty-three against harbour installations, shipyards, ships, and cranes; ninety-nine against German military installations and depots; twenty-four against electrical undertakings; eighty-seven against garages and vehicles; forty-four against oil and petrol installations; thirty-nine against restaurants catering for the Germans; thirty-six against laundries, uniform cleaners, and similar establishments; and seventy-four against Nazi business concerns. This summary takes no account of the railway sabotage outside Copenhagen, of the many raids on German and Danish arms stores, of the excellent work of the radio and propaganda sections, and of the specialist team who produced false identity cards, weapons permits, and similar documents, or of the grim activities of the liquidation squads who, together with Holger Danske, carried out most of the executions of traitors and informers.

The group's most spectacular achievement came on 27 March 1945, when Langebro, the larger of the two bridges connecting the island of Amager with Copenhagen, was put out of action. At that time more than forty big Danish merchantmen were lying in the South Harbour. Sixteen of them were about to be commandeered by the Germans for the transport of troops and coal supplies and it was feared that the remainder would suffer a similar fate, but the sailings could be prevented by making Langebro inoperable. The ships could not pass the South Harbour sluice and so would be bottled up until the end of the war.

In the afternoon of 26 March the Bopa leaders met harbour and ministry officials in a room at the ministry of transport to discuss the possibilities. The objective was to prevent the bridge from being raised while doing as little damage as possible to the structure. Langebro was used every day by many thousands of Copenhageners on their way to and from work. If the roadway were destroyed they would have to make a considerable detour and that, apart from all other considerations, might cost the Resistance dear in terms of public sympathy and understanding. The only practicable solution seemed to be to blow up the hoisting mechanism, which was housed in an engine-room in the bridge's superstructure. The problem was to get the explosive into the engine-room. Langebro was guarded day and night by twenty or thirty German military policemen. The police headquarters were at one end and there were German barracks and guard posts at the other, so that to try to storm the bridge would be hopeless. Scheme after scheme was debated and rejected and finally it was agreed that the operation could be carried out only by a volunteer working alone.

The plan involved the use of a truck powered by a gas generator, a type of vehicle conspicuously liable to mechanical failure. This, carrying two hundred kilos of explosive concealed in a sack of generator fuel, was to be driven on to the bridge and stopped directly beneath the engine-room, as if it had broken down. After tinkering for a time with the generator the driver was to pretend to give up the attempt to get the truck started again and walk off the bridge, telling the guards that he was going to ring for a repair van. Three minutes after he had got clear the explosive would go up, blowing the engine-room sky-high and the guards with it.

The job was given to Sven Jørgensen (Terkel), a nineteen-year-old apprentice who had come to Copenhagen from Sumatra, where his father was an engineer. Although with his round, owlish spectacles and perpetual broad grin Terkel looked more like a schoolboy than a saboteur, he was a seasoned fighter who had already been badly wounded in an arms raid in which two of his comrades had been killed. Shortly after two o'clock on the morning of 27 March he drove on the bridge and pulled up beneath the engine-room. But the planners had not reckoned with the boredom of the Germans on night duty. As soon as Terkel began work on the generator they crowded around him, offering helpful suggestions, and when he announced at last that he was going to ring for a repair van, they said: 'Don't bother. We'll give you a push.' They did. And he had no option but to drive away with his cargo of explosive.

That afternoon the group tried again. At one o'clock a party went to the marshalling yards at Islands Brygge, where trains for the harbour lines are made up. Sixteen wagons were being assembled into a goods train and after the railway workers had been held up for the sake of appearances the Bopa men took over the tail wagon, which was half-loaded with bricks. Above these they placed one hundred kilos of British PE2 and fifty kilos of donarit, together with a three-minute fuse. It had been intended that the action should be carried out early in the afternoon, while Langebro was comparatively clear of traffic, but there was an unexpected delay. A group with whom Bopa had no connection sabotaged a factory near Islands Brygge, with the result that Gestapomen, Hipos and police suddenly swarmed into the area. It was past five o'clock when the last of them left the yards. By that time—the peak of Copenhagen's rush-hour—Langebro was crowded with hundreds of cyclists, pedestrians and street-car passengers. All these had to be got off the bridge in the time it took a three-minute fuse to burn, and the alarm could not be given until the fuse had been lit. The crew of the engine-room had been warned in advance that something would happen during the course of the afternoon. They had been told: 'As soon as you hear shooting, it's up to you to get away.' Now they must take their chance; all efforts had to be concentrated on the urgent job of clearing the bridge of traffic.

Three men with sub-machine guns were sent to Christianshavns Vold, on the Amager side. A loud-hailer van 'borrowed' from the civil defence was placed in position on the embankment and a considerable force were spread around all the approaches to Langebro. At about half past five the leaders ordered the action to begin.

The train was manned by two Bopa men dressed in railway uniform. Holger Jensen (Gert), who had originated the plan, drove the locomotive and his friend John Georg Sand (Hans) sat in the tail wagon with the explosives. The train crawled slowly along the harbour and out on to the bridge, stopping when the tail wagon was under the engine-room. Then Hans jumped out and walked quickly towards the locomotive, which was now well towards the Copenhagen end of the bridge. The German guards watched them stolidly, suspecting nothing. No doubt they assumed he was going to inquire why the train had stopped. But the Bopa squads knew that the fuse had been lit.

The three men on the Christianshavns Vold embankment immediately opened fire on the bridge, shooting over the heads of the people. At the same time the loud-hailer van drove out, roaring: *'Alle væk fra Broen! Alle væk fra Broen!'* ('Everybody off the bridge!'). Pedestrians and cyclists rushed for safety while the German guards threw themselves flat or took cover as best they might. Some of them even crawled under the wagon containing the explosives. They could not see the attackers but they fired wildly in all directions. Meanwhile the Bopa men were stopping the traffic in all the approach streets. The street-cars were boarded and the drivers told to halt. Cyclists and pedestrians heard the loud-hailer and saw the street-cars stop. In half a minute all traffic was at a standstill. When the explosion came there was nobody on the bridge but the Germans and a few engine-room hands who had ignored the earlier warnings. The engine-room was blown to smithereens but the bridge itself was comparatively little damaged.

To add to the general confusion the Germans quite pointlessly closed Knippelsbro, the only other bridge connecting Amager with Copenhagen. It was reopened some hours later for pedestrians to cross in single file, waiting up to two hours to do so.

The Danish port authorities declared that Langebro could not be repaired and that the ships could not be got out of the South Harbour, but the Germans refused to believe it. They brought in their own specialists to inspect the damage. Since there was a chance that repair work might succeed, Bopa arranged with the Danish towing company to divert most of their tugs to Sweden, so that the ships could not be towed out of harbour. Further, to hamper attempts at sailing, two ships were sunk north of Knippelsbro. They were the derelict Dutch steamer *Wapu*, which had lain for some years at a quay on the Copenhagen side of the harbour, and the little Danish motor vessel *Japos*, which was berthed on the Amager side. A bomb was taken aboard the *Wapu*, her moorings were loosed and she was allowed to drift out into the harbour until the bomb exploded and sank her. The *Japos* had to be towed out into the fairway by a tug. There was a German guard aboard the motor vessel but he was overpowered and put ashore while the saboteurs made the tugboat's hawsers fast. Bombs were placed in the holds of the *Japos* but it was some minutes before they exploded and the hull filled with water. In that time the vessel drifted a little way from the place where she was supposed to go down, so the sunken ships did not completely block the entrance to the harbour. Nevertheless, the big merchantmen remained at their berths until after the capitulation.

Following the Langebro action Bopa received a congratulatory telegram from SHAEF: *Keep up the fine standard*. Only one man of the group never saw it. Terkel, who had so gallantly made the first attempt at the bridge single-handed, was killed in action a few days before the telegram arrived.

At the entrance to the Øresund, north of Copenhagen, the castle of Kronborg towers over the busy port of Elsinore. In one of its dungeons there is a statue of the Viking giant, Holger Danske (Holger the Dane). He sits sleeping in a chair, his white beard flowing into his lap, his sword and shield by his side. The legend says that should danger threaten Denmark, he will wake and stride forth to protect his country.

A legend, perhaps, but his spirit was surely abroad in the years of the occupation and it is fitting that his name should have been taken by an organisation of saboteurs who were to become dreaded by invader and traitor alike. That organisation, which between 1943 and 1945 grew from a handful of men to a well-disciplined force of more than three hundred, was founded by Josef (Tom) Søndergaard and Jens Lillelund.

Towards the end of 1942 Søndergaard, a veteran of the Finnish-Russian war, and his friend Carl Munck set up a printing operation for *De Frie Danske* in the back room of the Munck brothers' Star Radio shop on Istedgade, Copenhagen. There they were joined by Jens Lillelund, a cash register salesman, who from the beginning had been carrying on his own one-man war against the occupying forces.

'On the afternoon of 9 April 1940, I was cycling along Haraldsgade,' Lillelund said. 'I was sick and tired of looking at the Germans crowding the streets and when a company of *Wehrmacht* came tramping towards me, bawling *"Wir fahren gegen Engeland"*. I exploded. I spat at them and a couple of policemen grabbed me and hauled me off to a police station. The Germans there didn't know what to do with a fool like me and, after keeping me for six or seven hours, kicked me out of the back door. I felt stupid because I was the only one who had suffered. I decided that if I were arrested again it would be for something which had hurt the Germans as well as myself. So I started a bit of sabotage. A chemist friend showed me how to make incendiary bombs from calcium chlorate, granulated sugar and acid. Sometimes they worked and sometimes they didn't, but I managed to destroy quite a few German cars that way. My wife Ena bought the sugar and chemicals and acted as look-out while I was placing the bombs.

'In the autumn of 1942 I joined Søndergaard's team at the Star Radio shop but after a while we decided we were not doing much harm to the Germans just by printing newspapers and thought we would try something livelier. We got hold of some explosives from the stone-fishermen and a Bopa expert, Knud Børge Jensen (Spræng Schmidt), showed us how to use them. During the spring and early summer of 1943 we did considerable damage to factories working for the Germans and carried out a couple of big raids on military arms depots.'

On 27 July 1943, Søndergaard was arrested by the Danish police and sent to Vestre Fængsel. He was rescued eight days later by two of his comrades who, dressed in police uniform, marched up to the jail and demanded that he should be handed over to them 'for interrogation'. While sheltering in the home of Dr. H. Keiser-Nielsen, Søndergaard met the parachutist Poul Hansen and through him the saboteurs made contact with SOE.

'It was to facilitate communication with SOE that we took the name of Holger Danske,' Lillelund said. 'When I saw what they had to offer in the way of explosives and incendiary bombs it was like the first time I saw a Christmas tree. We organised a group of seven or eight people and began work in earnest.

'From a political point of view the most effective job we ever did was the destruction of Forum, the great exhibition hall in the centre of Copenhagen. In 1943 we were really fighting on two fronts—against the Germans and against our own govern-ment. We wanted to achieve what we called "Norwegian condi-tions", with positively no cooperation with the Germans. An undisguised Nazi government and Nazi parliament would have suited us better than an elected Danish government who just did what the Germans asked them to do. People were confused. They didn't know where they were. The government even en-couraged the recruitment of a Danish force to fight with the

Germans on the Russian front, and when the first contingent left Copenhagen the Danish commander-in-chief, General Ebbe Gørtz, stood beside the German commander, General Hermann von Hanneken, to give them an official send-off. That kind of thing was happening all the time.

'We heard that the Germans were going to move about five thousand soldiers into Forum and use it as a barracks. It occurred to us that if we blew the place up the Germans would be so angry that they would make demands which the government would simply have to reject. For example, if they demanded that Danish police should execute saboteurs who had been condemned to death, the government would have to say: "We can't allow it. Any executions must be done by Germans, not by Danes." In fact, that is just what happened. It might not have been the blowing-up of Forum which brought down the government but it was certainly one of the events which brought matters to a head.'

Seven men took part in the Forum action. They were Josef Søndergaard, Jens Lillelund, Max Bæklund, Mogens (Bob) Jarset, Jørgen Bjarnasson, Ewald Moesgaard and the taxi-driver Marcussen, who had often helped the group.

A few minutes before noon on 24 August 1943, as the air-raid sirens wailed over the city, Max Bæklund, dressed as a liquor store roundsman, rode up to Forum on a delivery cycle. In the carrier was a crate ostensibly filled with Tuborg lager, but under the bottles were packed twenty-eight kilos of plastic explosive. Max jumped off the cycle and stood looking around idly while he rolled a cigarette. By St. Mark's Church, near Forum's south door, Lillelund was sitting astride a stationary bicycle, reading a newspaper. Marcussen's taxi was parked in front of the main entrance on Julius Thomsens Plads. In the back seat was Bob Jarset, carrying the only sub-machine gun Holger Danske then possessed. Down the street came Søndergaard and Moesgaard, clad in workmen's overalls. All was ready.

The Danish artisans who were preparing Forum for the soldiers trooped out of the building, heading for their mid-day beer, and Søndergaard and Moesgaard went in. Two of the senior staff were standing just inside the door. The saboteurs drew their pistols. 'Don't try anything foolish,' they warned. 'This place is going up in a couple of minutes.'

While Lillelund and Jarset kept watch outside, Bæklund carried in the crate of explosive and placed it in the middle of the exhibition hall's vast floor. 'All clear?' he asked.

'Take this pair out,' Søndergaard ordered Moesgaard. 'I'll make sure there's nobody else around.' He ran down to the end of the hall where the offices lay. As he got there, a workman appeared in the south doorway. 'I forgot my bicycle,' he said. 'Can I get it?'

Søndergaard could not refuse. Bicycles were in short supply in wartime Copenhagen. He replied: 'Yes, but look sharp about it.' He watched the man retrieve his machine and then began to search the offices, washrooms and lavatories for possible stragglers.

'All clear?' Bæklund called again.

'Yes,' the man with the bicycle answered on his way out through the door.

Bæklund mistook his voice for Søndergaard's and immediately lit the fuse. A minute later came a blast that was heard all over Copenhagen as Forum disintegrated into a chaos of glass, concrete and shattered timbers.

The group counted heads. 'Where's Tom?' Lillelund asked. Nobody knew. Nobody had seen him since he walked into the offices.

Two of the saboteurs ran into the smoking ruins. Amid the piles of debris that had been the exhibition hall they saw Søndergaard crawling towards them, covered with blood and half unconscious. They carried him out to the taxi and Marcussen drove him to a nearby apartment block where he could be given first-aid.

Later, after treatment by Max Bæklund's brother, who was a doctor, Søndergaard was shipped to Sweden. Until the capitulation he helped to run one of the illegal transport routes between Gothenborg and Jutland, but he never recovered from the internal injuries he had sustained in the explosion. He died in 1947.

After the Forum action the group was so hard pressed that its members had to follow Søndergaard across the Øresund. 'I was the only one who was able to remain in Copenhagen,' Lillelund said. 'Poul Hansen, the parachutist, had also disappeared, breaking my contact with SOE. I was absolutely alone. That was a grim time; but the work had to go on. By good luck I met Svend Otto Nielsen (John), who taught mathematics at Skovshoved School, and we formed a new group of some half-dozen men. Through Mogens Staffeldt and Flemming Juncker of *Dansk Samling* we met another parachutist, Ole Geisler, and renewed contact with SOE. Shortly afterwards, through Jørgen Staffeldt, we established connection with the Freedom Council and with fresh funds and supplies of explosives we could expand.'

Geisler brought in two other parachutists, Jens Pedersen and Hans Johansen, to act as instructors, more groups were formed, notably group 2 under John's command and group 4 under Christian Ulrik Hansen, and sabotage was resumed. There were big actions against the Wedela footwear factory in Copenhagen on 15 October 1943, against the Danish Timber Industry's factory at Næstved on 28 October, and against the Rifle Syndicate's Hellerup division on 28 November. On 4 December Hartmann's engineering works in Copenhagen were blown up. Between these major engagements there were many smaller raids, usually to obtain weapons and other supplies.

'One of our bases at that time was Mogens Staffeldt's bookshop in Dagmarhus on H. C. Andersens Boulevard,' Lillelund said. 'That made very good cover. Dagmarhus was the Gestapo headquarters and it tickled us to think that we were being guarded by Gestapomen with machine-guns. They never had a clue that Mogens and his team were printing illegal newspapers and books in the basement while we used the place to store arms and ammunition. The Germans finally kicked Mogens out because he wanted to take over the whole building, so he got another shop on Kongens Nytorv. Right oposite there was a restaurant, the Opera Café, where we lunched regularly. The cloakroom was run by Mrs. Christensen, who also sold cigars and cigarettes in the restaurant. She would come to our table and whisper: "There are three pistols hanging in the cloak-room," and we'd drift out and take them. When the Germans discovered they were gone and asked what she knew about it, she would say: "I didn't see anything. I was in the restaurant, selling cigars."

'One day she told us: "There are at least twelve pistols in the cloakroom, but this time you'll have to make it look like a hold-up." So we held her up and she cried and threw her tray of cigars on the floor, and the Germans rushed out, but we were away with the guns.

'It was too good to last. When I next went to the Opera Café a girl from Staffeldt's shop was waiting outside. She said: "Don't go in there. The Gestapo are waiting for you. They've seen you in there. Their boss went to Mrs. Christensen and said: 'A man comes in here, tall, with no hair. What's his name?' She said she didn't recognise the description; she saw so many people that she couldn't remember them all. Then she nipped over to the shop to warn me."'

One of the men who served in Holger Danske's group 2 was Bob Ramsing, now a writer on the staff of Danish State Radio.

'In the summer of 1943 I was a cadet officer at the Danish Lieutenants' School,' he said. 'A few of us formed a group to smuggle out weapons. My best friend, Christian Ulrik Hansen, was the leader. We were interned for two months after 29 August but when we got out we made contact with Finn (Jens Lille-lund) and John, who were starting to rebuild Holger Danske after the Forum business. They formed two groups, one of naval cadets and medical students, among them the brothers Jørgen and Flemming Kieler; the other was the so-called lieuten-ants' group, to which I belonged. There were not more than twenty of us altogether. We were the new Holger Danske, under the leadership of Finn, John, and Flammen (Bent Fauerschou-Hviid), who was working more or less as a free agent. We were well-trained military people, so we merely had to learn the illegal way of life. That came easily and we started a few actions almost immediately.

'John took charge of the lieutenants' group. He was a born leader, a man we could trust. He was thirty-five years old, blond, blue eyed, and of middle height. His eyes were remarkable. They were normally warm and kind but in an instant they could get very, very cold. When that happened we didn't argue with him, but it took a great deal to ruffle him. He was a very calm man, who usually gave his orders with a smile. He was built like a hunter, heavy-set but agile, with fast and sure movements. He was a crack pistol shot and several times saved our bacon by blacking out a German searchlight with a well-placed bullet.

'Even before he became our leader we had heard about his exploits, like the time he went into a German airfield to steal a secret bomb-sight from one of the planes. On the way in he had to shoot a sentry with his silent pistol, and he got away from the airfield only after a hair-raising game of hide-and-seek in the darkness. He liked to dress up as a policeman or a doctor and for a long time he drove around in a car, which he had stolen from the Germans, bearing Danish medical plates. One day he was stopped and asked to help some people injured in a traffic accident. He did the best he could but no doubt some of the bystanders were amazed by the "doctor's" strange methods.

'John had a wonderful sense of humour, which meant a lot to us when we were in trouble. Once, carrying a bomb wrapped in brown paper under his arm, he was travelling on the platform of a street-car with Finn. Beside them stood a German soldier. John wanted a smoke but the parcel got in his way, so, with a polite *"Bitte"*, he dumped it in the soldier's arms. And while John got out his cigarettes and lit up, the German obligingly held a plastic bomb big enough to have blown up the street-car and a few nearby buildings with it.

'It's difficult to make anybody understand the confidence John inspired in us. When he took command of the group we were all between eighteen and twenty-one years of age. We had never seen him before. We knew his cover-name but we knew nothing else about him. Yet we obeyed his orders blindly—even when it meant killing somebody. We believed in him *without* knowing him. That was an important thing in the Danish Resistance, that incredible confidence between people. For me it goes back to four men: Finn, Jens Pedersen, Flammen and John. Pedersen, the SOE parachutist, was a small, tough man. We were

impressed by the fact that he was a British officer who had been
at Dunkirk and who had survived many commando raids. Finn
was a man you could trust. He was as cold as hell—a fine guy,
but cold. John was somebody you remembered from your old
school and your scouting days. He was like your old school-
master, but very tough and very brave when it was necessary.
Flammen was something else again, an adventurer, a deadly
"lone wolf". I doubt if anybody really understood him. We met
briefly every day, perhaps for only half an hour in Larsen's
tobacco shop, with interruptions when customers came in, or on
street corners and whatever. There was neither time nor opportunity to form close personal friendships, yet we built up that
unbelievable confidence in each other. It was a very strange
situation. You knew a man very well and yet you didn't know
him at all. In our army days we had known each other quite
well but during the illegal time I found out something about
my comrades which I'd never known. There were eight in my
group; now I'm the only one alive. At six o'clock one morning,
the others were taken. One of them realised that the Gestapo
were outside his house. He shut the door, locked it, and ran
to the telephone to warn the others. He never thought of saving
his own skin.

'My best friend, Christian Ulrik Hansen, was taken by the
Germans in Aalborg. We heard about it in Copenhagen and left
next day for Jutland to liberate him. Four of my comrades,
dressed as warders, got into the prison. They got to Christian's
cell and talked to him. They were ready to attack the German
guards and get him out. He refused. He said he had a responsibility towards the men he had recruited and who had been
taken with him, and he wanted to share their fate. He was
executed with them. Christian had been studying to be a priest.
He spent the last few hours of the night talking with his comrades, praying with them, and giving them courage to face the
firing-squad. He even found time to write ten letters, which I
and a friend later collected in a book. Here was a young man
of twenty-two, who had the chance to escape, giving up his life
to stay with his friends. Before his death he was tortured
viciously by the Gestapo but he said nothing. There were many

similar instances of men dying under torture rather than give away their comrades. John was one of the people who built up that spirit.

'A thing that isn't realised today about the Resistance is the loneliness of the man in the field. To read the stories, it seems as though we were always active, always doing things, but that isn't true. Out of twenty-four hours one was occupied perhaps for two. Night after night one was alone in a room, living under a false name, with a gun under the pillow, listening to every little sound. Hundreds of times I've jumped out of bed with my gun in my hand and gone to the window to see what kind of car was stopping in the street. Wherever I went, my first job was to find where the exits were, whether I could jump out of a window, and so on. It sounds dramatic, but it's not fun.

'Then there was the waiting. You would be going into action in the evening but all day you were alone. What the hell were you to do with yourself? My own way was to get out into the country. I was always a nature-lover. I got a lot of pleasure out of that. But sometimes the pleasure was marred by sadness, especially if you had just been on a liquidation. You needed someone to talk to—and there was nobody. I was lucky. I could talk to Christian, who was a marvellous person. John was another. You could talk to him, not directly but in a roundabout way. You were less scared of going into action if you were with John. It was like being on a school outing, confident that your teacher would arrange everything.

'John was taken only a few months after our group had met him. We were deeply shocked. We were unable to do anything for a week. Because it had happened to John. Anyone else, but not John. That was the beginning of a series of events which led you to the point where you said: "Next time it's me". He was the first of the group who got it. We realised for the first time what we were in.

'I was passing Dagmarhus when I saw somebody being carried in. Somehow I knew it was John. I went down to the tobacco shop and there was Finn, absolutely white in the face. Then we heard the story.'

On the evening of 8 December 1943, Lillelund had arranged

a meeting with John outside Oscar Davidsen's restaurant on Aaboulevarden. When they had finished their business, John asked: 'Where are we going to spend the night? We can't go to our usual hide-out. As I came past I saw several Gestapo types hanging around outside.'

'That's awkward,' Lillelund said. 'What do we do now?'

'Well, I know a Norwegian woman, Hedvig Delbo. She's a dressmaker. I've stayed with her before. Let's go there.'

'Ring her first, just to make sure,' Lillelund suggested. 'But we've got to get under cover soon; it's almost curfew time.'

John phoned from a call-box and came back. 'It's all right,' he said. 'We'll be welcome.'

The two men rode to the dressmaker's apartment on Faksegade and took their bicycles inside. Mrs. Delbo received them warmly. She sat with them for some time, listening to the news broadcasts from England and Sweden, and then showed them to a bedroom. Lillelund remembers that just before they fell asleep, John said: 'I hope I survive the war. I've been living underground so long that I can't remember what it was like not to be afraid. I'm always afraid. I'm scared every time a car pulls up outside the door or somebody comes up the stairs. I go cold if a man looks a bit too hard at me in a restaurant as I get up to pay my bill. It would be wonderful to walk around without having to be frightened of anything. I'd like to get back to my school and go hunting with my brother, the forester. But how big is the chance? Fifty-fifty? I don't know, but I suppose my chance is better than yours because you're so well-known. I don't think you'll get through, but it's just possible I might...'

The friends rose at seven o'clock next morning and said goodbye to Mrs. Delbo, but she protested that they could not leave with empty stomachs. 'I'll run down to the dairy and get some bread and milk for breakfast,' she said.

'Don't bother,' Lillelund replied. 'We're in a hurry. We can eat at a restaurant.'

'Nonsense! I'll be back in five minutes.'

She picked up a shopping bag and went out.

'I know now that she had gone to ring the Gestapo,' Lillelund said. 'She had probably warned them the night before, because

she had ten minutes in which to act between the time of John's
telephone call and our arrival. When we finally left the apartment she followed us to the door and shook hands with us. I'm
sure that was a signal.

'As we mounted our bicycles I saw four men in a car parked
fifty metres away. At that time petrol rationing was stringent
and one seldom saw a car in the street. I said to John: "They're
Gestapo."

'"Do you know if any of our people are living around
here?" he asked. We had no idea that the car was waiting for
us.

'We headed for Østerbrogade and the car started up and
followed. I said: "Hell! It looks as if we're the target. Ride on
normally and we'll see what happens."

'We pulled up at a red traffic light and the car stopped
immediately behind us. That was the longest red light I ever
had in my life. I said: "We'll make a U-turn and head back the
way we came. If they follow, then it's us they want."

'We turned, and the car turned with us. There was no doubt
now. We put on speed and tore down Ryesgade, a long street
with few outlets, with the Germans close behind us. A second
or two later the firing started. I turned round to see what was
happening to John. He was trying to get his pistol out. I yelled:
"Don't try to shoot," but he shook his head and called back:
"Ride on". I think he was already wounded.

'I pedalled on into Østerbrogade and looked round again for
John, but I couldn't see him. I took it that he had gone off on
his own. I rode through some side-streets and parked my bike
in a courtyard; then I went back to the entrance and looked out
cautiously. I saw a Gestapo car passing and it was clear they
were scouring the area for us. I went back into the yard and
climbed a back staircase to the third floor of an apartment
house. I was soaked with sweat under my heavy overcoat. I
was sick, too. I had a fever. I hadn't shaved for three or four
days and I was feeling rough. I was sitting on the landing, dead
beat, when a woman opened the door of one of the apartments.
The sight of me seemed to frighten her and she asked: "What
do you want?" I said I was looking for a man called Overgaard.

'She said: "There's no Overgaard here. And why are you looking for him here and not on the front staircase?" She went inside and locked the door. She had spoken with a German accent and I thought she might have heard the shooting and be calling the Gestapo. It was time to leave. I went down to the courtyard again and saw a milk van standing outside a shop. I whistled and the milkman came over. "Will you give me a lift?" I asked.

'He looked a bit surprised, but he said: "All right. I heard the rumpus. As I was coming along Østerbro a chap scorched past me on a bike, with the Gestapo shooting at him. Was that you?"

'He could have been a *stikker* but I took a chance and said: "Yes."

'"That's all right," he said. "Wait till I've delivered the rest of the milk. I won't be a minute." He disappeared into the shop and I waited for what seemed a long time. After a few minutes he came back and asked: "Where d'you want to go?"

'"Can you take me to Strandboulevarden?"

'"Sure thing. It's on my route."

'He dropped me there and I went into an apartment belonging to a friend. I rang the doorbell but he wasn't at home. I went down to the street and was lucky enough to find a taxi. I told the driver to take me to Larsen's tobacco shop at Farimagsgade 40 but to stop at a telephone kiosk on the way.

'As I did every day, I called my wife to make sure that she was all right. When she lifted the receiver I could hear voices in the background. I asked: "How are you?" and she replied slowly: "I am very, very well."

'That told me something was wrong. She was not very well; she had been out of sorts for some days. I heard her protest: "Am I not allowed to say anything at all?" Then the receiver was taken out of her hand and a man asked: "Is this Mr. Lillelund?"

'I said: "My name's Olesen. I want to talk to Mr. Lillelund."

'"Who are you?"

'"I'm from his office. I've a message for him."

'The voice said: "You're Mr. Lillelund. Why don't you come

home? We want to have a chat with you. We have your wife here and your youngest boy." Then the receiver was replaced.

'The Gestapo were in my apartment, but there was nothing I could do about it. Despite the implied threat in the man's voice I didn't think the Germans would harm Ena or the boy. I returned to the taxi and told the driver to go on to Farimags-gade. There were three or four of the group in the shop. I asked: "Where's John?"

' "He hasn't arrived yet."

'I said: "Then I'm pretty sure he's been arrested. For all I know, he may be dead. We'd better find out, quick."

'Flammen went down to police headquarters to ask one of our friends there whether they had any news. The officer told him: "We've just had a report from our chap on duty at the corner of Østerbrogade. Around eight o'clock he heard shooting in Ryesgade and saw two men coming towards him on bicycles. One rode past into Østerbro; the other fell on to the sidewalk. Our man recognised him as John and saw that he was wounded. As he ran to call an ambulance he saw a Gestapo car pull up. John was lying on his back but he managed to turn on to his chest and get his pistol out. His first shot smashed the car window and killed the driver. The second killed a man who was getting out of the car. Another Gestapoman cut loose with a sub-machine gun. John fell back and dropped his pistol. A Gestapoman grabbed it and knocked him unconscious with the butt. They picked John up and chucked him into the car. Now he's either in Vestre Fængsel or in Shellhus. I'm pretty certain —and I hope—that he's dead."

'On the following day I was called to police headquarters and the officer said: "I'm sorry to tell you that John's still alive. He's very badly wounded, eight bullets in his belly and one leg completely smashed. The Gestapo are giving him hell, trying to get names and addresses out of him."

'I knew nobody but Mrs. Delbo could have betrayed us but I thought it best that she shouldn't know I suspected her. I telephoned her and told her what had happened. I said: "When we left your place the Gestapo were waiting for us. They chased us and now John's dead."

'She said: "That's terrible," and I could hear her crying.

'I said: "I've got to go to Sweden. I'll be leaving this evening but I'll come to say good-bye at three o'clock. I'll give three long and three short taps on your door, so that you'll know it's me."

'"I'll do anything I can for you," she sobbed.

'I asked Peter Akselbo, a young lawyer who worked in the ministry of agriculture, to go out to Faksegade to see how the land lay. He took with him Mrs. Stubben Munk, a student married to a Danish officer, and they stood on the staircase of an apartment house across the street, kissing and cuddling. Outside Mrs. Delbo's apartment there was a pushcart loaded with Christmas trees for sale. Two men were standing by it. Gestapo cars were parked at each end of the street. Some of the men from one of the cars got out and walked over to the push-cart to chat with the "salesmen". They were obviously working together. Our couple left. As they strolled hand-in-hand past the pushcart they could see a machine-gun mounted under cover of the Christmas trees. They met me in the centre of Copen-hagen and told me: "You were right. The Gestapo were there with all the old Turkish music. Two cars, about fifteen men and machine-guns."

'I had a talk with our friend at police headquarters and he said: "There's only one thing for it. The Delbo woman must be shot. If she isn't killed, she'll go on informing."

'"That's all very well," I said, "but we've never killed any-body, and this is a woman you're talking about."

'"It can't be helped. She must be killed. *But don't do it your-self.* Get someone else, whom she doesn't know. Give me your word on that."

'I agreed, but I worried about it for the rest of the day. How could I ask any of the group to do my own dirty work? I knew I'd have to do the job myself. I was quite sick about it, but it had to be done.

'That evening I drove to Faksegade with Flammen and another man in a Gestapo car which we had stolen. We parked some streets away. The third man remained in the car, with the motor running, and Flammen and I went to the apartment.

I rang the bell and another Norwegian woman opened the door. I was in a very bad state, nervous and sweating. Almost in a whisper I asked for Mrs. Delbo. The woman stepped aside and let us pass.

'Mrs. Delbo came out of a door at the end of the long corridor. She just stood and looked at me, and then she screamed. I took out my single-shot silent pistol. I fired and she fell. I tried to reload the gun but I couldn't get the cartridge into the chamber. Flammen said: "Leave it. She's dead. Let's get out of here." We ran out to the street, jumped into the car and drove back to Larsen's.

'Next day I was summoned to police headquarters. When I walked into our friend's office his face was like a thundercloud. He said: "You're a damned fool."

' "Why?" I asked.

' "Because you did it yourself."

' "What does it matter? She's dead."

' "Dead?" he scoffed. "Don't kid yourself. You only hit her in the shoulder. Now she's in a room here with a bunch of Gestapomen and she's identified you. They've got a picture of you and they're in that room, making five hundred copies of it for circulation. You'll have to clear out to Sweden immediately, and you've only yourself to thank for it. You're a bloody fool— *a damned amateur!*" '

Under German protection Mrs. Delbo escaped to Norway. The Norwegian Resistance tried twice to liquidate her but failed. John's betrayal had to be avenged in other ways. Almost in desperation group 2, whom he had commanded for almost a year, began a series of hazardous actions which, without his cool and intelligent leadership, could end only in disaster.

'Finn was blown and had to leave for Sweden,' Bob Ramsing said, 'and we had only Flammen left as leader. He was young but he was trained, experienced, and damned tough. He became the symbol of the people we had believed in, the old guard who had enlisted us. Jørgen Kieler, a medical student, took over group 4. On Saturday, 5 February 1944, we went to Aabenraa, a town near the Danish-German border, to join local groups in an attack on the Hamag factory and the Aabenraa motor works.'

It was a foolhardy venture, for in that small town, with its many German inhabitants, the arrival of so many young strangers was quickly noticed. The raids were carried out that night. The Hamag factory was destroyed but at the motor works the charges failed to explode and the saboteurs had to fight their way out. Most of them retreated to the house of Peder Koch, an elderly motor dealer, at Styrtom and took shelter in an outbuilding; but German neighbours gave away their hiding-place. The Gestapo surrounded the house and in the ensuing battle Peer Borup, a pharmaceutical student, was mortally wounded. He died a few hours later in Aabenraa Hospital. Koch and his housekeeper were arrested. Subsequently Koch was deported to Neuengamme concentration camp, where he died on 16 November that year.

Four of the saboteurs tried to escape over the snow-covered fields behind the house but traces of blood showed only too clearly the way they had travelled. Two of them got clear but the others were surprised by a German patrol and shot down from behind. After prolonged torture at the local Gestapo headquarters they were sent to Copenhagen and imprisoned in Vestre Fængsel to await execution.

Jørgen Kieler was taken to a cell where he found John lying on a makeshift cot, very weak but still in good heart. He told Kieler that after his capture he had been subjected to the most inhuman treatment. During interrogation the Gestapo guards had repeatedly taken hold of his shattered leg, twisted it around and kicked it. 'But they didn't get anything out of me,' he said with a tired smile. 'They actually helped me, because they tortured me so terribly that I passed out and couldn't tell them anything. They chucked a bucket of water over me and started again from the very beginning, but I didn't talk. At last I was brought here and dumped in this cell, alone. I couldn't move and nobody was allowed to help me to get to the latrine. I couldn't get up to wash, so I tried to wash in the soup they gave me for dinner. I stopped eating to keep down my bowel-functioning; I hadn't any appetite, anyway. Within a short time the mattress and the blanket were so soaked in blood and excrement that there was a horrible stink in the cell. The

German doctor refused to come in here to dress my wounds because he couldn't stand the stench, and nobody was allowed to open the window. That was how I spent a month before some of the other prisoners were allowed to help me.'

John remained steadfast to the end. On the eve of his execution he wrote to his family:

Today I was taken to the German headquarters. The court-martial was at eight o'clock in the evening and I was condemned to death and taken back to my cell. At two-thirty the German judge came to say that the sentence was passed. It would be carried out at six in the morning, so that now I have three more hours to live.

So far I have taken everything calmly, almost with a smile, and—if God wills—I shall die in the same manner.

Dear friends, for the last time I am thanking you for what you have been to me, and I wish with all my heart that you may live happily together. It is to be hoped that you will have many more years to live; use those to forgive each other. You don't know when God may call for you, but then it will be too late to make good what you might have neglected.

Now it is the end of me. I wonder whether I shall hear the shot, or if I shall then be dead already? Soon I shall know. I am not afraid of dying and I hope that I won't be.

John was so weak that he had to be carried to the place of execution at Ryvangen; only by summoning the last remnants of his strength could he contrive to stand while the soldiers aimed and fired.

On the following day the newspapers carried a German official notice:

On 26 April 1944, Svend Otto Nielsen, a teacher of mathematics, born on 29 August 1908, a resident of Copenhagen, has according to the laws of war been sentenced to death and executed for sabotage and the murder of a German policeman.

In the same issues another notice appeared over the signature of General von Hanneken:

To any person who passes on to the German authorities information about a planned sabotage, or makes possible the arrest of saboteurs or the confiscation of stocks of ammunition, a rich reward will be offered. This reward will consist in each case of an amount of up to twenty thousand Danish kroner. Treatment of the informer will be guaranteed confidential.

That was the exact amount which Mrs. Delbo received for betraying John and Finn. Her infamy led to a hardening of the Resistance attitude towards the *stikkers*. Before the end of the occupation the execution squads of Holger Danske and Bopa had liquidated more than three hundred Danes working as informers for the Gestapo. Mrs. Delbo, who had been unwise enough to return to Copenhagen and resume her business as a dressmaker under a false name, was shot down in her apartment during the winter of 1944.

After the execution her body was taken to the Medico-Legal Institute and efforts were made to find a relative or friend who would accept responsibility for the burial. No one would admit knowing the woman. In desperation an appeal was made to the Gestapo, whom she had served so well, but they disowned her. The body lay unclaimed in the institute's mortuary for fourteen days. When all hope of proper burial had faded it was sent to the Institute of Anatomy to be used for dissection; but the medical students did not want it and the corpse was left lying in its tank of formalin until a way could be found of disposing of it discreetly.

The ill-fated Aabenraa expedition was followed by a long series of arrests which came near to destroying the Holger Danske organisation. Jørgen Staffeldt and his brother Mogens were taken at their bookshop, *Nordisk Boghandel,* on Kongens Nytorv, and after interrogation in Dagmarhus were sent to Vestre Fængsel. Mogens was released after eight months but

Jørgen was transferred to Frøslev concentration camp on 23 August 1944, and three weeks later deported to Neuengamme. From there he was sent to Porta Westfalica, where he was put to forced labour in the slate quarries and on the repair of bombed railway installations. He contracted tuberculosis and died on Christmas Day 1944.

Groups 2 and 4 had been very badly hit. 'By the late spring of 1944,' said Ramsing, 'there were only three or four of us left out of twenty-five. We were absolutely desperate and lost. There was nobody to believe in any more. What contacts we had were new and we lacked confidence in them. One of our group, Gunnar Dyrberg (Herman), changed addresses thirty times in six months. Three times he had to jump out of the window while Gestapomen were shooting at him. Can you imagine how a young man of twenty-one felt, never more than one step ahead of death?

'I got to Sweden in June 1944, and I was sent to jail for some days because I wouldn't say anything. Three nights after I was freed, I was walking along a street in Malmø with a saboteur from Jutland. A car came along and stopped at the kerb behind us. In a split second we had dashed for a doorway and flattened ourselves there. It was only a taxi, but that's the way we were. Our nerves were in shreds. Later on I joined Danforce. I had a special job and I had a good time but it took me three or four months to get calm again. Eventually I heard the news that most of my comrades in Denmark had been executed, all on the same day. I was very deeply shocked but my main feeling was shame. I was ashamed of being alive and in safety in Sweden.'

Following the arrest of Jørgen Staffeldt the over-all leadership of Holger Danske was assumed by the merchant Egil Barfod, one of the founders of *Dansk Samling*, with Lieutenant Knud Gamst-Pedersen as second-in-command. The Freedom Council and SOE had called a temporary halt to all sabotage activities and Barfod's chief task was to try to rebuild the sadly depleted organisation. In June 1944, a group led by Hans Edvard Teglers, who had a long career as a Bopa saboteur behind him, joined Holger Danske. Teglers, by virtue of his experience, proved a great asset to the organisation as instructor, leader and saboteur, Barfod remained in control until June but internal difficulties, partly of a political nature, arose and Lillelund was recalled from Sweden to continue the reorganisation and to carry out sabotage in Jutland. When he left for Aarhus, Police-Sergeant O. B. Bertelsen, of the Copenhagen CID, took over administration while the leadership of practical activities was assumed by Knud Larsen, a school teacher, and Christian Kisling, the head of a salvage corps station. At the same time Holger Danske broke their connection with *Dansk Samling* and affiliated with Frode Jakobsen's *Ringen*.

During the summer the organisation gained strength and grew steadily, thanks largely to the work of Knud Larsen. Not least of his contributions was the founding of a fictitious marine salvage company, through which he obtained legally large quantities of explosives and so solved one of Holger Danske's biggest problems. But his career was short. On 4 September 1944, the Gestapo received a tip that several Resistance leaders had been called to a meeting at Harsdorffsvej 9, Frederiksberg, the home of the merchant Gunnar Bomhoff. They stormed the villa and O. B. Bertelsen, who was staying there, was wounded. Bomhoff was not at home but his wife was arrested and later sent to Frøslev. The villa was blown up, killing Bomhoff's brother. Larsen had arrived for the meeting just as the Gestapo were moving in. He sought sanctuary at a nearby police station but was arrested and his attempt to take a cyanide pill failed. He was taken to Dagmarhus, where he died after a few days in circumstances which have never been explained.

Bertelsen was smuggled across to Sweden and shortly afterwards Lillelund, who was also being hunted by the Gestapo, went to Stockholm. Almost at once he was called to the British legation to discuss a problem which was making sabotage in Jutland so dangerous as to be almost impossible. During actions in the comparatively small towns of the peninsula the local saboteurs were easily recognised and the number of arrests was mounting steadily. Lillelund was asked to find a solution. After thinking the matter over for a couple of days he proposed that future actions in Jutland should be undertaken not by local groups but by flying-squads who would leave the scene as soon as possible. If a town were blockaded, they would hide in safe-houses until the blockade was lifted. The plan was approved and Lillelund returned to Jutland via Copenhagen, where he had meetings with Holger Danske, Bopa and the Freedom Council. Six months later, having established the flying-squads, he went back to Stockholm, whence he flew to England and joined the Parachute Regiment as a lieutenant.

After long and not always friendly discussions an outsider, Police-Sergeant Harald Petersen (cover-name Søren Jensen), took over the leadership of Holger Danske. A five-man council was established and the organisation, now some three hundred strong, was reformed on military lines in divisions, companies and sections. From that time on a long series of effective sabotage actions and an increasing number of liquidations were carried out. There were heavy losses. Many men were killed in action and there were many arrests which for those concerned meant prison, torture, deportation to German concentration camps or execution; but others took their places and at the end of the occupation Holger Danske was the country's biggest sabotage organisation.

Said Bob Ramsing: 'When the war was over some of us got into an old Gestapo car and drove up to Kronborg Castle and there, in the dungeon, our leader put the red, white and blue armband of the Resistance on the right arm of old Holger the Dane. And we thought of our sixty-one friends who had been killed during the fight—and of John, the first to die.'

13: CITRONEN

One afternoon towards the end of March 1944, Gunnar Dyrberg went to a garage in Copenhagen to help with the repainting of an Opel Kapitän stolen from the Gestapo. It was there that he first met Jørgen Schmidt, the already famous Citronen.

'I saw before me a dark-haired, well-built man of middle height,' he said. 'As he held out his hand and introduced himself, I looked at him curiously. He had a pleasant face, with kind brown eyes, and his smile was warm and friendly. He didn't look at all as I had expected. Citronen (The Lemon) was said to be fantastically daring, extremely fast in his reactions, and completely merciless when it was a matter of carrying out a dangerous mission. I shouldn't have dreamed that this man possessed such qualities. He looked like any ordinary family man of thirty-four, with no thoughts on his mind but keeping his job and looking after the wife and kids. I should have passed him in the street without a second glance. No one could have believed that he was one of the two most wanted men on the Gestapo's black-list. The other was his friend, Flammen.'

Jørgen Haagen Schmidt, the eldest of three brothers, was born into a middle-class family at Hellerup. After leaving school he was articled to a hardware merchant but the life was too tame for him and at the end of his apprenticeship he left to try his hand at a variety of jobs. Eventually he became stage-manager at Copenhagen's Zigøjnerhallen, where he remained for several years. In 1942 he was employed at the Citröen factory in the South Harbour, where German military vehicles were repaired, and began to amuse himself with minor sabotage against cars and lorries destined for the Russian front. For some time his efforts went undetected, but after blowing up two workshop trucks he had to go underground.

By chance he made contact with Søndergaard's group when he went to buy a radio set in Istedgade. At that time the Bopa saboteur Spræng Schmidt was working with Holger Danske as an instructor. To distinguish between the two, Jørgen was given the name of Citröen Schmidt, but later, after he had carried out a single-handed sabotage action against the Citröen factory, wrecking the workshops and destroying six cars and two military lorries, he was re-christened Citronen. After the Forum explosion he went with the rest of the group to Sweden but returned to join the new Holger Danske being organised by Jens Lillelund. During the following months, though he continued to work with Holger Danske, he became increasingly involved in the operations of *Speditøren*. His energy and endurance were incredible. He often worked around the clock, sometimes going two or three days without eating, taking off his clothes, or snatching more than half an hour's sleep. Because of his exceptional personal acquaintance with people in all branches of the Resistance, he was invaluable to the transport operators.

'This was a time when hundreds of refugees, couriers and shot-down Allied airmen were being sent across the Øresund by *Speditøren*,' Dyrberg said. 'Citronen personally took care of every single one of them. He picked them up and took them aboard the boats after dark, having first scouted the port area to make sure the German patrols were out of the way. He checked the identity of every one of the travellers very carefully. The presence of an informer could mean catastrophe. But once, despite all his precautions, he almost "bought it".

'A man called Bertelsen asked for a passage to Sweden. Citronen was suspicious of him from the start. Although the chap had got through a preliminary interrogation, he decided to question him once more and picked him up in a taxi. Bertelsen was carrying a suitcase. Two of our comrades were waiting on Vesterbrogade in the stolen Opel Kapitän. Citronen asked the taxi driver to stop at the opposite kerb. "We're getting into that car over there," he told Bertelsen.

'Bertelsen took a long time to get out of the cab. He looked nervous and while paying the driver Citronen watched him carefully. He picked up the suitcase with his right hand and put his left hand in his pocket as they started to cross the street. Citronen felt a bit easier; he thought that as long as the man had the suitcase in his right hand he couldn't start trouble. He didn't know Bertelsen was left-handed.

'When they were half-way across the street Bertelsen spotted the two men in the car. He whipped out his pistol and fired. Citronen threw himself to one side and pulled out his own gun. His bullet hit the mark and the *stikker* fell dead. Citronen raced across the street and made his getaway in the Opel.'

Citronen was an incorrigible practical joker. One afternoon he got into the Richhus, near the city hall, and rigged a portable gramophone and amplifier in the tower. A few minutes later the strains of *Tipperary* blared out over the city hall square, to the joy of the Copenhageners and the fury of the Germans in Dagmarhus.

But his tricks were not always appreciated. 'One day we were gathered in the back room of a candy store, chatting with the owner,' Dyrberg said. 'Suddenly there was a deafening bang. We whipped round, scared out of our pants, to see Citronen standing with a pistol pointing at our legs. "I ... I'm awfully sorry," he stammered. We bawled him out for his carelessness, but we were still more annoyed when we found that he had merely set off a fire-cracker behind us. He thought that was one hell of a joke.

'I always remember his quick tongue. Once he took a team to steal three cars from the Gestapo's own garage. As they entered he pointed his sub-machine gun at the belly of the elderly German guard. The poor devil thought his last hour had come. He kept repeating: *"Ich bin sozialdemokrat!"* ("I'm a social democrat!"). Citronen just looked at him. "That's all right, my old friend," he said. "Unfortunately we've no time to hold an election now."

'Actually that action was quite simple, once our men had got into the garage. They waited until the Gestapomen drove in, then held them up and made off with their cars.'

Like Flammen, Citronen frequently used Danish police uniform as a disguise. It was that habit which brought about his undoing.

'On 18 September 1944, Citronen and I spent the evening in the apartment of our friend Kis (Christian Kisling),' Dyrberg said. 'Citronen was in great form. He showed us his latest "invention". He had discovered that he could strap a small-calibre automatic on the inside of his thigh, where the Gestapo never looked for weapons. He thought that if he were frisked, the searchers would look no further when they had found the two guns he carried in a shoulder holster and in his pocket. "I'm prepared for any attack now," he said, laughing.

'It was late when the party broke up and Citronen drove me home in the black Opel. I asked him to stop the car a couple of blocks away from my hide-out. The silencer was broken and I didn't want the noise of the engine to attract attention in the quiet street.

' "Are you afraid?" he asked.

' "You bet I am," I replied.

'Citronen was never afraid. At least, he never showed it.

'At noon next day I was with a friend in an apartment in the centre of the city when the air-raid sirens started to wail. Shortly afterwards we heard cars stopping and doors slamming right under our windows and the clatter of heavy boots on the stairs. We knew the Gestapo had come calling and we prepared our guns and hand-grenades to give them a hot welcome. But they weren't after us. A police inspector was living in the same building. He was the one they had come to get. We listened to the commotion as they took him away and then relaxed. We were sorry for the chap but there was no way we could help.

'After the "all clear" had sounded we went down to the street and there we heard the news. During the "alert" the Germans had taken over the Danish police headquarters and arrested every policeman they could find. We saw some of the cars taking the prisoners down to the harbour to be shipped out to concentration camps in Germany. On that day the Hipos, the cruellest gang of criminals in Denmark's history, were turned loose on the public. The Germans had decreed that those thugs should continue the work of the Danish police.

'I was crossing the city hall square later in the afternoon when I heard the sound of a car with a broken silencer. I turned. It was Citronen's black Opel, but now it was full of Germans. I checked the licence plate and saw the D which I myself had transformed into a K and the 8 which I had turned into a 3. There could be no doubt. It was Citronen's car—and that could mean only disaster.'

By diabolical chance Citronen had decided to wear his police disguise when he set out from home that morning. He was carrying two pistols and there were two more, together with grenades and the briefcase holding his other 'tools', on the rear seat of the car. The air-raid sirens sounded as he was driving through Nørre Allé but he was going so fast and the broken exhaust was making such a din that neither he nor his companion heard them. As the car navigated the roundabout at Tagensvej and headed towards Sankt Hans Torv, he saw a line of soldiers blocking the road between Sankt Johannes Church and Sankt Hans Gade School. He slowed down and stopped in front of the line. A German sergeant walked up to the car and ordered the two men out. They stood on the sidewalk with their hands above their heads while a Schalburgman disarmed them. Citronen was not unduly perturbed. He had been in similar situations before and his police uniform had always got him out of them. It was not until they were marched into a yard beside the school, where other men were already standing under guard, that he realised something out of the ordinary was happening. Almost all the other prisoners were Danish policemen.

Half an hour passed, then the guards were relieved by Hipos. Citronen, his friend and a CB (Danish auxiliary policeman) were ordered into the adjoining schoolyard and lined up in an alleyway which looked out on to Nørre Allé. One Hipo was left to guard them. Citronen asked permission to smoke. He took out a packet of cigarettes and gave one to each of the other two men. Under cover of striking a match for his friend, he whispered: 'Don't forget: you stopped me on Lyngbyvej and asked me for a lift. You'd never seen me before. I'm getting out of here. I can't risk them recognising me.' As he stepped back into line, he nodded towards two dustbins standing by the alley fence and said: 'There's my springboard. I'm going to try it soon.'

A few minutes later another Hipo appeared at the mouth of

the alley. 'Bring those criminals out!' he bawled.

The CB went first. Citronen stepped back to let his friend pass and then bolted. He was half-way over the fence when the guard fired. The bullet hit him in the back and he fell down between the dustbins.

The shot and the clatter of the bins brought Germans pouring into the alley from the street and schoolyard. In the confusion they completely forgot about the other two prisoners, who promptly made their escape.

An employee of the Falck company was walking along the opposite side of Nørre Allé when the Hipo fired. He saw Citronen fall and, even at that distance, recognised him. He ran to a telephone kiosk and called his head office, where the saboteur was well-known. An ambulance was sent at once to Sankt Hans Torv. As it raced into the square, the Germans hailed it and ordered the driver to go to the school to pick up a wounded man. They did not suspect that it had been sent on just that errand.

Citronen was carried out on a stretcher. His face was grey and his jacket was soaked with blood. The Germans must have thought that he was dead or dying for they put only one Hipo into the ambulance as guard. He sat, nursing his rifle, with his back against the wall of the driver's cabin. Citronen lay with his head towards the rear doors. Despite the pain of his wound and severe loss of blood his mind was still clear and on the way to the German hospital on Nyelandsvej he tried to bribe the Hipo to let him escape. He offered him ten thousand kroner and a safe passage to Sweden, but the man would not listen. Citronen changed his tactics. He feigned a collapse and began to moan and plead for water. The Hipo had not lost the last spark of humanity. He ordered the driver to stop by a chemist's shop. Both the driver and his mate got down from their seats, leaving guard and prisoner alone.

With great difficulty Citronen dragged the 6.35mm automatic from its hiding-place on his thigh and pumped all seven bullets into the Hipo. When the ambulancemen returned, they found the guard dead and Citronen unconscious. They drove him to Frederiksberg Hospital and then took the dead Hipo back to

Shellhus, where they told his masters the prisoner had shot him while escaping.

That evening Nurse Ellen Christensen was sitting in her apartment, reading. Suddenly the telephone shrilled. She picked up the receiver, giving only her number. The voice at the other end of the line said: 'Go to Jægersborg Allé 184. You're needed urgently.'

Ellen did not ask for details of the case. The voice was that of a doctor high in the councils of the Resistance. She had no doubt what she had to do. A few minutes later she was pedalling quickly along Strandvej, heading northwards out of the city. Passing the towering buildings of the Tuborg Brewery on the outskirts of Hellerup, she smiled. Tonight, she thought, it would not matter if she were stopped by a German patrol. There was only surgical kit in the carrier of her bicycle. On other night journeys it had been different. Then the carrier had held revolvers, grenades or plastic explosive. It would do so again, if the luck held. Throughout the occupation she had been living a double life. A hospital nurse by day, at night she was an active, daring member of a sabotage group. From the beginning the doctors and nurses had been in the thick of the fight for freedom. Before the day of liberation more than one hundred doctors were to be arrested, thirty-five of them on one black day in June 1944. Most went to Horserød concentration camp but at least ten were deported to the German hells of Dachau and Neuengamme. Five died there. Dr. Jørgen Theilmann, betrayed by a neighbour, was shot for sabotage in Copenhagen. Twelve of his colleagues died in action in the streets. The roll of honour of the nurses was no less tragically glorious.

For Ellen, at first, it had been fairly easy. Nobody had suspected the gentle-faced girl of illegal activities. But the inevitable *stikker* had whispered her name. On the day of the mass arrests she too had gone underground, seldom sleeping in the same house for more than a few nights, hunted always by the Gestapo. To be caught meant the firing-squad or, still worse, the unclean horrors of the concentration camp. That was something she did not let herself think about.

She had reached Charlottenlund, home of some of the city's

wealthiest families. Pedalling slowly along blacked-out Jægersborg Allé, she stopped in front of a large modern villa. The
door opened at once. A student, his face older than his eighteen
years, said: 'Thank God you've got here. He's in a bad way.'

'Who is it?'

'Citronen. I think he's had his chips this time.'

He led the way into a room on the ground floor. A young
doctor was leaning over a bed. He straightened as Ellen came
in. He said: 'Good girl! I'll have to leave you with him. I've
been away from the hospital too long already.'

The man lying in the bed was plainly in a bad way. The
eyes in his chalk-white face were closed. His breathing was
laboured and irregular. A large paper dressing showed beneath
the open neck of his pajama jacket.

Ellen asked: 'How bad is it?'

'Rifle bullet. It went in below the right shoulder, followed
the ribs inside the spine, perforated the left lung and came out
just under the left armpit. The spine's not damaged but he's
lost a lot of blood. We gave him a transfusion at the hospital.
He's got a fighting chance—and that's all Citronen ever asked
for. We brought him here after he'd had the transfusion. You
can bet the Gestapo are combing the hospitals for him this
minute. That's why we've got to get back.'

He shrugged into a trenchcoat and followed the student to
the door. 'Good luck,' he said. Then they left Ellen with her
patient.

Amazingly, Citronen pulled through. By the first week on
October he was strong enough to sit up in an armchair. He
could even send a card to his friends. It read:

> *J. Schmidt*
> *pro tem. ill*
> *Wines, tobacco and flowers*
> *are being received*
> *No wreaths*

On 13 October Flammen called at the villa, lugging a heavy
suitcase. 'I'm off to Jutland in the morning,' he said, 'so I'll
leave this with you. It ought to be safe here.' He flung back the

lid and Ellen saw neatly packed in the case two Sten-guns, a Luger Parabellum 9mm pistol, a cluster of hand-grenades and a 6.35mm automatic.

Citronen smiled. 'All right,' he said. 'They'll be safe. In fact, they might come in handy.' He did not know how soon his joke was to become grim fact.

Saturday 14 October passed quietly enough at the villa in Jægersborg Allé; but while Ellen and her patient chatted in the garden, swift, efficient action was being taken at Shellhus. A member of *Speditøren* had taken a chance and paid a visit to his home, to find a Gestapo squad waiting for him. Following his arrest a raid was made on the group's head office on Gammel Mønt and vital records, stamps for false papers and other compromising material were seized.

Aage V. Ström Tejsen, the official tenant of the office, was also the owner of the villa in which Citronen was convalescing. He returned to Jægersborg Allé, knowing nothing of the raid, and joined Ellen and Citronen at dinner. They had reached the coffee stage when the telephone rang. Tejsen picked up the receiver, listened briefly and frowned. 'Would you believe it?' he said. 'At this time of the evening! I've got to get back to town at once. As far as I can see, it will be about midnight before I come home.'

Had he known it, that telephone call was to save his life.

It was about an hour after Tejsen had left the house when the telephone rang again. This time the call was for Citronen. Replacing the receiver, he grinned. 'There's been an "accident",' he told Ellen. 'They finally caught up with that damned *stikker* Gilbert. He's been liquidated.'

At eleven o'clock Ellen ordered Citronen back to bed in the room with the French windows opening into the garden. Shortly afterwards the telephone rang for the third time. Ellen took the call. 'It was Tejsen,' she said. 'He'll be here in an hour's time.'

'Good!' said Citronen. 'If it's all the same to you, I'll stay awake until he comes home.'

It was in fact a few minutes past midnight when a sharp knocking sounded at the front door. Ellen said: 'He's here.'

She walked out into the hall. The low-powered bulb, shaded to conform with the black-out regulations, hardly scattered the darkness. Ellen called: 'Who is it?' A male voice answered something that might have been 'Tejsen'. She opened the door and two men stepped swiftly inside. They wore the familiar trenchcoats of the Gestapo.

One of the men said 'Sicherheitspolizei. Is your husband in?'

'I'm not married.'

'Your brother, then.'

'I have no brothers.'

The man made an impatient gesture. 'All right. Well, where is he?'

'Who?' Ellen asked.

'Tejsen. The owner of this place.'

'I don't know. I'm merely taking care of the house. I'm here alone.'

'You're lying.' The man moved towards her, saying to his companion: 'Search the place. See what's in that room behind.'

The other man nodded. He started up the hall. And as he did so Citronen fired. The German staggered backwards with a yell. His hand clutched his shoulder, which was streaming blood. A second shot came from the bedroom as he stumbled towards the door.

Both men had drawn their Lugers but they did not return Citronen's fire. The sudden attack seemed to have thrown them off balance. For a few seconds they stood there, staring along the hall.

Two more shots came from the bedroom. The bullets smacked into the wall, scattering fragments of plaster. Ellen flattened herself in a corner. The Germans had forgotten her. The man who had been doing all the talking muttered: 'God knows how many of the bastards there are. We'll have to get reinforcements. Open that door.'

His mate fumbled with the Yale lock but his wound made him clumsy. He said: 'The bloody thing's stuck. I can't move it.'

The other shoved him aside. 'Here, let me do it.' He swung

the door open and shouted an order into the darkness. Ellen heard the sound of running feet. A second later two more Gestapomen burst in with pistols drawn.

'See if you can make it to the bedroom up there,' the leader ordered. 'That's where they're holed up.'

But Citronen had already shifted his ground. He was now in a dressing-room from which he could cover both bedroom and hall. As the two Germans edged cautiously towards the bedroom, keeping close to the wall, he threw the first grenade. The Germans dropped just in time. There was a blinding flash and a crash which rocked the villa. Glass shattered in the windows and the bulb in the hall went black. Wildly, blindly, the Gestapomen sent shots up the dark hall. There was no answering fire from the dressing-room. In the pregnant silence Ellen heard the crackling of burning woodwork.

The muzzle of a Luger jabbed viciously into her ribs. 'One move out of you, you bitch, and I'll cut you to pieces,' the leader snarled. 'How many of the swine are there?'

'I don't know.'

'You're lying. It's obvious they're sniping from every room. How many?'

'I don't know.'

At last he gave up. 'We're wasting time,' he said. 'Get her out of here. Put her on the steps outside the house and hold her there. If she tries to run, drop her.'

Big hands grabbed her arms and she was hustled out. As she went, she called loudly: 'All right. No need to break my arm. But why have I got to stand out on the steps?'

That was for Citronen's benefit. She was letting him know that he had a clear line of fire. He heard and understood. She was barely out of the front door when he opened up with one of Flammen's Sten-guns. One of the Germans, hit mortally, screamed like a baby. The others, yelling and cursing, emptied their Lugers into the dressing-room door.

The shooting and excitement were too much for the man who had been left to guard Ellen. When another burst rattled from Citronen's Sten-gun he deserted his post and bolted up the steps into the house.

Astonishment held Ellen rooted for an instant. But only for an instant. Then she darted into the garden and round to the back of the villa. A thick hedge gave her shelter while she thought out her next move. Escape into Jægersborg Allé was impossible. There were already German military vehicles in the road and more were arriving. The hard-pressed Gestapomen were getting the reinforcements they had requested from the Jægersborg barracks. The firing in and around the villa was now practically incessant. The bedroom into which Citronen had thrown the grenade was blazing fiercely and in the light of the flames licking through the broken windows Ellen could see soldiers and Gestapomen moving about the garden. If she remained, capture was inevitable.

Hardly feeling the sharp twigs which tore at her face and thin dress, she forced her way through the hedge into the neighbouring garden. Cautiously she made her way to the big house which stood shuttered and silent, as if deserted. Her knocking brought no response. If the owners were at home they were too frightened to get mixed up in Resistance business. She tried a second house and a third with no better luck. At any second she expected to feel a Gestapoman's hand on her shoulder or hear the pistol shot which would spell her death. Almost despairingly she raised her hand to knock at a fourth door. It opened and a woman's voice whispered: 'Inside! Quickly!'

She stepped into an unlit hall. A soft bundle was pushed into her hands. The unknown voice said: 'Here's a coat. Put it on. There's money in the pocket—enough to get you into town. Now, please go. And God go with you.'

Ellen was grateful. She did not expect shelter. The woman was already risking enough. Maybe she had small children in the house, and the Gestapo were not gentle with Danes found harbouring fugitives. Moving stealthily as a redskin she made her way from garden to garden. The sky was crimson with the flames from the burning villa. The rattle of machine-guns, rifles, and pistols was punctuated by the crump of grenades. Citronen was still fighting his impossible one-man war.

At last she reached the home of a family of Resistance sympathisers, and there, from a first-floor window, she watched the closing scenes of the tragedy.

Leaping tongues of flame, brighter than the Northern Lights, silhouetted the skeleton rafters of the villa. A thunderous rumble and a burst of sparks told her that at least one of the walls had fallen. But still the firing continued.

Not until three o'clock did silence come. And Ellen knew that Citronen was dead.

When she left the safe-house dawn was breaking grey over the listening streets. The sour, acrid smell of wood smoke hung in the damp air. As she hurried through Jægersborg Allé, huddled in her borrowed topcoat, she saw that nothing remained of the villa but a bleak, charred shell.

One man, who saw the last stage of the battle, said: 'There were at least two hundred Germans in the attacking forces and for hours in that blazing furnace Jørgen Schmidt kept them at bay. I saw the Nazis haul away eight dead men. At least four more were stretcher cases.

'Alone, in agony from his wounds, Jørgen fought on until the walls began to cave in around him. Then, suddenly, he charged through the smashed French windows, a wild, slight figure in blood-soaked blue-and-white pyjamas. He rushed out on to the lawn, the Sten-gun at his hip still firing.

'He got only a few steps before they cut him down. He looked like a pathetic doll crumpled on the grass.

'But he went out as he would have wished—fighting to the last.'

14: FLAMMEN

Erik Schousboe Poulsen, merchant and amateur astronomer, was one of the transport group operating from the old Snekkersten Kro in the autumn of 1943. One day he went to the inn with O. B. Bertelsen to make contact with a saboteur from Holbæk who had asked for passage to Sweden. Henry Thomsen, the innkeeper, brought bottles of beer to their table. 'There are two suspicious characters at the bar,' he said. 'One's tall and dark, an unpleasant type. The other's a lanky, fair-haired kid with freckles. I've never seen either of them before.'

Bertelsen and Hans Christian Kiding, another Copenhagen CID man, took the dark stranger to a room upstairs. He was searched and found in possession of a fully-loaded Luger pistol. He presented his credentials, his story was confirmed over the telephone with a police contact in Elsinore, and he was put on the list for transport.

Bertelsen and Kiding went back to their seats at the table with Thomsen and Poulsen. 'I'm supposed to be vetting another chap,' Bertelsen said. 'It must be that curly-headed lad over there.' He nodded towards the young man standing by the bar, who responded with a cheerful grin. He was casually but expensively dressed and Poulsen noticed that his white hands were carefully manicured. When he was questioned he replied in a soft, almost effeminate voice that his name was Bent Fauerschou-Hviid, that he was twenty-two-years-old and that his father owned the Birkegaarden restaurant at Asserbo, in North Zealand. He said he had been involved in illegal work, including small-scale sabotage, in Holbæk and was now on the run from the Gestapo.

After another telephone call had established his bona fides he was told he could go to Sweden.

'Thanks a lot,' he said, 'but I'm planning to come back as soon as possible.'

'You'd better think twice about that,' Bertelsen warned him.

'Normally we provide only one-way trips. You might find it wiser to stay out of trouble.'

Since the transport was not sailing until the following day, Poulsen took the young man home to dinner and gave him a bed for the night.

'In the morning,' he said, 'a telephone call in code came from our doctor friends, Grete and Jørgen Gersfelt. It was to tell my wife Lise and me that we should see Bent off on the boat, as already arranged; but Grete must have got the code tangled because as the three of us were walking along the coast road with Coco our Scots terrier, Jørgen drove up in his car and announced that he had come to pick up the passenger. A bit of an argument developed and in the finish Bent refused to leave. He said he wouldn't go to Sweden; Snekkersten looked like a peaceful haven where he could make himself useful. We told him that was impossible; he was classed as a refugee and he'd have to go.

'But the luck was bad that morning. Jørgen hadn't driven far when he was stopped and warned that a German patrol were searching the area. There'd been no time to provide Bent with identity papers—usually the last thing needed by a traveller to Sweden—so he had to be transferred in his beautiful suit to the interior of a garbage truck. To add to his troubles he was put into the wrong boat, but at last he got safely across the Øresund.

'Ten days went by and then, just as we were sitting down to lunch, Bent arrived back on our doorstep. He was too young and active to settle as a refugee in Sweden; further, the Swedes would have sent him out into the woods, which meant hard labour, felling trees. He and Lise decided that he should live with us and he at once became a member of the group operating from the inn.'

Lise Poulsen said: 'Bent was a tall, slender young man. He had blue eyes and strong white teeth with which he was apt to remove the caps of beer bottles if I weren't there to stop him. His hair was blond when he came to us but he decided to disguise himself by changing the colour to a darker brown. O.B.'s wife Agnes volunteered to do the dyeing and she made a mess of it. Bent's hair came out of the bowl a screaming carrot-red. He managed to wash out a little of the dye but red it remained for the rest of his days. When he presented that horrible mop at the inn, Henry Thomsen spontaneously christened him Faklen (the Torch), which was most appropriate. In the following weeks we called him sometimes Faklen and sometimes Flammen (the Flame), but Flammen it became.'

Flammen settled quickly into the circle at the Snekkersten Kro. Most of the members were older than he and it is probable that they were sometimes irritated by his cocky manner, but his immense charm and cheerful acceptance of the most gruelling assignments won them over. There was a steady coming and going of Holger Danske men at the inn and he inevitably gravitated towards them.

'I met Flammen through John,' Jens Lillelund said. 'He came to me one day with this very young, very pale, red-headed young man who wanted to join the group. I took John into another room and said: "We'll try the chap, if you like, but he looks like a cissy to me." John said: "I'm sure he's good enough." So we took him on and he was absolutely formidable—a born leader.'

In Holger Danske, Flammen had as tutors such experienced saboteurs as Mogens Jarset, Carl and Børge Munck. Poul Moesgaard, Max Bæklund and Citronen. He was quick to learn and soon distinguished himself by his fearlessness in action. He seemed to be without nerves and as time went on his recklessness made him a problem-child for the policemen in the group. He made friends in too many circles and it was frequently necessary to impress on him the overriding importance of security. Though he was urged repeatedly to memorise all instructions, he had a dangerous habit of carrying incriminating notes and sketches in his pockets. He was frisked twice a day but, despite all promises, there was always a harvest. Equally disturbing was his carefree practice of parking his stolen German car directly in front of the entrance to any house he might be visiting, a practice as potentially disastrous to his hosts as to himself.

To Lise and Erik Poulsen, with whom he lived for eleven

months, Flammen was like a son, 'a charming mixture of child and grown-up, sensitive and good, with a becoming shyness'.

Said Lise: 'There was nothing he enjoyed more than sitting down in a dinner jacket to a good meal with red wine, and in those days of strict rationing he could organise better wines than people who had no restaurant connections. But he also liked cosy evenings with just Erik and me, sitting around in slippers, chatting freely and pleasantly or reading a book. His manners were unusually gentle and he never became boastful. He seldom laughed but one learned to read his moods. There was a soft, hissing sound which he made when he was amused or feeling happy. I never once heard him raise his voice in anger.

'When he was on a job for Holger Danske he always wanted Jørgen Schmidt with him. They were inseparable friends. It was funny to hear Bent ordering Jørgen about, persuading him to carry the heavy suitcases full of guns and bombs, despite the fact that the famous saboteur was his instructor and ten years his senior. They made a strange pair. Bent was always smartly dressed and a little demanding about his clothes. Although soap was rationed, he insisted on having a clean white shirt every morning. Jørgen was completely different. Half his collar was always sticking out and his tie was always askew. But nobody minded that. One only remembered his kind brown eyes and his modest bearing. Something I liked about both men was that they never complained. Whenever we asked Jørgen how things were going, he invariably answered with a wry little smile: "Splendid, as always".

'Bent's fastidiousness had its comical side. I remember a morning when he was going out on a factory sabotage action. He came downstairs dressed in what he imagined to be a typical workman's get-up. His beautifully-cut jacket was encircled with a broad leather belt. His pants had a knife-edge crease. He wore no tie but his freshly-laundered shirt was almost dazzlingly white. He looked perfectly ridiculous and I told him to go and change into some of Erik's old gardening clothes.'

Flammen's skill as a chef is acknowledged by all his friends but occasionally, like the best of cooks, he had his failures.

There was the time, for example, when he decided to celebrate Erik Poulsen's birthday with a special dinner.

'He went hunting in Ørstedsparken with a pistol fitted with a silencer,' Poulsen said. 'He must have known that hunting in the parks was a serious crime; nevertheless, back he came with a huge white swan. He plucked it himself and the feathers flew everywhere. Our black terrier, Coco, was running around like a little white ghost. Bent cooked that bird for hours, but it must have been a veteran of many winters in the Nile delta. It was absolutely uneatable. But there was one slight compensation —the wine was excellent.'

Gunnar Dyrberg recalls a similar fiasco. On that occasion the main dish on the menu was a duck which Flammen had shot on the lake in Ørstedsparken. 'He prepared it according to the finest recipe,' Dyrberg said, 'and as the aroma spread through our apartment our appetites grew. But anything tougher than that duck would be hard to imagine.'

Flammen was always willing to lend a hand with the washing-up and other kitchen chores, but, said Poulsen, 'he was definitely best at supervising, inspecting, and keeping others busy. He must have been terribly spoiled and waited upon at home. He loved nothing better than having breakfast served on a tray in bed. Neither Lise nor I was an early bird but Bent simply hated to get up in the morning. However, if he had an appointment with danger he would be up and dressed in no time. He had a large wardrobe of German and Danish uniforms and forged gun-permits and identity cards to correspond. He also had doctors' papers and a complete kit of surgical instruments. Of course, looking after such things was other people's business. He left ammunition, grenades, pistols and Sten-guns strewed about the place for us to pick up. He really needed a team of assistants to tidy up, run his errands, move his car, take messages which couldn't be entrusted to the telephone, and perform a thousand and one other chores. I used to compare him to a bomber plane with ground crew facilities. He was as careless and untidy in the house as any schoolboy; yet in action he was coolly methodical, planning every move in meticulous detail. His boldness was phenomenal.

'On one occasion a transport of explosives had been reported to us. We knew the strength of the escort, the number of the railway truck, and the times of departure from the naval depot and arrival in the freight yard. Bent put on his police uniform and drove to the freight yard, followed by a lorry. The railway truck was parked right in front of the shed housing the German guards. Bent went straight to the goods manager and declared: "This shipment was made in error. I've got orders to remove the freight." The manager protested and demanded to see the authorisation but Bent ignored him and ordered the crew to start transferring the explosives on to the lorry. He followed the manager into his office and said: "It's no use phoning the depot. My colleague's on the way with the documents. He'll be here any minute." His air of authority was so convincing that neither the manager nor the guards dared argue. The lorry was loaded and driven to our secret storehouse. Unluckily, two days later an informer alerted the Gestapo and the goods, a beautiful shipment, were recaptured.'

In April 1944, Erik Poulsen was arrested. He was taken to Dagmarhus, where four Gestapomen positively identified him as a participant in the hold-up of three German cars. During the ensuing interrogation he was confronted with damaging evidence of other illegal activities.

'If we put you in front of a court-martial, you're finished,' the Gestapo chief said, 'but that's not what we want. We're holding you as a crown hostage. You're the man we're going to use to get Flammen.'

That was the beginning of an intensive man-hunt which was to continue throughout the summer and autumn. To the Germans Flammen was one of *die böse Leute*, to be captured at any cost. They put on his head the highest price ever offered for any Resistance fighter. But the hunt opened with an episode of sheer farce.

Immediately after Poulsen's arrest the Gestapo sent squads throughout Copenhagen and rounded up at least a hundred and fifty young Danes whose only offence was that they had been born red-headed. Stunned by seven hours of interrogation and beatings Poulsen was taken down to the foyer of Dagmarhus and posted in the entrance facing the statue of the Little Bugler in H. C. Andersens Boulevard. There he saw a strange assemblage of hatless, red-haired citizens. They were ordered to march along the sidewalk and Poulsen was told to point out Flammen. That was typical of the Gestapo mentality. It never occurred to them that the wanted man might not be among their haul.

'I was held in Dagmarhus for four months,' said Poulsen, 'then Vilhelm Leifer, a Danish police official, bribed the Gestapo officer Walther Rothe to set me free. Two days later I met Bent in a street doorway. He was jubilant about my escape and insisted that we should have a celebration dinner that night at the home of Erik Nygaard. "Forget it," I said. "As far as you're concerned, I'm poison." I begged him not to see me again and to contact me only through O.B. or Little Peter. He thought I was crazy. He refused to understand why I had cold feet. He couldn't see that if we were caught it would probably be because I'd been tailed. He was pretty angry and that was the last time I saw him.'

With Poulsen in Gestapo hands and Lise under constant surveillance, Flammen found a new home with Helmer and Liz Bomhoff.

'A friend brought him to us one rainy evening because he had nowhere to go,' Liz Bomhoff said. 'We'd heard all about his courage and skill as a saboteur, but to us he was just a big boy, sensitive, gentle, and considerate. When we think of the joy he brought into our home during the last seven months of his life, we give thanks that we were privileged to know him. No doubt the war had hardened him but it also brought out the best in him. He loved having happy people around him; he loved music; he loved life itself.

'He enjoyed cooking meals for us, though his extravagance sometimes shocked me. He thought nothing of using six eggs and a bottle of rum to make three helpings of sago pudding or a pound of butter to make a dish of Bearnaise. He went to endless trouble to get what he needed. During the general strike he drove around the countryside in his stolen German car, risking his life recklessly to get food for the house and for all the stranded, hungry saboteurs who came there.

'During the strike, when even the saboteurs had to lie low, his favourite occupation was to play with our two pets, Busser the miniature poodle and a little stray black cat. He would crawl with them all over the lawn, ruining his light trousers. That never worried him; *somebody* would take care of the mud and grass stains.

'He loved all animals and once, while we were staying at Tisvilde, he waded fully-dressed into a cold, stormy sea to save a wounded crow. He brought the bird carefully ashore and the unlucky "sportsman" who had shot it got a tongue-lashing that terrified him. When I was being interrogated after Bent's death I told the Gestapomen about that little incident. Naturally it didn't interest them. One man shoved his face up to mine and snarled: "Well, he might have been an animal lover but he was no lover of humans. *He liked killing,* do you understand? *He liked killing!*"

'That wasn't true. Bent never took pleasure in his work. To him it was only a dirty job which had to be done. I think from the beginning he knew how it must end but his sense of duty would give him no rest. A couple of times when things got too hot for him he was sent off to Sweden, but that didn't suit him. Before long he would be heading back across the Øresund, in a rubber dinghy if all else failed. He felt it was at home, not in Sweden, that he was needed. As time passed he made a number of trips with *Speditøren.* I remember the last time he returned. He came running across the lawn, his arms full of parcels and red and white carnations, his eyes sparkling with delight. He stood shuffling from one foot to the other, with his hands behind his back, while we unpacked his gifts; and as I unwrapped one package he said shyly: "That's for you, little mother. Do you like it?" '

It is a charming picture, but few saw that softer side of Flammen's character. Bob Ramsing first encountered Flammen in November 1943. 'There hadn't been a liquidation up to that time—at least, officially,' he said. 'We were at a meeting in Larsen's tobacco shop. Jørgen Staffeldt was then leading the group, having taken over after Finn left for Sweden. He said:

"We've been ordered to do two liquidations. I don't like it, but it has to be done. Any volunteers?"

'Before anybody else could speak, Flammen said in his gentle voice: "I'll do it."

' "What, both of them?" Jørgen asked.

' "Yes."

'I was appalled that this quiet boy should be so ready to kill two people whom he'd never seen. Next morning I read in the newspapers about the two liquidations. One was a former captain in the Danish army who'd been serving the Nazis; the other was a journalist. The previous evening, within half an hour, somebody had rung the doorbells at their apartments and when they opened up said: "This is from the Resistance movement," and shot them.

'I saw Flammen again that afternoon. You can imagine the way I looked at him. He frightened me.'

A few weeks later Gunnar Dyrberg and his friend Paddy (Patrick Schultz) took part in an action against another informer.

'I clutched the revolver in the pocket of my trenchcoat as we stood waiting under a street lamp and I had a sick feeling in my stomach,' Dyrberg said. 'Paddy had been a member of Holger Danske for three weeks and was getting to be an old hand, but I'd been a saboteur for only a week and this was my first action. I'd never even fired a gun and in fact I'd had to borrow one for the occasion. Perhaps it was as well we were only part of the cover-team.

'Paddy nudged my elbow. "Flammen's sitting over there with a Sten-gun," he whispered.

'A little further down the street a yellow Adler was parked and inside it I could see a man wearing a soft felt hat. So that was Flammen, the chap who kept the Gestapo jittery day and night, I thought. I wished I could get a closer look at him. When he cut loose with that sub-machine gun we'd be all right...

'But suddenly the street was full of Danish policemen who'd been called out by a nervous businessman who thought we were planning a hold-up. Most of us got away and the *stikker* was allowed to live a couple of months longer.

'That was the first time I saw Flammen. Not long afterwards I got my wish to inspect him at closer range.

'Paddy and I were ordered to get rid of one of the Gestapo's top informers. He lunched every day at the Lumskebugten restaurant and while he was eating his smørrebrød we were to shoot him with a Sten-gun which we were to carry in a badminton racket case. Flammen had promised to drive us to the restaurant and look after us. We sat waiting for him nervously. It was our first execution job and we didn't know how we'd make out. But when Flammen arrived, there was nothing more for us to do. He'd intercepted the informer on his way to lunch and emptied his Sten-gun into him. Unfortunately the man survived. His panzer-vest had protected him and the bullets had only smashed his ribs.

'That was the beginning of our close association with Denmark's most famous saboteur. We were a strange team. There was the tall, elegant, experienced Flammen, twenty-two-years-old. There was Citronen, a dark, muscular fellow with a never-failing sense of humour. At thirty-four he was the old one, even more experienced than Flammen. He was married but his wife was in Sweden with their two-year-old daughter; their second daughter was born there and never saw her father. Finally there were Paddy and myself, both twenty-two and mere fledglings in the tough world of the Resistance.

'Flammen was unique. Many things have been said and written about him, mostly pure fable. The Germans called him a sadistic murderer who killed for the fun of it. He was never that, though he was certainly a killer; he started killing as a boy, hunting with a bow and arrows in the woods around his home. He joined the Resistance because he loved his country and he took his work as a kind of adventure. His dream was eventually to join the United States forces and continue his fighting in the war against Japan. He was clever, a brilliant marksman, lightning-fast in his reactions, and quite fearless. During his comparatively short career he killed more traitors than anyone else in Denmark but he always gave his adversary a sporting chance. There was a story about him finding some Gestapomen in the Latin quarter of Copenhagen and shooting

it out with them. It was probably true. He seemed to be engaged
in a perpetual game of Russian roulette.

'He only once met his equal. SOE had ordered the liquidation
of SS Obersturmbanführer Seybold and he was given the job.
The action was carefully planned but somehow the wires got
crossed and Little Peter (the naval engineer Peter Pedersen),
who was to drive the car, failed to show up. Flammen picked
up the SOE agent and drove to the rendezvous. In the ensuing
gun-battle Seybold was so badly wounded that he became a
wheelchair case and Flammen was hit in the knee and hip. The
SOE man couldn't drive a car so Flammen dropped him and,
almost blind with pain, made for home alone. There was nobody
in the apartment and he would have bled to death if Little
Peter hadn't seen the bullet-riddled car outside the building and
summoned help. The group's doctor couldn't be found but
O. B. Bertelsen managed to get in touch with Dr. Paul Thygesen,
the eminent neurologist. No anaesthetics were available but
Flammen didn't utter a sound while Thygesen probed for the
bullet which had entered at the left hip and buried itself behind
the spine. Afterwards he was transferred to a private clinic,
where the SOE man saw that he had all the attention and
comforts money could buy. It was a couple of months before
he was fit for action again.

'Flammen was a good comrade and, despite the stories, a
man with feelings like the rest of us. At times his miserable
"speciality" depressed and disgusted him. He would then go
off to do the work he preferred, helping Citronen to organise
the transport to Sweden of shot-down Allied fliers. In a way,
that seemed to compensate for the liquidation of several dozen
traitors, who were after all human beings, however despicable.'

Even in the grim business of the executioners there were
sometimes moments of comedy.

'One afternoon in April 1944, we were ordered to eliminate
Dr. Wäsche, one of the most dangerous examining judges in
Dagmarhus,' Dyrberg said. 'We weren't very happy about it;
it was the second liquidation job we'd been given that day and
the strain was getting to us. The plan was straightforward
enough. Wäsche lived on the fourth floor of a fashionable apart-

ment building. Flammen was to ring his doorbell, pretending to be a workman sent by the administrators of the building. As soon as he was in the apartment Citronen, Paddy and I were to follow. Now we were sitting in Erik Poulsen's apartment, waiting for Citronen to arrive. Paddy and I were already in workmen's clothes. Flammen had taken off his jacket and placed it neatly on a hanger while he got into paint-stained overalls. I looked at his shoulder-holster and the sight of it chilled me. I'd seen that kind of holster in plenty of American gangster films and automatically connected it with criminals. It was a nasty feeling. Shoulder-holsters were rarely used by Holger Danske people. It was easier to carry one's gun in a pocket or stuck in the waistband of one's trousers, where it was ready for action. But Flammen always carried several pistols; the one in the shoulder-holster was a reserve.

'At last he was ready, but Citronen still hadn't turned up. "We won't wait any longer," Flammen said. "If he can't get here on time we'll go without him."

'We set out on bikes for Wäsche's home. On the way Paddy's trouser-leg got caught up in the cycle chain and he lost balance. As he fell his pistol dropped out of his coat pocket and slid across the sidewalk, much to the surprise of the passers-by. He picked the gun up quickly and remounted. Soon we were climbing the back stairs leading to Wäsche's apartment.

'Flammen went first. Paddy and I followed, half a landing down, walking slowly so as not to attract attention. I was carrying the tool-bag holding our Sten-gun and silent pistol. When Flammen reached Wäsche's door I started assembling the Sten. The parts clanked together and Flammen hissed: "Quiet!" He rang the doorbell. We heard footsteps and then the door was opened by an elderly woman.

'Flammen explained that we'd come to do some repairs but she didn't like the idea. She told us to come back when Wäsche was at home. We were on our way down the stairs again when she called: "Oh! painter, since you're here anyhow, will you help me to fix the sitting-room curtains? They're stuck."

'Flammen couldn't very well refuse, so Wäsche had his curtains put right by the man whom the Germans feared and hated more than any other Resistance fighter.'

The Gestapo often came close to capturing Flammen but his amazing luck, iron nerve and deadly marksmanship got him out of the most impossible situations.

While he was staying with the Bomhoffs the Germans arrested a man named Johansen. Through intermediaries Flammen received word that Johansen had been freed and had important information to give him if he would call at a certain address.

'That sounded highly suspicious,' said Dyrberg. 'Since when had the Gestapo started letting convicted Resistance men loose? We knew through our contacts in Dagmarhus that Johansen had confessed and probably given names. We strongly advised Flammen to stay away from him but he wouldn't listen.

'We checked the proposed meeting-place in the evening and on the following morning, half an hour before the appointed time, we were on our way. Flammen and Citronen were to go into the apartment building while Paddy and I wandered around on the square outside, looking at the shop windows. It was a lovely spring day and there were plenty of people around. Some of them were trying so hard to look like casual strollers that they stuck out a mile as Gestapomen. That was a nasty shock, and after twenty minutes we began to sweat a little. We didn't feel happy walking around in broad daylight amongst more than a dozen Gestapomen. Flammen and Citronen were supposed to ride past us in a street-car when they'd left the apartment block by a back entrance. What in the world was keeping them? Each time a street-car passed we looked after it hopefully. It seemed an hour before we saw Citronen standing on a rear platform with a wide grin on his face. We slipped away discreetly and went back to Poulsen's place to hear what had happened.

'Flammen and Citronen had gone to Johansen's place and when he opened the door they had asked him to go to a neigh-bouring apartment, where an old friend of Citronen lived. There the conversation had been very short. Johansen, who was shaking with nerves, had nothing to tell and our friends left him quickly.

'It had indeed been a trap. After the war I spoke to the

German who had led the action. He told me the signal had been that Johansen should step out on to the balcony as soon as Flammen was inside the apartment. Paddy and I were lucky. There'd been so many Gestapomen in the square that they didn't all know each other and they'd taken us for colleagues. When the trick failed Johansen was taken back to Vestre Fængsel. He died later in a German concentration camp.'

Early in July 1944, Dyrberg had an appointment with Flammen at a greengrocery shop kept by Bent Hoegsbro Østergaard, known as Gemysen (the Vegetables). He was cycling along the street when a small black car overtook him and stopped outside the shop. Automatically he looked at the Danish licence plate. It bore one of the Gestapo's forty secret numbers. Dyrberg pedalled on past the men who were getting out of the car, noticing out of the corner of his eye that the shop windows had been drilled by bullets.

'I heard the explanation when I met Kis,' he said. 'A radio group had held a meeting in a nearby restaurant, Davidsens, and had asked Gemysen to join them. But an informer was also present. All of a sudden the Gestapo surrounded the restaurant and arrested everybody, including the *stikker*.

'Flammen, knowing nothing of this, walked into the greengrocery a little later. "Three pounds of potatoes," he said, as usual.

'"Yes, *sir*," said Gemysen's wife, and Flammen knew something was wrong. He paid for the potatoes, left the shop and went into the tobacco shop next door to find out what was going on. But the Gestapomen hidden in the back of the greengrocery had become suspicious. It wasn't every day that a dandified young man entered a greengrocery to buy potatoes. They followed him into the tobacco shop.

'Flammen drew his gun and began shooting before they'd crossed the step. He ran out of the door, grabbed a woman's bicycle which was propped by the kerb and raced across the street towards an alley, with the Germans shooting wildly after him. A Gestapoman posted at the entrance to the alley threw up his sub-machine gun, but before could pull the trigger Flammen put a bullet between his eyes. That wasn't bad shooting by a man zig-zagging along on a woman's bike. When he got back to the Bomhoffs' house, where he was living, Flammen was as calm and unruffled as ever. He didn't even bother to mention the incident.

'A few days later the *stikker* reappeared, claiming that he'd run away from the Gestapo. Since he suffered badly from asthma and couldn't run two metres, that story didn't wash. After prolonged questioning he admitted the truth and was liquidated immediately.'

On 13 October 1944, Flammen left Copenhagen for Jutland, stopping on the way to visit Citronen in the villa on Jægersborg Allé. Why he made that journey is not clear. Erik Poulsen said that he went to Jutland to carry out an execution on direct orders from SOE in Stockholm. Bob Ramsing and others believe that he went to get guns and explosives for Holger Danske.

'This whole arms question was more important than people realise,' Ramsing said. 'Weapons were coming into Denmark but we weren't getting them. There was a deliberate policy behind that. The active groups were kept short while the so-called "waiting groups" of the underground army had plenty of arms stored in secret depots. I remember that we staged a "phony" action, exploding a few small mines in Ørstedsparken to celebrate Princess Benedicte's birthday. Bopa were as mad as hell with us for using explosives for such a stupid purpose. Jespersen was furious about the waste. That shows the situation. In March 1944, Jens Pedersen asked our group to take part in an action at Vestre Fængsel. A VIP—SOE wouldn't say who—had to be freed. Through a Gestapoman in their pay they knew that at seven in the morning on a certain day two cars would leave the prison. In the first car would be four Gestapomen and in the second the VIP with some guards. There were eight men from our group, together with Leif Pedersen from Søborg, who was later killed in the city hall square. We met in the evening in a cellar on Sønderboulevard. At six in the morning we were at our posts. The idea was that I should drive a lorry and block the street so that the cars couldn't get through into Vesterbrogade. I was to have a Sten-gun and blast the Gestapomen in the first car; the rest of the squad would then

Above: Svend Otto Nielsen (John) and Bent Fauerschou-Hviid (Flammen)

Jørgen Haagen Schmidt (Citronen)

Top: Unpacking a container of arms dropped by the R.A.F. Centre: Illegal
manufacture of weapons. Bottom: At a group meeting before an action,
explosives are issued to the saboteurs

Top: This roadsweeper is really a saboteur. His dustcart is packed with weapons and explosives. Centre: Railway sabotage was one of the most effective ways of hampering the German war effort. The first successful action was near Espergærde, 6 November, 1942. Bottom: Sabotage of Langebro by Bopa, 27 March, 1945

Above: The French school in flames after the disaster during the R.A.F. raid on Shellhus, 21 March, 1945. Below: *Retribution* Two photographs of Shellhus, the Gestapo headquarters in Copenhagen, after the R.A.F. raid (from a film by Hans Gjerløv)

tackle the second car and rescue the prisoner. The Sten was the only automatic weapon we had. My comrades had only pistols. Some of those were very old and the owners weren't even sure they'd fire. Imagine sending nine youngsters, not very well trained, into such an action with only one sub-machine gun! That was the first Sten I ever had in my hands—and the last—during that period. Bopa were no better off than we were. Wherever the arms were, we weren't getting them. As late as February 1944, I was in an action to steal guns from the Germans, because they were desperately needed.'

Jens Lillelund confirms Ramsing's opinion. 'I was in Aarhus, organising the flying squads, at that time,' he said. 'I was ill and very tired. I'd been up for several nights, working with the reception committees collecting supplies dropped by the RAF. One of my friends told me that a man was looking for me and said it was vital I should meet him.

' "What does he look like?" I asked.

' "He's tall and pale, with red hair and freckles."

'I said: "Go back and ask him the first name of Mr. Bomhoff, junior. If he says Helmer you can bring him here."

'Half an hour later the man came back with Flammen, as cheerful as ever and burdened with flowers, food, and three bottles of red wine. "I heard you were sick," he said.

' "What can I do for you?" I asked. "I can't do much because I really am ill."

'He said: "We've no weapons and no explosives in Copenhagen. We need your help. If you can let me have some stuff, I'll get it back by fishing-boat."

' "Of course I'll help you," I said, "but only if you promise to come straight back here when you've delivered the goods. If you stay in Copenhagen you'll be dead within three weeks. You're a marked man. Even here in Aarhus and Aalborg you're well-known. The Gestapo know all about Flammen. They even know your real name."

'We knew that because one of our friends, the chairman of the Red Cross in Jutland, was allowed into the Gestapo headquarters to visit the prisoners and take them food. Naturally he was able to get us a lot of useful information.

'Flammen said: "All right. I'll come back, but only if you'll give me some real work to do."

'"You have my word," I said. "Go to Copenhagen, deliver the supplies, and come right back."

'The last I saw of him, he was standing in the doorway, saying: "You'll see me back here on Tuesday of next week."

'Two or three days later I saw on the posters, TERRORIST ARRESTED. I bought a paper and read that Citronen had been killed, that Flammen had been arrested at Erik Nygaard's home, and that Holger Danske were finished.

'I said to myself: "That's not the end of Holger Danske. It may be true that Citronen and Flammen are gone but there are still some of us left. If one's killed, there'll be ten others to take his place." I moved from my apartment because if Flammen were still alive and under torture he might reveal vital names and addresses. Since he'd been with me only three days before, he might have given my address away and the Gestapo might be on their way to pick me up. I moved to another safehouse but nothing happened and I knew Flammen was dead.'

Flammen returned to Zealand on the night of 17 October and sought out the Bomhoffs, who were then staying at the Belevue Strandhotel at Klampenborg. He was completely unarmed. He had left all his weapons at the villa in Jægersborg Allé before going to Jutland.

'18 October dawned like any other day,' Liz Bomhoff said. 'We were still suffering from the shock of Citronen's death, but on the following morning we were going to move to a new residence in Holte. Everything was ready and we were looking forward to having a new "home" and getting Bent safely back to Jutland.

'Bent spent the morning at meetings in Copenhagen and later the rest of us went up to town. We all met for lunch in the restaurant at the National Museum and afterwards strolled through the galleries. Bent was relaxed and happy, playing "Bags this" and "Bags that" as we looked at the collection of antique furniture. He joked about his "dream" hotel, in which he would have "shooting" doors and where the dessert every day would be a *bombe glacé*. But when we visited the "church room" with its wonderful carvings he fell silent and his face was sad. I'm sure he was thinking then of Jørgen's death and of his own uncertain destiny.

'Had we known it, his fate was already sealed. The Gestapo had taken some of our contacts and they had been made to talk.

'We returned to the hotel for Bent's favourite dinner of golden pea soup and pancakes. Then Bent went out and telephoned Erik Nygaard at his home. He came back and told us that we were to go there for coffee. It was raining, so we took a taxi to the villa, Strandvejen 184. There were four of us: Bent, my father-in-law Gunnar Bomhoff, my husband Helmer, and me.

'The evening passed quietly and rather sadly. The shadow of Jørgen's death was on all of us and though we tried to be cheerful we didn't really succeed. Bent had put the pistol he got from Nygaard into the inner pocket of his jacket, which was hanging over the back of a chair in the dining-room. That carelessness was to prove fatal.

'At ten o'clock, as we were getting ready to depart, the door-bell rang long and loud. We looked at each other, startled. We knew what it meant. Then came the first kick on the door from a Nazi boot, and the shout "*Aufmachen!*" which always brought death with it.

'I still believed in the invisible lucky horseshoe over Bent's head. I *wanted* to believe in it, however hopeless the situation seemed. So, as he ran past me, coatless, to seek shelter on the first floor, I called: "So long! We'll all meet at the hotel." Then we had to open the front door.

'A pack of Gestapomen led by Kriminalrat Bunke milled into the entrance hall and reception rooms, howling and firing their pistols. They were scared stiff—terrified of an ambush which didn't exist. I remember one hulking brute bawling and cursing at me and shoving the muzzle of his machine-pistol almost into my face. It was quite ridiculous, a heavily-armed German frightened of a woman with her hands above her head; but I didn't think of that. I was trying to make out above the din what was happening to Bent.

'He had tried to get out through a bedroom window but a

salvo from a machine-gun in the garden made him withdraw hastily. The shooting brought return fire from the Gestapomen in the house. Everything was confusion. The Germans thought the house was full of saboteurs. They herded Mrs. Nygaard and me up the stairs on to the flat roof. They wanted to make sure we'd be the first to die if there were anybody up there. As we were forced upstairs we saw the Nygaards' two sons, about nine to ten years old, sitting up in their beds, their eyes dark with terror, holding a blanket like a shield in front of their faces. We could not see Bent. He was hiding behind the door. Then we were pushed down again and Bunke rushed up the stairs to the bedroom with a couple of his thugs at his heels. As they burst into the room Bent swallowed a cyanide pill and ended his own life. A Gestapoman stood over him with raised gun, yelling: *"Sind Sie Flammen?"* and kicking repeatedly at his body.

'The Gestapomen dragged Bent down to the hall by his feet. I heard the thud of his head hitting each stair. They threw him down in front of me and forced us to get some milk from the kitchen to try to counteract the effect of the poison, but it was too late. He was beyond their reach.

'His face was calm. I longed to kneel beside him and close his eyes but the Germans kept their guns trained on us all, ready to fire at the slightest excuse. I could only stand there, looking down on the boy who had come to mean so much to us and thanking God that his brave spirit was at last at peace.'

On the morning of 19 October 1942, shortly after his seventy-second birthday, King Christian set out from Amalienborg Castle on his horse, Jubilee, for his usual ride through Copenhagen. Unluckily the day was a school holiday and the press of too-enthusiastic young loyalists following on bicycles made the horse restive. The king, a fine rider, managed to maintain control for some time, but on the railway bridge behind the English Church on Langelinie the animal shied, got the bit in its teeth, and bolted. It careered down the slope towards the Gefion Fountain, then made a sudden swerve. The king was thrown, gashing his head on a boulder. He was taken to the Diakonisse Institution, where his injuries were found to be serious. To complicate matters, pneumonia supervened and for several days it was doubtful whether he could survive.

From the German embassy came an order that in the event of the king's death, no flags were to be flown at half-mast. He was the paramount symbol of national unity and the Germans hoped that his passing would remove a major obstacle to German-Danish collaboration. They wanted, therefore, no public expressions of mourning.

On Sunday, 25 October, prayers for the king's recovery were offered in churches throughout Denmark. Two days later the nation heard with joy that following two blood transfusions and treatment with the new sulfanomide drugs, the crisis had been passed. The king's condition gradually improved and on 27 November he was able to return to Amalienborg.

During his absence there had been important changes on the political front. Cecil von Renthe-Fink had been recalled to Berlin after the 'birthday telegram' incident, leaving P. G. L. Barandon to function as acting ambassador. Hanneken had replaced General Erich Lüdke as commander-in-chief of the German occupying forces, and on 5 November Dr. Best had arrived in Copenhagen as German plenipotentiary. Neither Best nor Hanneken visited the king after his return from hospital. He had been shelved, and thereafter the Germans dealt only with the politicians.

Hanneken's avowed objective was to get rid of the last remnants of the Danish military forces as quickly as possible. He was saddled with the task of preparing against the expected Allied invasion and he had very few troops in Funen and Zealand, where the Danish forces were concentrated. He knew and had reported to Berlin that the Danish military intelligence officers who were spying on him had established lively connections with Britain. Something had to be done, and the government's total rejection of the German ultimatum on 28 August 1943 gave him his opportunity. During the night, without warning, the small, widely-scattered units of the army and navy were attacked, disarmed and interned.

The king and queen were spending the summer at Sorgenfri Castle, a few miles outside Copenhagen, protected only by one officer, one non-commissioned officer and nineteen men of the Royal Life Guard and two policemen. The king was still a sick man. A wound in his foot had not healed and he was forced to spend most of his day in a chair.

At half past five on the morning of 29 August a strong detachment of German soldiers, commanded by Air-General Ritter von Scheich and guided by a Danish traitor, stormed Sorgenfri. The guards were hopelessly outnumbered and after a short fight the king ordered the cease-fire.

Scheich, accompanied by two soldiers, marched into the castle and demanded an immediate audience. The king, meanwhile, had been carried down to his study, angrily denouncing 'this paltry assault'. Sitting in his chair, he received the German commander with the contemptuous greeting: *'Guten morgen, mein tapferer General!'* ('Good morning, my brave general!'). Why, he asked coldly, had it been necessary to stage this attack under cover of darkness? With all the power at their disposal, why could not the Germans have come to the castle in daylight, in a manner worthy of soldiers?

Scheich may well have wondered whether that might not have been the safer course. The raid had been costly for the

attackers. Seven German troopers had been killed and one
wounded. The Life Guard's only casualty was one wounded
man, who later recovered completely in the military hospital.

From that time on the king was a prisoner in his own castle,
guarded by troopers under an officer who formerly had been
head of the German State Railways tourist bureau in Copenhagen. He could not even go for a drive without first obtaining
German permission.

On 6 October the military state of emergency was ended
and the German guards at Sorgenfri were replaced by Danish
police, but otherwise the king's situation remained unchanged.
He still regarded himself as a prisoner, cut off from all participation in the affairs of his country.

Throughout the winter and summer of 1944 unrest increased
throughout Denmark. The steadily growing campaign of the
Resistance groups against collaborating factories, shipyards and
workshops was backed by spontaneous public demonstrations
like the great general strike in June and July. The Germans
retaliated by unleashing on the population the murderous Peter
group, headed by the German Otto Schwerdt (Peter Schafer),
and gangs of thugs led by the Danish criminals Henning
Brøndum, Bothildsen-Nielsen, Nedermark Hansen, and Ib
Birkedal Hansen.

The indiscriminate slaughter of prominent Danes by these
terrorists aroused fears for the king's safety and the Danish
police chiefs advised him to return to Copenhagen, where he
could be better protected. Accordingly, on 5 September the
royal family moved back to Amalienborg Castle.

The guard on the four palaces at Amalienborg numbered
about fifty policemen, among them the former Royal Life
Guardsman Frank Zorn (now a detective-inspector in Copenhagen). Zorn had joined the police force in 1940 and while serving with the coastguard division had worked with the illegal
transport groups on the Jewish evacuation. Afterwards he remained an active member of a police underground group.

'The Germans had long been threatening to disband the
Danish police,' he said. 'Most of us resented having to work
alongside the Gestapo and they feared, quite rightly, that at the

first hint of an Allied landing we should go over openly to the Resistance.

'On the morning of 19 September 1944, they struck. Shortly before eleven o'clock the air-raid sirens blew in Copenhagen, Odense, Aarhus and Aalborg. It was a false alarm. While the streets were empty the Gestapo and German troops took the police stations by surprise and arrested men on patrol or going on or off duty. After the action Police-General Pancke, the Gestapo chief, announced that the Danish police had been disbanded because they could be trusted no longer. That same evening all the arrested men under fifty-five years of age were deported to Germany. They were sent first to Neuengamme and Buchenwald and from there to various prisoner-of-war and labour camps. At least eighty were to die in captivity.

'Some two thousand men were arrested, but seven thousand escaped the round-up and went underground to form an illegal police force.

'Shortly after the sirens sounded in Copenhagen, a party of German marines marched into Slotspladsen, the great central courtyard of Amalienborg. They tried to act like casual sightseers but we weren't taken in. Real sightseers don't carry submachine guns and carbines. We fired a volley over their heads and they retreated in disorder.

'It was about an hour before the Germans moved on the castle in strength. We heard later that there had been a dispute among the German authorities as to whether the king should be arrested. Pancke finally made his point that the police guard should be taken first and that they could then decide what to do about the king. The delay gave us plenty of time to get ready. As soon as the order came to defend the castle, we blocked every entrance to Slotspladsen with "Spanish riders" (prefabricated steel barricades topped with barbed-wire) which we'd kept in store for just such an emergency. The public, particularly in the harbour district, joined in enthusiastically. Dock labourers, clerks, shopkeepers and errand-boys worked like beavers, filling hundreds of sandbags and packing them around the Spanish riders and in the windows and doorways of the palaces. They blocked Toldbodgade, between the palaces and the harbour, with old cars, barrows, timbers, and similar junk, and stretched steel cables from one side of Amaliegade to the other to prevent German vehicles from getting up the street. A big lorry was parked between the central pillars of the Colonnade, effectively blocking access to Slotspladsen from that direction. The Danish Red Cross set up a first aid post in the yellow palace, Amaliegade 18, and the rest of us took up positions covering all approaches to the castle. Then we settled down to wait.

'I can't say that we were feeling particularly happy. Our entire defence force was fifty policemen, a few CB men and the castle officials. Some of the dockers wanted to fight alongside us, but we simply hadn't the guns to give them.

'At a quarter past twelve somebody yelled: "They're coming!" and we saw a column of about a hundred German marines trying to get up Amaliegade from Langelinie. They were having a rough passage. Half-way up the street there was a big Tuborg warehouse. A party of Danes had carried crates of beer up to the roof and were bombarding the Germans with bottles. They showered down in hundreds, bursting like hand-grenades. In places there was a litter of broken glass about two feet deep on the roadway. The young lieutenant leading the marines was almost dancing with rage. He ordered his men to set fire to the warehouse. They chucked hand-grenades and incendiary bombs through the windows and doors and the building went up in flames. Several people died in the blaze.

'The Germans continued their march on Amalienborg. When they neared the main gates they spread out and advanced in open order. Our chief, Police-Commissioner Nielsen-Ourø, went out and shouted: "Halt!" They took no notice. Captain Poul Henningsen, the king's adjutant, had no better luck. While the body of the force lay down in the street with six machine-guns trained on the castle, some of the marines went forward and started to cut the barbed-wire on the Spanish riders. We made no move. For a few minutes there was a strange, deadly silence. Then a trigger-happy marine fired a couple of shots. It was enough. Captain Henningsen shouted "Fire!" and we cut loose with a fusilade from our rifles and sub-machine guns.

'From my post behind the sandbags on the right-hand corner

of Amaliegade I could see that most of the Germans were boys of sixteen, seventeen and eighteen, who probably had never been in action before. We could hear them screaming "*Heil Hitler!*" and "Mother, help me!" when they were hit. They took cover in doorways and cellar entrances, and when they stuck their heads out we shot at them. Three times they tried to advance, and each time we drove them back.

'At a quarter to one, another detachment tried vainly to get up Amaliegade from Sankt Annæ Plads; and so it went on for more than an hour. The Germans were getting nowhere, but our own situation was precarious, for our ammunition was running low. To add to our troubles, just after two o'clock a German gunboat arrived at a quay opposite Amalienborg and began shooting over Larsens Plads towards Ny Toldbodgade, on the eastern side of the castle. We had to reform our forces to deal with this new attack and repel a landing-party from the ship.

'In Frederiksgade, on the eastern side of the castle, stood the German-occupied Damehotel. A gang of naval ratings and their Danish girl friends had gathered on the roof to watch the battle and they decided to join in. They started shooting down into Slotspladsen, so that we were now under attack from three sides. Once more we had to regroup our small forces. We could expect no help from outside. The Germans were bombarding Amaliegade with cannon and hand-grenades and several buildings were on fire. A number of civilians were burned to death or were shot by the half-hysterical young marines. As we fought on, we could see Danish policemen being taken in lorries to the ship which was to carry them to concentration camps in Germany.

'There was a moment of light relief when Crown Prince Frederik came out of his palace and down to the gates to ask how the battle was going. He brought us cigarettes and beer and we told him that no German was going to get past us. But when we were attacked from the fourth side by two panzer cars stationed in Fredericiagade, it began to look like the end. We had only a handful of cartridges between us and our sub-machine gunners were reduced to firing single rounds to conserve our stock. Then, in the nick of time, some Resistance men drove up in ambulances and threw supplies of ammunition into the castle gardens.

'After three hours of hard fighting the Germans decided the only way to get us out was to smash down the walls and roofs of the castle with shellfire. That was too much for the king. When he heard that artillery was being brought in, he sent his aide-de-camp and the palace steward, Captain Schlichtkrull, to parley with the German authorities. Incredibly, the Germans capitulated and ordered the shooting to stop. They claimed the attack had been a mistake! Word came from Pancke's head-quarters that the Amalienborg guard would not be disarmed and could carry on their duties unmolested.

'The Germans had sixteen dead and forty wounded. Our casualties throughout the entire action were three policemen, a volunteer and the palace steward wounded. Not one of the defenders was killed.'

After the battle the resident police guard at Amalienborg was increased to one hundred men, maintaining a round-the-clock watch. On Christmas Eve the king went with the queen and the crown prince to the guardroom, greeted all the police-men individually and presented every man with a silver match-box engraved with the royal monogram.

'In December restrictions were relaxed and we were allowed to live outside the castle while off-duty, going back again to stand our watches,' Zorn said. 'As soon as we left the castle we took off our uniforms, donned civilian clothes and went under-ground to work with Holger Danske, Bopa and the illegal transports. I worked with a team of saboteurs who were also responsible for collecting arms and distributing them to the other groups.

'The Germans unwittingly made our job easier. We had told them: "We can't guard our king without weapons." They agreed and not only allowed us to keep our rifles, sub-machine guns and pistols but issued us with personal firearms permits, enabling us to carry our guns at all times. A firearms permit was a useful document to have when one went underground.

'In one of the castle buildings not used by the royal family and their entourage we had a secret armoury, where we kept a large stock of heavy weapons like machine-guns and bazookas for use by the Resistance groups. Fresh supplies of guns and ammunition were brought in regularly by food lorries and ambulances making their legitimate calls at the castle. Of course, the king never knew anything about that.'

The guard on Amalienborg could never be relaxed. There were strong and probably well-founded rumours that the Nazis still planned to seize the king and his family and deport them to Germany. The military never again attacked the castle but there were several abortive night raids by gangs from the *Hipokorps*, commanded by the renegade policeman Erik V. Petersen.

The last battle at Amalienborg came in the hour of liberation.

'Shortly after nine o'clock on the evening of 4 May 1945, when the news of the capitulation came through, we were all mustered in Slotspladsen,' Zorn said. 'Suddenly the Germans in the Damehotel and in a nearby house started shooting at us. We were under fire from three points and two of our men, a policeman and a soldier of the Royal Life Guard, were killed. It was sad that they should have died at the very moment when thousands of Copenhageners were massed in the streets around the castle, cheering the end of five years of German oppression.'

On a wall in Politigaarden, Copenhagen's police headquarters, a roll of honour bears the names of one hundred and fifty-seven policemen who died during the occupation in battle, on sabotage missions or in the concentration camps. Seventy-six were killed in action. The others died from disease, brutality or starvation in the camps.

16: THE HIDDEN EYE

From 9 April 1940, all photography in Denmark was strictly controlled. Any citizen caught taking pictures of *Wehrmacht* or Danish Nazi activities was punished severely and even Press photographers could operate only within prescribed limits. Early in the occupation newsreel cameramen of the Danish Film Review were summoned to the UFA headquarters in Copenhagen and asked whether they would supply material for the official news bulletins shown in Danish and German cinemas. They refused. They had seen already how the Nazis could distort their work for propaganda purposes. A glaring example had been the splicing of film of Goering's visit to Copenhagen with shots of the crowds celebrating King Christian's seventieth birthday. When the cameramen refused to cooperate, they were told that in future they would not be allowed to buy any more film stock.

The restrictions had little practical effect. Supplies of film were obtained through underground channels and throughout the country amateurs and professionals, working often in conditions of extreme danger, continued to take pictures which eventually were to produce a complete photographic record of the five years of occupation.

At the outbreak of war Hans Gjerløv, a newsreel cameraman with the Danish Film Company, was stationed in Jutland. 'On the morning of 9 April 1940, I left Holstebro to do some filming in Viborg,' he said. 'It was a lovely day and I was feeling on top of the world. The war was far from my thoughts. It didn't touch us at all. We were neutral and always would be.

'The first intimation of trouble came when I reached Viborg. People were standing around in the streets, reading the newspapers and arguing heatedly. When they told me the Germans were crossing the border and invading Denmark, I couldn't believe it. I drove on south towards Kolding and there I met the first German troops—a column of tanks, escorted by armoured cars and motorcycles. I stopped the car, got my camera out and stood at the side of the road, filming them as they approached. Nobody stopped me. I suppose they thought I was one of their own people. I shot a lot of pictures in the district and sent them back to my firm in Copenhagen.

'Later I was recalled to the capital and went on filming there —the big German parades and that kind of thing. On 17 November the Danish Nazis had the cheek to stage a full-scale parade in H. C. Andersens Boulevard in memory of the Danish soldiers who had fallen on 9 April. That was something the Copenhageners couldn't take and the show ended in a near-riot. I got some first-class film, and not all of it went to the German censors. In the summer of 1941 all news photographers and film news units were ordered to the central railway station to see the so-called Danish Free Korps depart for the Russian front. Fritz Clausen and all the Nazi big-shots were there to give the heroes a send-off. That was another parade we were happy to shoot, since it enabled us to put the faces of so many collaborators on record.

'Towards the end of 1941 a few of us got together to make illegal films. We had Jess Jessen in Aalborg, Svend Aage Thomsen, a teacher, in Vejle, and in Copenhagen Olaf Malmström, Erik Frost Hansen, Finn Patik and Gunnar "Nu" Hansen. We used 16mm cameras, which could be concealed fairly easily, and Finn processed the negatives. Gunnar, who was news editor of the Danish State Radio, tipped us off to likely stories and stored our films. We weren't alone in the game. Several other small groups began making 16mm films at about the same time.

'When the RAF bombed the Burmeister & Wein shipyard on 27 January 1943, we were there. It was too dark to film the actual bombing but we got many good shots of the fires raging after the raid.

'On 29 August 1943, we organised a big party to film the events of the day. By eight o'clock in the morning I was sitting up on top of a big building on the corner of the Raadhusplads and I stayed there until eight in the evening, shooting everything that happened in the square. When I came down, a

Gestapoman obligingly helped me to lug all my stuff to my office in the Palladium Cinema.

'As time went on, our organisation got better and better. More people joined us and we established excellent contacts with the Resistance sabotage and fighting groups, so that we were usually on the spot when the lads went into action. We never had much trouble in getting supplies. A great deal of our 16mm film came from German soldiers. As they were going through the customs posts on the border, any spools they carried were taken from them and later a customs officer would ring us and tell us to come and collect the haul.

'Svend Thomsen made many good films of the railway sabotage in Jutland. He went out with the young saboteurs and shot whole actions from the placing of the charges to the wrecking of the trains. On several occasions he escaped capture by a hair's breadth.'

Gjerløv, too, had his bad moments, when only sheer chance saved him from arrest.

'In the spring of 1944 I was living in a *pension* at Hellerup and became friendly with a young man who had the room opposite mine,' he said. 'One day in March he rang me at my office and asked: "How are you? All right? Well, if I were you, I should stay in Copenhagen for a while." That same day the Gestapo raided the *pension* and arrested everybody there. My friend was taken with the others. He was a member of our group, and I'd never known it. It was then that I went underground.

'I was very lucky that I was never picked up, for I was out and about all the time, taking pictures, and I had to carry my equipment with me in a hold-all. At that time I was using a Bell and Howell 16mm camera, taking 100-foot spools. Many people knew me and knew what I was doing but I was never denounced.

'On one occasion a group I was working with told me I was being watched, so I went to stay with an uncle at Vordingborg until things cooled down. After I'd been there a couple of days I went to the railway station and saw a large party of Germans getting off the train from Copenhagen. I hurried home and warned my uncle and his friends that there'd be trouble that night. They wouldn't believe me. I couldn't risk staying there and took the first train to Roskilde. Next day I heard that the Gestapo had raided the house. Many people were taken.'

The problem of keeping out of the hands of the enemy was not the film-makers' only preoccupation. All too often the risks they took were ill-rewarded.

'After Kaj Munk's murder in January 1944, a funeral service was held in the old church at Vedersø, in West Jutland,' Gjerløv said. 'Despite German threats, several thousand people attended. The small building could accommodate only a few but the others were content just to stand outside and take part in the prayers and hymns. The congregation included the priests of many Jutland parishes, led by the Bishop of Ribe, and the Rev. Dr. Niels Nøjgaard, of Slagelse, gave the address. I managed to get to the ceremony and made a fine film, but the place where it was stored was sabotaged and it went up in flames.

'That was only one of several strokes of bad luck. Another came when I went to film a sabotage action in Copenhagen's south harbour. A youngster in my group had packed the lens of my camera with tissue paper to prevent it being broken. In the excitement I didn't notice the tissue paper (there was no through-the-lens focusing in those days) and so I didn't get a single picture.

'During the general strike I went to Nørreport to film the building of the street barricades. Three of the workers grabbed me and demanded: "Why are you taking pictures? Have you come from the Germans?" They would have smashed my camera if Sven Gyldmark, the Danish composer, who happened to be in the crowd, hadn't intervened. He got me away safely, but it was a near thing. Life was very difficult at that time. Nobody knew who could be trusted.

'The best arrangements sometimes went wrong. Before the raid on the Heiber Service factory at Lyngbyvej 165, Copenhagen, Poul Overgaard Nielsen of Danish State Radio asked me to go with him to "a little meeting". There I met the sabotage group and sat in on the discussion of the plan. It was decided to stage the action at nine o'clock in the morning on Sunday, 5 March 1945. Just before the appointed time I went with Nielsen to the office of a tobacco factory, from which I could get a clear view of the Heiber works. There was no sign of sabotage activity. Men were standing about and coming and going, but nothing happened. However, the job was pulled off on the following Sunday at the same hour and I got good pictures.'

Many of the best photographs and films of incidents in the streets—Hipo brutality, the daylight hold-ups of German soldiers for weapons, and popular demonstrations—were taken not by the film groups but by amateurs serving with Holger Danske, Bopa, and the other organisations. Some were taken by people who had no active connection with the Resistance but just happened to have a camera handy when something happened. Gjerløv himself was sometimes blessed with luck at that kind.

'All the places we'd been using were blown up by the Schalburgmen and Hipos and we had to move to new offices in Gyldenløvesgade, from which we had a perfect view of Shellhus,' he said. 'Just before eleven o'clock on the morning of 21 March 1945, I was sitting in the office when I heard the sound of unfamiliar aircraft engines. I looked out of the window and saw RAF Mosquitoes approaching low over the city. I grabbed my camera, rushed down into the street and started shooting just as the first bombs hit the Gestapo headquarters in that historic raid.'

Henrik Sandberg, owner of Merry Film Production, Copenhagen, became involved in illegal activities early in 1943. 'At that time my mother had the Merry Cinema on Amager and I managed it for her,' he said. 'A friend asked me if I could find a place to store paper for *Frit Danmark*. He had about a year's supply—enough to fill two fair-sized living-rooms. We took the bales down into the cinema basement and packed them into the channels of the air-conditioning plant. For the next year or so our patrons didn't have very good air but nobody ever complained.

'Since I'd now become embroiled, willy-nilly, in Resistance affairs, I thought I might as well do something constructive, so

I got in touch with Leif B. Hendil, who was running his escape routes across the Øresund and who had good contacts with Britain and America. Through him I had films brought in from Sweden and with these we were able to make good propaganda and, at the same time, raise much-needed cash for the movement. The first was Steinbeck's *The Moon Is Down* and this was followed by Frank Capra's films of the North African campaign, and many others. I had from fifty to sixty screenings, with audiences of from two to a hundred. Some of the showings were in my mother's cinema, others in cellars and anywhere else we could rig up a projector. And we had some funny experiences. Once we had a showing in the Metro-Goldwyn private cinema in Hammerichsgade. There was a club for German soldiers on the ground floor. We were screening a very serious picture and there was a hell of a noise downstairs because the Germans were dead drunk. I sent somebody down to tell them to shut up —and they did!

'The showings had to be kept secret and it was difficult to get people to come because they were afraid, but we got admission prices ranging from ten to five thousand kroner. We made no fixed charge. We said: "Pay what you like. It's all going to a good cause."

'There were only five or six people in my group but we were helped greatly by cinema owners and other good friends who provided places for us to show our films and by some who acted as projectionists. I don't know exactly how much money we raised with our shows, since we daren't keep written records, but it was certainly a considerable amount.

'I was never a saboteur. I was approached several times to do other jobs but my orders were to confine myself to showing the films. That was sensible. If you were picked up, the less you knew, the less you could tell, and if you were under torture, sooner or later you did tell. In my group, as in many others, there was an arrangement that if one of us were picked up, he tried to keep silent for twelve hours to give the others a chance to get away. After that he could talk. We had a special telephone number which we had to ring at fixed intervals. If one man didn't get through on time the rest of the group knew something was wrong and acted accordingly.

'All went well until Sunday 28 August 1944. We had a screening that morning in the basement of a house on Amager. There were only about ten people in the audience and one of them was a *stikker*. All of a sudden the house was surrounded. I'd seen the films so often that I couldn't stand looking at them again and I was out in the courtyard, smoking a cigarette, when the Germans arrived. There were about fifty of them in cars. I could see we'd no chance of getting away. None of us had a gun, so we couldn't put up a fight. We were all taken to Shellhus and locked up. I told the Germans that I accepted full responsibility. I said I had organised the show and the customers knew nothing about it; they thought they were going to see blue films.

'On the following evening, after hours of interrogation, I was taken into the office of SS-stürmbannführer Karl Heinz Hoffmann, then the Gestapo chief in Copenhagen. It was a very hot evening and the windows were wide open. Hoffmann was sitting at his desk, smoking a fat cigar, and the films were stacked all around him. That gave me an idea. Cinema film is highly inflammable and can be extremely dangerous in loose coils; but in tightly-wound reels it's safe enough. Hoffmann was unlikely to know that, and I thought: "Here's my chance of surviving." I snatched the cigar out of his mouth and chucked it out of the window.

' "What the hell d'you think you're doing?" he roared.

'I broke off a short strip of film, took a match and lit it. The film flared up immediately. I said: "You see? Your cigar could have sent up the whole building."

'He believed me. After that I was quite well treated. He thought I'd saved his life.'

After further interrogation Sandberg and his customers were sent to Vestre Fængsel, and in October Sandberg was transferred to Frøslev concentration camp, on the Danish-German border.

'I was lucky,' he said. 'I was put in with some good men. Our room was called the Goat Stall because it stank to high heaven, but that was no fault of ours. My room-mates were excellent "organisers" and I asked whether they could get me an old camera. I'd hoped only for a second-hand Kodak or Agfa, but what eventually reached me was a Minox sub-miniature camera —the first I'd ever seen—and a 16mm cine-camera, complete with films. They were smuggled into the camp in flour sacks by the Danish food contractor. (Because Frøslev was supplied by the Danish prison authorities we got much better food than the muck dished out in Vestre Fængsel.)

'One of our fellow-prisoners, Lieutenant Leif Feilberg, helped me with the filming. We got some marvellous shots of the huts and the guards, of guards chasing Danish prisoners and of the early-morning roll-call of prisoners who were being deported to concentration camps in Germany. As there was nowhere in our room to hide the exposed films we passed them to a man who worked in the hospital section. Unluckily he knew nothing about photography and hid the spools in the X-ray room. More than two-thirds of our work was completely ruined.

'On the day of liberation I still had enough film left to take plenty of valuable shots of the happenings inside the camp. I got pictures of the stool-pigeons who'd been planted among us (naturally, we knew most of them) and of collaborating Danes who'd got themselves into Frøslev during the last months of the occupation because they thought that would be the safest place to hide. Some of those shots provided useful evidence when the time came to bring the traitors to trial.

'On the evening of 6 May 1945, I returned home to Copenhagen, taking my films with me. The negatives were processed and a set of prints was sent to London. The material was used in several British and American newsreels and in the Danish documentary films produced after the war.'

Henrik Sandberg and Feilberg were not alone as jail and concentration camp photographers. Men in Vestre Fængsel and in Horserød operated with equal ingenuity to produce a comprehensive record of the prisoners' daily round. Many moving examples of their work can be seen today in the galleries of the Freedom Museum in Copenhagen.

17: THE CHURCHILL CLUB

In the summer of 1942 a tonic gale of laughter swept Denmark following the capture of the Churchill Club, eight Aalborg schoolboys who, with the slogan *'Vi maatte gøre det, naar de voksne ikke ville'* ('If the grown-ups won't do something, we will'), had infuriated the Germans by a series of arms thefts and sabotage actions. Their legend has grown through the years and it is tempting to believe that they were a serious thorn in the side of the occupying power. In fact, the amount of damage they inflicted on the Germans was negligible. Nevertheless, their escapades drew attention to what might be achieved by well-organised, determined groups of saboteurs and undoubtedly inspired their elders to try their luck at the game.

Knud and Jens Pedersen formed the club, early in the occupation, at Odense, where their father was a priest. The family moved to Aalborg towards the end of 1941, when Pastor Pedersen was appointed to a post at the cathedral. The boys were sent to Aalborg Cathedral School and lost no time in reorganising the club there. Among those they recruited were the brothers H. U. and S. J. Darket, now pilots with the Scandinavian Airlines System.

'Jens Pedersen was in the top form, preparing for his degree,' Uffe Darket said. 'Knud was in a lower form with my brother. At that time Jens was eighteen and Knud sixteen. I was sixteen and studying at another school.

'Jens was the leader of the club. The rest of us were a year or two younger. Our youngest member was only fourteen. When eventually we were arrested he was too young to be punished.

'We began operations early in 1942. We had an anti-Nazi sign, a swastika with an arrowhead at the tip of each arm, which we painted on walls, in stairways, and wherever we could. It wasn't a success because most of the townsfolk didn't know what it meant. More usefully, we compiled news-sheets with the aid of a toy printing set. Some of our information came from BBC broadcasts but a lot of the stuff we printed was sheer rumour. We had no way of checking our facts. Very soon we started to collect weapons in the hope that we'd be able to join the liberating forces when they arrived from Britain. We never doubted they'd come.

'Getting guns was no trick at all. The Germans were incredibly careless with their weapons. We'd accost soldiers after a parade or at the railway station and while a couple of us engaged them in friendly conversation, the others would steal the rifles they'd propped against a wall or bench. Our best hunting-grounds were the restaurants. The German officers hung their belts and holsters in the cloakrooms and we'd pinch the pistols from there. The local barracks was another good spot. When the troops had left for a route march, the place would be empty except for a few guards. While they were in the huts, polishing their equipment or busy with other chores, we'd lift their rifles through the open windows. Once a postman caught us at it. He thought we were after money and opened his mouth to shout, but when he saw that we were only taking rifles he just went on about his business.

'Among my friends at the Aalborg gliding club was a youth of about nineteen. He wanted to join us but he was too old and we wouldn't take him. One day he told me that he could get us six mortar grenades. His elder brother and a friend who lived at Bränderslev, a small town north of Aalborg, had stolen them from a troop train. He said we could have them only if we allowed him to join our club, so we accepted him. Once we'd got the grenades we didn't know what the hell to do with them. We had vague ideas about dropping them from the church steeple on to the square during a *Wehrmacht* parade, or of dumping them on to a German ship from the harbour bridge. Neither plan was feasible, so the grenades were stored with the rifles and pistols in the cathedral crypt.

'The Churchill Club in Aalborg carried out some twenty-five sabotage actions but we did little real damage. The Odense section were more efficient. One night they burned an old Danish drill hall and destroyed at least twenty German army lorries. Our best job was the burning of a freight train loaded with war materials. We'd made friends with the guard by running errands for him and he told us what was in the different sections of the train. He pointed out one wagon which contained aircraft wings. We went back to the yard after dark, poured petrol over the wings, and set them alight. Meanwhile our youngest comrade had found another wagon containing military supplies. In the best Boy Scout tradition, he set fire to it with only one match. When we left, the whole train was ablaze.

'There was a steep hill in the town which was tiring to climb on our bicycles. We used to make the ride easier by hanging on to the tailboards of lorries. We saw a German truck going up the hill with a load of war materials hidden under a camouflage of straw. We hung on to the tailboard and set the straw alight, then slipped away. By the time the truck reached the crest of the hill the load was blazing. That incident was never reported to the police because nobody could understand how the straw had caught fire.

'Officers' barracks, where Danish firms were working for the Germans, were major targets. We resented the collaborators more than the Germans themselves. To us they were plain traitors. We burned out two or three barrack sheds while they were closed for the week-end.

'We were too young to understand the risks we were taking. When we found an unguarded lorry, the main thing was to make sure there was fuel in the tank; otherwise we couldn't destroy it. We had no explosives. One evening we found a lorry but we thought the tank was empty and started looking for another. However, our youngest comrade unscrewed the cap, struck a match, peered into the tank and said: "Hold on! There's petrol here." It's a miracle it didn't blow up in his face. We stuck a bit of rag into the tank, lit it and the lorry burned.

'Our biggest disappointment came when we went into a German barracks and found a large box, marked *Krudt*. That's the Danish word for gunpowder. We spent a whole evening lugging that box down to the cathedral crypt, and when we opened it, it contained nothing but boots and old uniforms. Krudt was the name of its owner.'

The game came to an end on 8 May 1942. A cloakroom

attendant at one of the restaurants had seen the boys going in and out and suspected that they were petty thieves. She noticed particularly the care which Knud Pedersen gave to his hair. When the loss of a pistol was discovered and the police were called, the girl told them to look for a tall youth with long hair which he was always combing. The police kept watch outside the Cathedral School and saw Knud leaving. The girl identified him and he was arrested. Within two or three hours the police had the names of the entire group.

'When I got home in the late evening I saw two cars outside the house,' Uffe said. 'I guessed what had happened. I went in and said: "Here I am. Are you looking for me?" Afterwards I wished I'd run away to Sweden, flown to England, and joined the RAF—my dearest ambition. Instead I was arrested. None of us escaped. We sat in Kong Hansgades Arrest, the local jail, for two months and then we were all sent to Nyborg to begin sentences ranging from one and a half to three years.

'The three older chaps from Brønderslev, who'd stolen the mortar grenades, were arrested with us but they were kept in a different part of the jail. They were given sentences of four and a half and five years. There was some doubt about which prison to send them to, so they stayed in Aalborg for about six weeks longer than we did. The two brothers had another brother outside and they asked him to smuggle a file into the jail. On his next visit he brought them two. Within a fortnight they'd filed through the cell bars in such a way that they could take them out and replace them undetected. A week after we'd left for Nyborg they started going out at night as soon as the guard was changed. There was no cell inspection during the night hours but just in case the guard happened to look through the peephole in the door they arranged dummies in their beds. That first night the three went to the brothers' home, where the father said he'd try to arrange for their escape to Sweden. Since he had no direct contacts with Resistance people, it took more than a week to fix things. During that time the three went out every night, did a bit of sabotage, and returned to their cells unchallenged.

'The Germans and the Danish police couldn't understand

what the hell was going on. They'd caught all the saboteurs in Aalborg and still they were getting trouble. The German commander warned the police that if they didn't catch the culprits, his men would take over. Meanwhile the three lads were happily burning military supplies and throwing German cars into the harbour.'

On the night of 24 August, when they went to the brothers' home for a meal of bread, cakes and coffee, they were told that plans for their shipment to Sweden were well advanced. They left the house in high spirits; but as they were walking through the town on their way back to jail, the air-raid warning sounded.

'That put them in a proper fix,' Uffe said. 'They knew the sirens would wake the guard at the jail. They had a talk in the entrance to an apartment building and decided the only thing was to go on and try to climb into their cells unseen. But their luck had run out. As they left the building two policemen saw them and shouted to them to stop. They ran on and got into another apartment house but the policemen found them and asked what they were doing there. Since they could produce no identity papers they were taken to the police station, where they were recognised. Their sentences were increased to fifteen and twenty years and they were sent to a German prison camp, but six months later they were returned to Denmark and put into Horsens state prison. There they stayed until the liberation.

'The rest of us were kept away from the other prisoners in Nyborg. For the first two months we were put on handicrafts; but when term started we got on with our school work in jail. We had an hour's tuition in the morning and two hours in the afternoon, followed by two hours' private study in the evening. Scholastically, we probably did better than we might have done in the classroom, because in our cells we had no distractions and had no option but to concentrate on our work.

'By the time we were released sabotage was better organised and what we'd done was just peanuts. Two months after we got out I joined a group which was handling sabotage with real expertise I had to report to the police every week and I was warned that on the merest suspicion of illegal activities I'd be sent to Germany. That didn't stop me. During one action, when we blew up a repair shop servicing German cars, I was recognised by the Danish sentry and had to go underground. I went to Sweden and joined Danforce. I returned on 5 May 1945, and served on the border for two and a half months. There, to our joy, my brother and I were reunited. When Danforce were disbanded I went back to the Cathedral School in Aalborg, graduating in the following year. After twelve months' service in the army I was commissioned and transferred to the Royal Danish Air Force.'

Sven Juul Darket's association with the Churchill Club was brief. 'Five lads in my class were involved, including Knud Pedersen, the younger brother of the leader; but I left the group shortly after they began operations,' he said. 'One reason was that they talked too much; they weren't security-minded. It seemed to me that they were bound to run into trouble.

'After I'd finished my studies at the Cathedral School I began reading to be an architect. I did practical building work during the summer and attended technical school in the winter. Towards the end of 1943 I made contact with a butcher named Knudsen who was the leader of a Resistance group. That was my introduction to real sabotage. Later, when we got more weapons, I formed a couple of new groups and became an instructor to the so-called underground army.

'One night the Knudsen group attacked a Danish-owned garage used for the repair of *Wehrmacht* vehicles. The raid was a failure. The sentries were too alert for us. We didn't wreck any cars but we killed three Germans, and we had to run. That was my first shooting and I didn't like it. We were lucky none of us was taken because the garage was in the centre of the town.

'On another occasion we went to a small shipyard where torpedo-boats were repaired. We wrecked the cranes and put them out of action for some months. We got one of the boats later on, after it had been repaired and was lying in the basin of a yacht club near the shipyard. There was only one guard on board. We held him up and scared him stiff. After we'd planted our charges we took him ashore and told him to run when the bang came; then we bolted in the opposite direction.

'The Peter gang were active in Jutland at that time and there were reports that they were heading for Aalborg. We stood watch all night, every night, for more than a week, with a grenade in one hand and a pistol in the other, but the gang didn't show. That was a big disappointment.

'I was on my way to my first arms-dropping when the Gestapo picked me up. Some of the reception committee used to meet outside a cinema, mingling with the audience leaving after the first evening show. We carried pistols and a package of sausages and bread and butter for the night's meal. That's where it happened, on the street. We were very lucky. Knudsen arrived just as the Gestapo descended on us. He saw the whole thing and was able to warn the rest of the group. Only three of us were taken. I didn't know the other two, though I'd met one of them once before and had been in his room. We were taken to the Gestapo headquarters in an hotel only five hundred metres down the street from the cinema. It was then about nine o'clock and we were interrogated for most of the night. The agreement in our group was that if we were taken we'd try to hold out for at least three hours. Though I was badly beaten up I managed to stick it out until three in the morning. It was pretty rough, but nothing to what some of the lads went through. I knew Knudsen would be far away by the time they'd finished with me. I had to go with a party of Gestapomen and point out where he lived. They poured hundreds of machine-gun bullets into the house and then blew it up, but by that time the butcher and his family were well on their way to Sweden. I was thrown into jail and had a few more beatings but the Germans didn't get anything more out of me. It helped that the other two men and I didn't know each other, so we couldn't give much away; and since I'd never taken part in a dropping, I couldn't say anything about the reception committee's activities.

'I sat there in jail. There were eight of us in a cell meant for one prisoner. We had to take it in turn to sleep on the one cot. I couldn't sit or lie down for the first couple of days because of the pain from the beatings. The Gestapomen had done pretty grim things with the nail on my left thumb and they'd torn great patches of hair from my scalp.

'I remained in jail for eight or nine weeks, awaiting trial and sentence. Eventually I was taken into a big room and there, in the presence of my father, I was sentenced to death. My father fainted, but I wasn't allowed to go to him. A couple of Gestapo-men hustled me quickly back to my cell.

'I couldn't complain of my sentence. It was reasonable, in view of the shooting at the garage when the three Germans had been killed. I hadn't shot any of them but I'd been there.

'I was transported with a party of other prisoners at the end of February 1945. Chained together, two by two, we were put into a prison train and I felt sure we were headed for Shellhus in Copenhagen. We were kept at Fredericia railway station for eight hours or so and then taken on to Frøslev. I was lucky again. We arrived on the day after the last transport left for Germany. Because I was under sentence of death I was kept in a special barrack inside the camp for the first week; then I was transferred to another barrack, where I met some of my friends from Aalborg who'd been captured earlier. It was a barrack for carpenters and other craftsmen and we had certain privileges. One of my friends was working in the kitchen, which helped a lot. The kitchen was under the administration of the Danish Red Cross and was run by Danes, so most of the people in Denmark fed no better than we did. I must admit we were a little cramped for space. The camp had been built for two thousand, four hundred prisoners but at the peak there were eight thousand of us. We slept in three-tier bunks, two to a bunk. My bed-mate was a burly policeman and as I'm not exactly a midget there wasn't much room to spare.

'I was in Frøslev until 5 May. As soon as news of the capitulation reached us, we disarmed the German guards and Gestapomen and escorted them to the border; then we took over the camp and rounded up all the *stikkers* and others who had worked for the Germans. There were special huts for informers and their wives and children who had taken refuge in the camp. We saw to it that they stayed there, together with the collaborators who were being picked up throughout southern

Jutland. Later I volunteered for service with the border control, a job that had its moments. At intervals Tiger tanks would appear, loaded to utmost capacity with soldiers and their guns, kitbags and suitcases. We tried to stop them, and occasionally we succeeded, but it isn't easy to halt a juggernaut driven by a man half out of his mind with hate and desperation. We had better luck with officers who tried to get across the frontier in their cars. We took their cars, their weapons, their field-glasses, and anything else that appealed to us. It was a comical thing to see a party of four or five British soldiers controlling a column of thousands of dispirited German infantrymen. They collected great stacks of rifles and pistols and sacks full of currency notes and watches. Not all those watches got to their official destination. The Tommies would take a jeep, drive to the Russian posts and flog them there. In those days a Russian soldier who owned a wristwatch felt like a millionaire.

'There was a similar lucrative trade in horses originally stolen by the Germans. Some of the artful dodgers among the Allied border patrols developed such misguided ingenuity that a farmer could easily buy back his own horse three times over. Of course, those racketeers were a very small minority, and they risked heavy punishment if they were caught.'

18: THE RECEIVERS

When Ole Geisler went to Jutland in the spring of 1943 as SOE's regional leader, to prepare for the reception of parachutists, explosives and weapons from Britain, he found a small but very efficient band of helpers waiting for him. Since the previous year Flemming Juncker, a *Dansk Samling* member who owned an estate near Randers, had been working tirelessly to establish contacts in Frederikshavn, Aalborg, Randers, Aarhus, Viborg, Esbjerg, Varde, Tønder and Aabenraa, and through them to form groups who would undertake full-scale sabotage.

The first delivery of supplies was made by the RAF Halifax which brought Flemming B. Muus and three other parachutists to Denmark. The reception was planned some days in advance in the home of the widow Boje at Brødregade 23, Randers. There Juncker and Geisler met the five-man reception committee (Henning Brøchner, Jørgen Boje. Svend Aage Frederiksen, Peter Jensen and Eigil Thornsberg) and explained what had to be done. On the evening of 11 March the BBC's Danish service relayed the expected code-signal and that night fifteen containers of sabotage materials were dropped in a plantation at Trinderup Hede, near Skrødstrup.

On the following evening Geisler and Juncker went to the Hvidsten Kro, a thatched, half-timbered inn on the highroad between Randers and Mariager, and talked to the innkeeper, Marius Fiil, and his friend Dr. Thorup Petersen. There was an important cargo lying hidden in the Trinderup plantation, they said. It would be dangerous for strangers to try to retrieve it; but the innkeeper was well-known and could travel through the district without arousing too much curiosity. Fiil agreed to help. He took a horse-drawn wagon to Trinderup Hede and with the aid of the wagon-driver the containers were loaded and carried to a building owned by Andreas Stenz, near the inn. From there the materials, packed in Hertz shoe boxes, were taken in Dr. Petersen's car to Henning Brøchner's warehouse at Randers.

Geisler had supervised the packing in his usual methodical fashion and had prepared a stock-sheet showing where everything was stored. Boxes marked 'Men's shoes, size 37' contained plastic explosive, those marked 'size 37½' held detonators and those marked 'size 38½' contained fuses. A couple of days later Geisler met Flemming Muus at the warehouse to discuss the distribution of supplies to the sabotage groups.

'Ole had a habit of putting his half-smoked cigarette down on end, with the burning tip uppermost,' Muus said. 'Suddenly he started swearing because he'd forgotten where he'd put it. I spotted it just in time. It was smouldering away on top of a box of detonators and it had already burned almost through the cardboard lid. And there were about five hundred pounds of explosives in that room!'

The Hvidsten Kro now became the centre for the reception of weapons and sabotage materials. Although well past middle-age, Marius Fiil took control of the work with energy and enthusiasm. He quickly organised a group of people whom he knew and could trust. Among them were his son, Niels; his son-in-law, Peter Bergenhammer Sørensen; the miller, Henning Andersen; an auto mechanic, Johan Kjær Hansen; the veterinary surgeon, Albert Carlo Iversen; a radio merchant, Niels Nielsen Kjær; and the coachbuilder, Søren Peter Kristensen. The group was augmented by people from Randers and by Geisler's parachutists. Fiil's wife, Gudrun, and his two elder daughters also gave willing service when need arose.

A new dropping-zone closer to Hvidsten was established at Allestrupgaards plantation, north of Spentrup, a hilly, thickly-wooded area with deep pools into which the containers could be dumped after they had been emptied. The first delivery there was made on the night of 17 April, when arms, explosives and a parachutist were landed. During the spring and summer further supplies were dropped near Hvidsten and Djursland in Jutland, at Enebærodde and Rugaard in northern Funen, and at Gyldenløveshøj, a well-wooded area between Roskilde and Ringsted in Zealand. A score of parachutists were also landed to act as instructors to the sabotage groups. The importance of these operations was out of all proportion to the moderate quantities of materials received. They boosted Danish morale, helped to popularise sabotage, and correspondingly worried General von Hanneken and his regional commanders.

Droppings over Denmark became fewer during the autumn of 1943. Such weapons and explosives as Britain could spare were more urgently needed in France, in Italy and in Jugoslavia, where Tito's partisans were harrying the Germans. Consequently, between August 1943, and March 1944, Denmark had deliveries of only forty-five containers carrying a total of five tons of materials.

The Hvidsten group had a serious setback in October 1943, when a German aircraft was signalled in mistake for the expected Halifax. Following that incident they had to abandon reception work and confine themselves to taking care of the Resistance fugitives who sought shelter at the inn.

In December Flemming Muus, who had been to London for discussions with SOE, was to be dropped at Glydenløveshøj. As his aircraft was nearing the dropping-zone it was spotted by a German night-fighter and shot down in flames. Muus landed safely and made his way to Copenhagen, but thereafter all operations in Zealand were suspended and the few droppings which followed were made over Jutland.

December was a bad month for the Resistance. Three parachutists were trapped in an apartment at Aarhus, with disastrous consequences to the groups who had been in contact with them. Ole Geisler, among others, had to leave Jutland to escape capture. Despite the many arrests throughout the peninsula, the Hvidsten group stuck to their posts and even prepared to resume reception work. It was a fatal decision. On 12 March 1944, a Gestapo squad from Aarhus arrested the innkeeper, his son, his son-in-law, and several other men. On 17 March all but two of the rest of the group were taken. Three months later Marius and Niels Fiil, Peter Sørensen, Henning Andersen, Johan Hansen, Albert Iversen, Niels Kjær and Søren Kristensen were condemned to death by a German military court in Copenhagen. On 29 June 1944, they were executed at Ryvangen.

In December 1943, disagreement between Flemming Juncker

and Muus had reached such a stage that Juncker was on the point of abandoning Resistance activities; but following Geisler's enforced departure he agreed to take over the leadership of the reception work with Christian Ulrik Hansen, of Holger Danske, as his assistant. New dropping-zones were found, district leaders were appointed, and a wide range of contacts was established.

A skilfully carried out sabotage action at Skive, in north-west Jutland, drew Hansen's attention to Anton J. Toldstrup, a customs officer in the town. He introduced him to Juncker, who set him to work organising military groups in the region. When Hansen was arrested at Aalborg railway station on 29 February 1944, Juncker appointed Toldstrup as his successor. There could have been no more fortunate choice, for the job called for outstanding qualities of leadership and organisational ability. The newly-formed 'waiting groups' of the underground army were demanding weapons in large quantities and at the same time supplies had to be found for the sabotage groups and, in particular, the railway sabotage groups on whom the Allies were relying to disrupt German troop movements. Despite the lull in droppings during the winter months, London insisted that the necessary materials would be forthcoming and urged that efficient preparation should be made to receive them. That called for the reconnaissance of suitable dropping-zones, formation of reception committees, arrangement of storage depots and transport and organisation of radio communication between the groups and with London. Toldstrup set about the task calmly and confidently. When Juncker, hard-hunted, went to London in the middle of April to join SOE's Danish section, with special responsibility for droppings, he knew he was leaving the work in safe hands.

As from the summer of 1944, Denmark was divided into three reception regions, each with its own autonomous headquarters. Region 1, Jutland, was headed by Toldstrup; Region 2, Funen, by the engineer Erik Frandsen; and Region 3, Zealand, by the newspaper editor Stig Jensen. All three men were dynamic, courageous leaders but they differed greatly in temperament. Stig Jensen, at 46 the eldest of the trio, was a sober, meticulous administrator, working from his Copenhagen headquarters with key men distributed throughout Zealand. Frandsen, an unparallelled organiser, balanced, far-seeing and punctilious, also preferred to direct operations from his head-quarters in Odense. The younger Toldstrup, like Frandsen a brilliant and imaginative organiser, was happiest out in the field with his men, by whom he was universally loved and respected. There was a touch of the swashbuckler in his character and sometimes, when occasion called, he could be reckless. Brigadier Mockler Ferryman, of SOE, has described him as the most efficient receptions leader in Western Europe; but Dr. Jørgen Hæstrup, the Resistance historian, maintains that Erik Frandsen deserves at least equal recognition. Jutland, nearer to England and topographically most suited to droppings, was undoubtedly the most important of the three regions; but Frandsen's area of operations, though smaller, was more densely populated and receptions were correspondingly more difficult and dangerous. Yet, thanks to magnificent organisation, Funen was unique in suffering no losses either of men or materials.

Between March 1943, and June 1944, one hundred and ninety-six containers, carrying twenty-three tons of materials, were dropped over Denmark. After June, as aircraft became available following the liberation of France, droppings became more frequent and from the beginning of August mass deliveries were made from England. With the Allied forces thrusting through Europe, Denmark's military importance had increased, not least because of German troop transports to southern Norway, and supplies were needed urgently for Jutland's railway saboteurs, for the industrial sabotage groups and for the rapidly-growing underground army. That meant that there had to be constant readiness for receptions at scores of places throughout Denmark and on 'big nights' there could be more than twenty locations on the schedule. In Jutland there were two hundred and eighty prepared and acknowledged dropping-zones; in Funen, thirty; and in Zealand, eighty. Actually used in operations were two hundred in Jutland, twenty-five in Funen and fifty-seven in Zealand. Some places took several droppings and one zone in Jutland was used seven times. The total delivery between August 1944, and April 1945, was six thousand, four hundred containers carrying six hundred and fifty-five tons of materials. Of these, three thousand, nine hundred containers were received in Jutland, eight hundred in Funen, and one thousand, seven hundred in Zealand.

The main problem in all three regions was the distribution of the supplies once they had been received, for Denmark's road and rail transport systems were in a state of disruption. There was a general shortage of cars, lorries and fuel, while the enthusiastic destruction of lines and rolling-stock by the railway saboteurs created almost as many difficulties for the reception groups as for the Germans. An additional hazard was the ever-present menace of the informers and prowling Gestapo and *Wehrmacht* patrols. Hence, deliveries had to be determined more by possibility than by wish and need. Toldstrup, Frandsen and Jensen solved the problem by creating special transport organisations and well-developed radio and intelligence services, to such remarkable effect that by the spring of 1945 interference with reception operations and losses of goods in transit had dwindled into insignificance.

F. Ahlgreen Eriksen, now a senior airlines executive, took an active part in the reception work in Middle Jutland.

'In the autumn of 1943, as a youth of eighteen, I was working at the railway station in Nørre Snede, a busy traffic centre on the main road A13 through Jutland,' he said. 'A bank clerk with whom I was friendly introduced me to Dr. Malmstrøm and his wife, who were in the illegal newspaper business, and I joined their little group. It was small-time stuff, really. We didn't do any printing; we just distributed papers. In the spring of 1944 a military intelligence unit asked us to get some information about what the Germans were doing in the area. They were at that time building a big airfield, Grove, north of Herning, and ammunition depots in the forest north of Nørre Snede. The waybills and other railway documents which came into my office told us a lot about those projects.

'A couple of months later Kai Linde Laursen, a student-teacher, contacted Dr. Malmstrøm and suggested that we should try our hands at reception work. We built up a group of fifteen to twenty farmers, farm labourers and artisans from the surrounding villages, most of them around thirty years old but some in their forties and fifties. Laursen was our active leader, with Malmstrøm as our link with Toldstrup's headquarters. Our code-name was "Yvonne".

'We chose as our dropping-zone an open moorland area north of a small lake called Rørbæk—a very easy target for aircraft to find on a clear night. We arranged to "steal" a truck whenever we wanted it, on the understanding that it would be returned to the owner in the morning, and got petrol supplies by holding up a garage which catered for the Germans. Then, with our plans prepared, we waited for the signal to get to work.

'At last the message, "Greetings to Yvonne", came over the BBC. We went out to Rørbæk an hour before midnight and at one o'clock we heard the sound of aircraft engines. We lit our flares, three in a line, indicating the direction in which the pilot should approach the field, and a red one showing wind direction, so that he could make a swing and come in towards the wind. It was a lovely night, with a cloudless sky. The Wellington bomber roared over and dropped its load. We collected the twelve containers and parachutes, stacked them in the truck, and drove along minor roads to a farmhouse where we had an agreement with the owner. We hid the stuff and went home. A few evenings later we went back to the farm, emptied the containers, and dumped them with the parachutes into a lake. We'd made some wooden crates and hidden them in various places, and when the order came we packed the weapons and explosives into them and drove them to the railway station. Since I was in charge of the place, there was nobody to ask awkward questions. We put the crates into rail wagons and what happened to them after the train left Nørre Snede was none of our business.

'The second delivery was made on a rather windy night and it gave us plenty of trouble. Nørre Snede lies at a pretty fair elevation, affording on a moonlit night a very good view south to our dropping-zone. The Germans had just come to the town and their patrols were altogether too zealous for our liking. We knew they wouldn't be able to see our flares but they would certainly hear the aircraft circling, so we posted sentries around the fringe of the zone to give us warning of possible attack.

When the dropping started, the wind blew the parachutes off-course. We counted ten containers coming down but we couldn't find two of them. We had a hell of a time, scouring the heather in vain. Finally we gave up and decided we'd have to continue the search in daylight. On the following afternoon I went out with two other men to try to locate the missing containers. As we were cycling towards Rørbæk a German patrol stopped us and asked where we were going. We said we were out for a ride, and since that was quite a usual pastime for youngsters, they let us go. We found the containers, hid them more securely, and picked them up a couple of nights later.

'We took three deliveries at Rørbæk and then started looking for new dropping-zones. We formed another group at Bryrup, on the road to Silkeborg, with a convenient reception area close to a lake, and there we had two droppings in the late autumn and beginning of winter. We also planned a zone further west, to the north of Ejstrupholm, a thickly-wooded area with no water. One dropping failed because German activity prevented us from getting to the place on time. We heard the Wellington come over and circle several times, but as no one was there he went away. We learned afterwards that he'd dropped his load on another zone further south. We took six successful droppings during that period. In all, our groups collected about sixty containers of carbines, Bren-guns and explosives.

'Most people in our area were Resistance sympathisers but there were a few collaborators and others who were too friendly with the Germans. Sometimes we had to throw a scare into them. Two farmers who made no secret of their liking for the soldiers had a nasty habit of passing on too freely the rumours they'd heard about droppings. We decided they had to be stopped. One night five or six of us went out and surrounded the farmhouses. One house had a telephone. We cut the wires; then we rapped on the windows and called the man and his wife outside. We stuck them up against a wall, trained our guns on them and warned them that if they didn't stop gossiping they'd regret it. We had no further trouble with them.

'Towards the end of 1944 a *stikker* betrayed Dr. Malmstrøm to the Gestapo. He was arrested and sent to Frøslev, not for his

work with the reception groups but for distributing illegal
newspapers. We were very lucky. So little could have brought
disaster. I remember going home in the small hours of the morning after a dropping. I had my Sten-gun under my overcoat. To
get to my room I had to pass the German headquarters on the
main street of Nørre Snede. I had a cold feeling in my belly
but I consoled myself with the thought that the Germans knew
I was a railwayman and would expect me to keep odd hours.
As I passed the sentry at the entrance, I said: "Hi! How's the
night going?" He grinned. "Bloody slowly," he said, and waved
me on. I got home safely, but if he'd noticed that slight bulge
under my coat, it would have been curtains for me.

'Some of the weapons we collected from the later droppings
went to our own people. By that time, in addition to our reception work, we were trying to build up a fighting force and also
doing some minor sabotage on the main trunk line serving
central Jutland. We weren't particularly skilled for that job; it
was more important for us to keep the dropping-zones in
operation.

'Two months before the capitulation I left the railway service
to concentrate on full-time intelligence work in the area. The
Resistance movement paid me and I went around on my bike
every day, checking on what the Germans were doing. Nobody
asked me why I'd left my job. I'd been ill and was supposed to
be on extended sick leave, with a genuine medical certificate to
prove it!'

19: PRIEST MILITANT

Pastor Harald Sandbæk served as chaplain to the thousand-strong Danish volunteer brigade during the Finnish-Russian war. When he returned home to Hersom, in central Jutland, Denmark was in the hands of the Germans. For the first two years of the occupation there was little he could do in his quiet parish, but in the spring of 1943 the chance came for him to take an active part in the fight for freedom.

'I was asked to find ten people who would be prepared to go out in the middle of the night and receive supplies dropped from England,' he said. 'The first man I spoke to refused. He was a bachelor but he had an old mother. He said: "It's impossible. There are too many houses around here. We couldn't go out and get home safely. Sandbæk, you read too many books. I'm a practical man and I know we could never do it."

'I then approached a farmer, a man of my own age, thirty-nine. He was a very bright man and a good Christian. He liked to dance, play cards and go to the theatre but he also attended church regularly. We were very fond of each other. I asked him: "Will you go with me?"

'He said: "Sandbæk, Sandbæk, I have three children."

'"I know that well," I replied, "but I've asked a young man with no children and he refused. Don't you think we should tackle the job?"

'He glared at me. "Have I said I wouldn't? But why ask me, with three kids?"

'"Well, this is a matter for grown-up people. If we're caught, we'll be killed. Make no mistake about that. You know something about life and death. I came to you because I daren't go to people who'd say no, good people though they are."

'"Of course I'll come," he said. "Say no more. I'll do what you want."

'We went to his farmhouse, down a little lane, and his wife gave us coffee. He didn't tell her what we'd been discussing. A Jutlander won't do that. He'll say: "Later". We drank our coffee,

chatting about the newspapers and many other things. Afterwards he walked with me to the highroad, talking generalities,
as Jutland people do. Then he shook my hand and said: "Good-
bye, Pastor Sandbæk. I could wish you hadn't come today, but
you can count on me."

'That was a real man. He didn't like what we had to do, but
he felt it was his duty. He was called, as we say. I found ten
more, all people of my church. They all said yes. I was happy.
I'd never been so proud of my congregation. They were typical
Resistance men, not like those who came in at the last minute.
They knew the job would be dangerous but they didn't flinch.
They said simply: "You ask me. I must come."

'Ours was one of the first reception groups. We got our signals
in Morse code. Only later were we given cover-names like
"Henrik" and "Christian".'

Shortly after the formation of the reception committee a
man from a group selling illegal books, with whom Sandbæk
had worked a few months earlier, was arrested by the Gestapo.
Under torture he revealed the pastor's name but he succeeded
in getting word out to his friends. Warned in time, Sandbæk
left his parish and joined Anton Toldstrup in Aalborg. In September 1944, he took over from the police officer A. J. Jørgensen
the leadership of one of Toldstrup's flying-squads, a group of
eight saboteurs, and established headquarters in Hadsten High
School, about fifteen kilometres north of Aarhus. By arrangement with the headmaster, the group were enrolled as students
of surveying and Sandbæk took the cover-name of *landbrugskandidat* (graduate surveyor) Hans Hansen.

A few days later Toldstrup called him to Aalborg to discuss
plans for the liquidation of a troublesome *stikker*. After the
meeting he was sitting on a bench at the railway station, waiting for his train back to Hadsten, when he saw a Resistance
man walking along the platform towards him.

'Good day, Tage,' he greeted him.

'You're just the chap I was looking for,' the other said. 'We've
got to get three of our people out of north Jutland in a hurry.
They're all trained saboteurs. Can you take them into your
group?'

Sandbæk shook his head. 'I've got all the men I need, and I can trust them. Who are these three, anyhow?'

'You can be absolutely certain they're all right,' Tage said. He took a postage stamp from his wallet and tore it in half. 'Look. Take this. When three chaps come to you and produce the other half, you can rely on them.'

Some days later three men appeared at the high school and asked for *landbrugskandidat* Hansen. Sandbæk, who was in a classroom on the first floor, went down to see them.

'I didn't like their faces,' he said, 'but I asked them: "Are you looking for somebody?"

' "Yes. We want to see Hans Hansen."

' "What do you want with him?"

' "We'd like to meet him, that's all."

'I said: "I'm Hansen."

'One of them produced half a postage stamp. I took out my own piece and the two halves fitted. I still didn't feel happy, but what could I do? Tage had vouched for the men. I took them up to the classroom, where the rest of my group were sitting. Immediately the three men drew revolvers and shouted: "Hands up!" I ran to the window but a fourth man was standing in the courtyard with a sub-machine gun. We were trapped.'

The disaster was no fault of Tage's. The three hunted saboteurs who were to have joined Sandbæk's group had been seen by a *stikker* when their train passed through Hobro station. He rang through to Randers, where they had to change trains, and there the three were arrested by the Gestapo. The half-stamp was found and, weakened by torture, they told all about their mission. Their places were taken by a Danish collaborator and two Gestapomen. The fourth man, who stood in the court-yard with the sub-machine gun, was *Kriminalrat* Werner, the Gestapo's deputy chief in Jutland.

'We were taken under heavy guard to the German jail in Aarhus, and there we were treated very badly,' Sandbæk said. 'At least two of us were tortured in the Gestapo headquarters. I could see the situation was hopeless and eventually I con-fessed. If the torture had gone on longer, I'm sure I should have confessed more. It was awful. At one time I was interrogated for thirty-nine hours without pause. I was given nothing to eat or drink and beaten and whipped continually. I went completely out of my mind.

'Half an hour before we were taken prisoner I'd written two letters, and I'd left them in my apartment. One was to a man in my parish whom I'd recruited into the reception group. The Gestapo found other compromising things in my apartment, too, and I suffered for them all. The Gestapo thought I was a much more important man in the Resistance than was actually the case.

'One thing eased my conscience. I thought I'd at least ensured that most of our friends would have been warned that we'd been taken. As we stood handcuffed in the classroom at the high school, the wife of one of the teachers had walked in. I said very loudly and distinctly: "I am Pastor Harald Sandbæk." My comrades gasped. They'd never known my true identity and least of all suspected that I was a priest. I gave my name then because I wanted the girl to spread the news of my arrest. Unhappily, it didn't occur to her to tell anybody and it took several days for the word to get around.'

Every single day from 15 September to 31 October, and often at night as well, Sandbæk was taken from his cell to the Gestapo headquarters in Aarhus Unviersity and interrogated mercilessly. Usually it was *Kriminalrat* Werner whom he had to face.

'I hated and feared that man,' he said. 'He was mentally sick but he had a razor-sharp brain and could put the most infamously cunning questions. As a lawyer he'd been accustomed to conducting interrogations in Germany and ill-treating his own countrymen. He was a devil—sadistic, ruthless, and very, very skilful. Some interrogators were so stupid that one could tie them up in knots, but never Werner!

'Once, as I was taken into the room for more questioning, I saw out of the corner of my eye that the window was ajar. I thought desperately of jumping through it and ending things once and for all. But Werner read my mind. "Try it," he said, "and I'll put a bullet in your guts, and then stick my finger in the hole and twist it round." '

At nine o'clock on the morning of 31 October Sandbæk was

taken again to the interrogation room on the third floor of the Gestapo headquarters. This time, to his astonishment, the handcuffs were taken from his wrists.

'Outside my cell I'd never been without handcuffs,' he said. 'I felt like a dog let off its chain. I thought: "What devilry are they up to now?" I was still more puzzled when I found that the questioning was to be conducted by a Dane. Hitherto, all interrogations had been in German, which I speak fluently. Later the reason was made clear. The editor of the Nazi *Færdrelandet* was to be present. He was to write an article in which I should "confess all my sins".

'The interrogation began, with Werner sitting beside the Dane. Suddenly, about mid-day, there came a series of explosions and I wondered what was going on. I knew it was impossible for the Resistance to stage an attack on the university. We'd neither the manpower nor the resources. It could only be an air-raid, though I could hear no sound of aircraft. Werner, chalk-white in the face, jumped up and made a dash for the door, with the rest of his gang at his heels. I sat there all alone—and unfettered. They'd completely forgotten me. I considered jumping out of the window and killing myself. I believe suicide is permissible for a Christian in such a situation. I knew a lot more than my torturers had got out of me and maybe they could force me to further confessions. By ending my own life I might still save many others. Yet there might be another way.

'I ran to the door and looked out. The Germans were crawling on their bellies towards the stairs on the right of the corridor. I got down and started to crawl in the opposite direction. I knew there was another staircase at the end of the corridor. Before I'd gone ten metres another bomb came down and the roof caved in on us. Werner and most of the other Gestapomen were killed instantly. I remember clearly that as I heard the bomb screaming down, I thought: "Now it's finished. It's all over." Then I passed out.

'I don't know how long I was unconscious. When I came round I'd forgotten everything and I had a hazy idea I was back in my cell. I was lying on my stomach and that puzzled me, because I always slept on my back. I tried to turn over and couldn't. It felt as if I were completely bound. I could move my head a little and that was all. My first thought was that the Germans had tied me up and that, now I'd come round, they'd resume the torture. I was worried sick that I'd reveal certain things and I was as full of fear as a man could be. Then I came more fully to myself and realised that I was buried in the rubble of the college building. I think I must be the only man in the world to have discovered he was buried alive and to be so happy that he could have cried. I knew I couldn't be tortured again. I thought: "You'll die soon. The air will give out and that will be the end of you." I just hoped it would happen quickly. I prayed to God for my wife and our two children, for my friends, and for myself. I didn't look forward to death with pleasure but I was ready for it. I'd done what I thought should be done and I was sure my friends would help my wife and the children.

'Somewhere a man began crying in Danish: "Oh! God. Oh! God help me." I forgot I was buried and said the Lord's Prayer very loudly, so that he could hear it. He said nothing, but as soon as I said "Amen" he started crying again. I said the prayer again and he shut up, but soon he began to moan once more. I recited some verses of scripture and he was silent. I suppose he'd fainted or died. I fainted, too, and the next thing I knew, I heard the sound of digging. I shouted frantically. I was afraid the diggers were going to drive a spade through my head. Finally they got near enough to free my face and hair and I heard a voice say in German: "There's another one here." They dug me out and, because I wasn't wearing handcuffs, they took me for a German or a *stikker*. That was a miracle. It was the one day in six weeks that I hadn't been in handcuffs while being interrogated. That saved my life. If I'd been manacled they'd have taken me back to jail and more torture. It helped, too, that I could speak German.

'I was taken to a Danish hospital, where my wounds were dressed by nurse Esther Prip-Buus, a sister of the senior physician. I told her: "I am Pastor Sandbæk."

' "That's not true," she said.

' "It is true. Get the doctor here."

'She called her brother and I convinced him without much difficulty of my identity. They knew what would happen if the Germans recognised me, so they took me to their apartment. They'd scarcely closed the door when the Gestapo came.

' "Have you brought a man called Pastor Sandbæk here?" the leader demanded.

' "No. A Dane named Jensen, yes. Nobody else."

'That lie could have cost them their lives, and they knew it. They were very brave people. The doctor rang Børge Rasmussen, the Red Cross director in Aarhus, who took me to his own home in an ambulance. Shortly afterwards my wife arrived at his door. She had tried to get permission to visit me, dreading it might be for the last time. When she saw the devastation at the university, she had gone at once to the house of Rasmussen, the only man who might be able to tell her what had happened to me. Rasmussen drove us both to Aabyhøj, where the municipal treasurer, Axel Sørensen, took us in.

'We lived in the Sørensens' small apartment for two weeks. My head was badly injured and I still had blood in my ears, but the doctor couldn't come to me in case he were seen and questions asked. Neither my wife nor I dared go to the lavatory during the day because we might have been heard by the tenants of the apartment beneath. We had to stay in one room with nobody to look after us until the young Sørensens came home in the evening. For fourteen days they sat in chairs so that we could sleep in their bed. I can never forget their kindness.

'At last Jens Lillelund came and took us to the house of Pastor Otto Andersen in Karlby-Voldby, north of the coastal town of Grenaa. From there we were taken to Grenaa Strand and transported by fishing-boat to Sweden.

'There is one thing which sticks in my mind. On the evening before the bombing of the university I'd been sitting in my cell, reading the Psalms. The Gestapo sometimes let me have a Bible and sometimes took it away from me. The psalm I was reading made a great impression on me. It said that if a man trusted God, his enemies would always be defeated. I felt that God was speaking directly to me, and I said to myself: "You're mad, old boy. Now you're really frightened. You're not the old

Sandbæk if you think you can get private messages from God. D'you think He's got nothing better to do?" But next morning, when they came to fetch me for interrogation, I took with me the photograph of my two children. As I put it in my pocket I said to myself: "You really are crazy. Why take this picture? You know it's impossible for you to get free." Still, I took it. And when I was dug out and had the picture of my children in my pocket, I was very happy. If I'd left that photograph in my cell, the Gestapo would have found it and had it reproduced in the newspapers, forcing me to give myself up because I couldn't leave my family to the mercy of the Germans. Nobody can fathom God's ways or prove anything about Him and His designs. God is higher than all our proofs and counterproofs. But I feel that He gave me a gift—a second life.

'In Sweden I became chaplain to the men and women of Danforce and after the liberation I returned to Denmark to become a vicar again. I don't understand why I should have been saved when men like Kaj Munk and Christian Ulrik Hansen and so many others who did ten times more good than I were killed.

'In the bombing of the university most of the records of the interrogations were destroyed, among them mine and those of the members of my group who had been arrested. I am thankful that not one of my good comrades lost his life.'

To encourage the Germans to believe that Pastor Sandbæk had died in the ruins of the university, the Resistance published his obituary notice in *Kristeligt Dagblad* on 10 November 1944. Only a few weeks later his voice was heard on the Swedish radio, telling of his experiences at the hands of the Gestapo.

Twenty-four RAF Mosquito bombers, escorted by twelve fighters, took part in the raid on Aarhus University. The buildings were completely destroyed, most of the records burned, and about one hundred Germans killed, together with many Danish collaborators. It was the first of three precision-bombing raids on Gestapo headquarters in Denmark. On 21 March 1945, Shellhus in Copenhagen was reduced to rubble, and eleven days later the Smallholders School in Odense suffered a similar fate.

20: DAY OF VENGEANCE

In the years before the war Shellhus, on the corner of Kamp-mannsgade and Farimagsgade, was Copenhagen's most modern office building. Completed in 1934 it was a landmark which could be seen far away over Sankt Jørgens Lake; but in the third year of the occupation it was to become a symbol of horror and dread.

On 15 May 1943, Gestapomen from all parts of Germany moved into Dagmarhus, the German administration head-quarters in Copenhagen. Neither the weak German police nor the *Wehrmacht* had been able to stem the rising tide of sabotage and now Hitler had decreed: 'Terror must be met with terror.' Within a year Dagmarhus had become too cramped for its motley population of civil servants, military officials, Gestapomen and collaborators, and more space had to be found. The *Sicherheitsdienst* (Security Service) were given offices in Vesterport and the Gestapo took over Shellhus. The six-storey building, heavily camouflaged, was transformed into a fortress, with concrete pillboxes and barbed-wire barricades to guard against attack by the Resistance, and there Dr. Karl Heinz Hoffmann installed himself with his departmental chiefs. These included Dr. Erich Bunke (Jews and sabotage), Elpert (espionage and Danish military affairs), Dr. Westphal (border control), Schweitzer and later Jessen (Danish Resistance affairs), Preisser (intelligence) and Hans Hermannsen, Hoffmann's deputy and right-hand man. Hermannsen was an enigma. He could hardly have attained his position without convincing his superiors that he was a sound and energetic Nazi party member, yet during his service as chief of the border control Resistance men found singularly little difficulty in crossing the Danish-German frontier when need arose. After his appointment as Hoffmann's deputy, many Danish patriots arrested by the Gestapo suddenly found themselves released without any apparent reason—a 'miracle' perhaps not unconnected with the fact that 'Uncle Hans' had copies of Hoffmann's signature and was himself in charge of *Haftkartei* (the Gestapo files of arrests and releases). Whatever his motives, Hermannsen was a good friend to the Resistance. He died, almost forgotten, in Hamburg in 1952.

In October 1944, the sixth floor of Shellhus was converted into a prison for Resistance hostages. There were twenty-two small cells, each furnished with a two-tier bunk and mattresses, three blankets per man, a desk, and two wooden chairs. On 11 November the first prisoners arrived. They were Captain Fritz Jørgensen,* Lieutenants H. P. Gregersen and Bent Nordentoft, Police-Inspector C. Lyst Hansen, Alf E. Olstrup and Tage Hartmann-Schmidt. Soon they were joined by Professor Mogens Fog, Rear-Admiral Carl Hammerich, Commander Hans Nyholm, Lieutenants J. Chr. Lunn and N. J. Mølgaard, Baron Karl Wedell-Wedellsborg and his brother Ebbe, Aage Schoch, Poul Sørensen and J. Palm Petersen. In the New Year 1945, the rest of the cells were filled with the arrival of Professor P. Brandt Rehberg, Lieutenant-Colonel E. C. V. Tiemroth, Commanders Børge Clausen and Ebbe Wolfhagen, Captain Poul Borking, Police-Inspector L. H. Christiansen, Poul Bruun, Hans Heister, William Jørgensen, Erik Crone,† Ove Kampmann, P. Ahnfeldt-Mollerup, Jørgen Nørup, O. G. Pedersen and W. Zohnesen.

Alf Olstrup has recorded: 'We were allowed as exercise only fifteen minutes' walk under heavy guard in the corridor each afternoon, but conditions generally were better than in Vestre Fængsel. We had better beds and we could go to the W.C. when we liked, not, as in Vestre Fængsel, when it suited the Germans. We managed to swap bits of news in the washroom, especially on Mondays, Wednesdays and Fridays, when we could shave and were allowed to stay in the washroom for up to half an hour. But there were drawbacks. We lived in the lions' den, and that wasn't comfortable. When we'd settled down for the night the guards came every hour to inspect us by first switch-

---

* Jørgensen was transferred to Frøslev and thence to Dachau, where he died on 28 March, 1945.

† Crone, after terrible torture, was executed at Ryvangen on 27 February, 1945.

ing on the cell light and then looking through the peep-hole in the door. Our food was brought from Alsgades School, which also supplied the German section of Vestre Fængsel, so we knew the menu: Mondays, Tuesdays, Thursdays and Saturdays, some kind of soup; Wednesdays, gravy, potatoes, and some sort of meat; Sundays, a small piece of steak. Fridays were days of horror; we got fish, we never discovered what kind, boiled up in a hash with potatoes and gravy. Dinner was served very irregularly, usually any time between two and three o'clock. Christmas was no exception. On Christmas Eve we had pork at half past two; on Christmas Day beef at four o'clock, but they'd forgotten the potatoes; and on Boxing Day it was sausages at half past one. Supper on all three days was a slice of meat sausage. Luckily the Danish Red Cross had sent us each a Christmas parcel containing a pound of butter, a salami, a wedge of cheese, a box of mixed sweets, a box of toffee, apples, cigarettes, and a book. A very good thing about Christmas was that we weren't taken downstairs for interrogations. Presumably the Gestapo were off-duty during the holiday.'

Just what that respite meant is made clear by Professor Rehberg, who was arrested in February 1945, with Lieutenant-Colonel Tiemroth, commander of the underground army in Copenhagen, and Mogens Prior, of *Frit Danmark*. The three men were at a meeting in the Technical High School when they were surprised by the Gestapo. While they were being taken from the building, Rehberg managed to get rid of most of the compromising papers he was carrying.

'When we arrived by car at Shellhus,' he said, 'all I had left was a little diary full of meeting-times and initials. It wouldn't be good to be questioned about that, so I threw it between two cupboards. When the Gestapo searched me they found only my wallet with my false identity papers and some false visiting-cards, something they'd never come across before. I confessed at once who I was, and my name was greeted with shouts of triumph by the Gestapomen, who had been hunting me since December. They thought they'd made a good catch. So they had, with Tiemroth, but from the very beginning they put too much importance on me. They believed, quite wrongly, that I was a member of the Freedom Council.

'On our way up to the sixth floor I agreed with Prior that we'd admit only our part in organising financial aid for dependants of patriots, but our plan came to nothing. From my keys the Gestapo discovered my three addresses. During their search they found a copy of a report from Thomas Døssing in Moscow, a list of members of the Scavenius cabinet, with various comments, and some notes on the Freedom Council's views about compromising members of the central administration. I couldn't talk myself out of that.

'The interrogations on the first two days were conducted fairly correctly. They were led by a CID man from Hamburg, assisted by a Danish former lieutenant, Erik Nielsen. Some Gestapomen were present as observers. It was really rather amusing. The interrogators were so excited about the papers they'd found that their questions weren't very clever and they were easily side-tracked. Unfortunately I irritated them a bit too much and they threatened to take me downstairs "in the evening, when we'll be alone". Their one aim seemed to be to make me confess that I was a member of the Freedom Council, and that I couldn't do. They waved the documents in my face and claimed they had all the proof they needed. At one stage the Gestapomen started arguing about the size of the Freedom Council. One man even thought it had a thousand members! I had to confess that I had some contact with the council and knew the names of three members. That made them do a war dance of joy, but it turned to rage when I said the three men were Fog, Schoch and Arne Sørensen. Everybody, including the Germans, knew that.'

On the following evening Rehberg was taken downstairs and the fooling came to an end.

'They told me my life was of no importance; they'd get the information out of me even if they had to torture me to death,' he said. 'Three or four men began to beat me with sticks. I almost fought back, but I calmed down. When I turned on them and said the whole business was ridiculous, they lashed at my face and broke my jaw. They tore my clothes off and chained me across a table with my head touching the floor and my hands tied to a bar beneath the table-top. Then they took it in turns to beat me up. I don't know how long it went on. When one was exhausted he'd hand the stick to another man, with the words *"Nun du"*. They behaved like savages, racing across the room at me, spitting with rage. I got the impression that they had to work themselves up before they could go on with the cruelty. I think it's wrong to call them sadists. That's not a defence of them, quite the contrary. Sadists are abnormal, sick people who are only partially able to control themselves. These were normal human beings cynically using torture in an attempt to get information. They had to work themselves up to it and afterwards they were almost pitiable. While I was still hanging there, chained and only semi-conscious, one of them came up to me and muttered that I shouldn't think he liked doing it. Later I overheard two of them saying that they'd never be able to tell their wives of the things in which they'd taken part. For all their brutality, they were little people.

'Nevertheless, they forced me to say something, mostly irrelevant trivialities which I retracted next day. I gave them one piece of truthful information, the name of the woman through whom I sent letters to Frode Jakobsen, of the Freedom Council. She was arrested at once, but just as promptly set free when she insisted that I was a liar. They probably thought that since everything else I'd told them was a lie, that was, too. When I'd given these apparently important pieces of information the beating stopped and I was dragged upstairs to my cell in rather poor condition. I was bleeding profusely and the next day I was black and blue from the waist down to the knees, with several blood patches under the skin. I demanded a doctor but no one came near me for several days. Then a German medical orderly treated me as best he could.

'During that night of misery I made up my mind that I couldn't stand much more punishment. I'd have to give some sort of explanation of the papers without disclosing anything of importance to the Resistance. I worked out a plan which I carried out through the following days. I told the interrogators at inordinate length about the Rockefeller Institute's help to the Jewish refugees, about our relief work for the Jews in

Theresienstadt and about our other relief projects. I went on so long that in the end they put their hands over their ears when I offered to give them a few more examples. In that way I got through a whole day without being lured on to more dangerous ground. When I'd finished, the chief interrogator's summing-up was excellent. At some points he skimmed so smoothly over what might have been awkward admissions that I couldn't help feeling he'd suddenly developed a blind eye. That the Danish interpreter did so is beyond doubt. But they were both snobs and seemed to be impressed by the fact that I was a member of the Association of Sciences.

'There was a tricky moment when they started to talk about my connection with *Informatión*. They knew that I took two copies of the paper and that I'd contributed to it. Actually, at that time I was receiving thirteen copies but by rambling on about the traditional "unknown men" I got away with it.

'The ensuing days were worse. To account for my presence at the Technical High School meeting I said I was against the Resistance movement, but in order to obtain knowledge of their plans I'd had to get inside their organisation. I explained away the documents they'd found partly by my connection with secretary of state Koch in the central administration, on whose behalf I'd tried to avert action from the Resistance, and partly by claiming intended discussions with Jørgen Jørgensen about post-war problems—"and surely that wasn't against the German interests?" I was playing high but succeeded in keeping the Resistance proper out of the questioning. The sessions ended in a relatively friendly atmosphere, when the chief interrogator declared that he believed eighty per cent of what I'd said "and that's a great deal, I can tell you; you've no idea how we've been cheated and deceived". I was told I should be kept in the Shellhus prison until the end of the war. The interrogations had been interrupted frequently by long discussions in which different SS officers had taken part. One of the latter was quite pleasant to me and sometimes appeared to see my point of view. It was strange, however, how often the chief interrogator, when dictating for the official record, made his comments with a slight bias in my favour.

'Unfortunately for me another department, who'd been hunting me earlier, got mixed up in the proceedings. They knew, among other things, that reports of tapped German telephone calls had been delivered to me. They also knew of a letter asking me to try to get a Danish aircraft brought back from Sweden and put on a route to Germany for the benefit of the British intelligence service. That didn't look good, especially in the light of my explanations during the interrogations. Luckily for me, before the new grillings could get started the RAF intervened.'

During the latter months of 1944 the Resistance forces were in grave difficulties. The Germans knew altogether too much and as a result the freedom fighters were suffering heavy losses. In December Hoffmann called the Swedish ambassador to Denmark, Gustav von Dardel, to Shellhus and placed on the table before him a brand-new Husqvarna sub-machine gun. How, he asked sarcastically, could the ambassador explain this evidence that his neutral country was taking part in acts of war against the Reich? A few weeks earlier the Resistance had received a shipment of two thousand Husqvarnas from Sweden. The Gestapo had captured six of them in a battle with a sabotage group in Frederiksberg.

Hoffmann's interview with Dardel finally convinced the Resistance leaders that an attempt had to be made to put Shellhus out of action. The destruction of the building with its all-important files could cripple the Gestapo for many months. But that could be achieved only with the help of the RAF. An appeal was sent to England.

Svend Truelsen, at that time intelligence chief in SOE's Danish section, relates: 'After the successful RAF raid in the autumn of 1944 on the Gestapo headquarters in Jutland, similar raids on the Gestapo headquarters in Odense and Copenhagen were often discussed at Special Forces headquarters in London. Such raids were never carried out without a direct request from the Resistance organisations concerned because of the risk to prisoners and for political reasons. In December the Resistance asked for a raid on Shellhus and their request was passed on to the British air ministry. As usual, the reply was that no firm

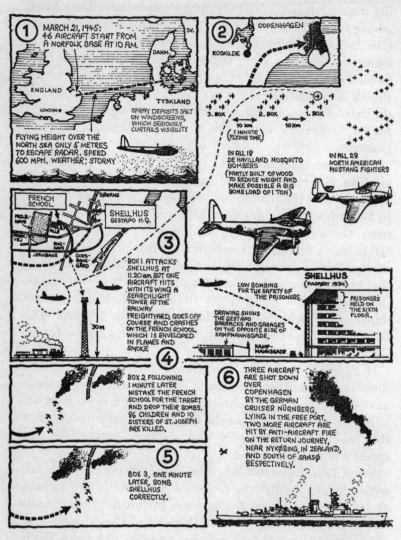

R.A.F. raid on Shellhus

("Besættelsens Hvem-Hvad-Hvor," Politikens Forlag, Copenhagen)

date could be given; the RAF were busy on other fronts. Nevertheless, we asked Copenhagen to supply us with all available
maps and photographs and with continuing information about
the Gestapo's activities in Shellhus, the location and changes in
position of anti-aircraft batteries, and so on.

'A second request came from the Resistance and Special
Forces took the matter up again with the air ministry. Once
more we were put off. Holland and Belgium had "air priority".
Since the raid on Aarhus I had been personally in touch with
(then) Air Vice-Marshal Basil Embry and this led to a discussion
between Embry and the air ministry. The ministry left the
decision to Embry, who in turn again asked for a clear request
from Denmark, stressing that an attack on Shellhus would
involve grave danger to the prisoners and to the occupants of
the surrounding buildings. The request came, and I had a meeting in France with Embry and Air Chief-Marshal Sir Arthur
Coningham, chief of the Tactical Air Force. The raid was on.

'The planning was based on excellent information from the
military intelligence in Copenhagen. We knew the purpose for
which the Gestapo used every single room in Shellhus and every
detail of the building's construction. We knew the exact
locations and strength of the German anti-aircraft batteries in
Copenhagen and throughout Denmark; we knew all about the
listening and direction-finding systems everywhere in the
country; and we had full details of the airfields, their manning
strength, and the types and numbers of aircraft in service.'

The raid was to be made by eighteen Mosquito bombers
escorted by twenty-eight US Mustang fighters, flying in three
waves with six bombers in each box. Each Mosquito was to
carry one ton of bombs, timed for maximum destruction and to
avoid the aircraft being blasted by their own bombs in the low-
level attack. To minimise risk to the prisoners on the sixth floor
of Shellhus, few incendiaries were to be carried. For the same
reason, the bombs were to be aimed at the ground floor and first
floor of the building.

The route was to be directly across the North Sea, South
Jutland, the Baltic, South Zealand, north-east to north of
Roskilde, and then along the main road to Copenhagen. The

aircraft were to turn above the New Theatre and proceed along Sankt Jørgens Lake directly to Shellhus. Over land the flying height was not to be above one hundred metres and over sea not above five metres, maintaining a speed of 580–600 kilometres per hour. Height at attack was to be fifty metres. Each box was to make one attack and then fly off across North Zealand, over Nykøbing, the southern tip of Samsø and back to England, flying low to avoid radar and anti-aircraft fire.

'The attack was timed for a quarter past eleven in the morning,' Truelsen said. 'We knew that at that time there would be most Gestapomen in the offices and the files would be in use and therefore most vulnerable.

'The pilots and navigators, picked forty-eight hours earlier and unaware of the task ahead, were taken to a base in Norfolk. There we had prepared an accurately coloured scale model of all the buildings within a square kilometre of Shellhus, with gun emplacements marked in red. There were also contour models of the Danish countryside, with German positions marked, for the routes out and back. About seventy airmen, all officers, including some of England's best, met in the operations room for briefing. Among the material with which they were provided were photographs of the cruiser *Nürnberg*; then lying in Copenhagen harbour, with details of her heavy guns. Squadron-Leader Sismore, leading navigator for the raid, went over the routes and gave co-ordinates for the out-and-back flights.

'While I was giving instructions for the actual attack, a Mosquito flew low over the operations room. A few minutes later Embry and his navigator, Squadron-Leader Peter Clapham (later to become air attaché at the British embassy in Copenhagen), stood by my side. I had been ordered to introduce Embry as "Wing-Commander Smith". He was not allowed to take part in operational flights because of his high rank. The Germans had put a price of seventy-five thousand marks on his head. He took every chance of hitting the Gestapo personally because of the brutalities they had inflicted on some of his men who had been shot down. Embry and Clapham took part in all three raids on the Gestapo headquarters in Denmark and in one on Holland. Now they sat down with the other officers to receive their instructions. Embry was to lead the first box but the over-all commander was Group-Captain Bob Bateson, who later was to lead the raid on the Smallholders School in Odense.

'On the morning of 21 March the Mosquitoes and Mustangs rolled out to begin their mission. Embry was first away and circling over the base radioed the signal for the rest of the aircraft to take off, two by two. Fifteen minutes later the formations set off for Denmark. Our best wishes went with them in their effort to give the Resistance a helping hand. We knew that usually twenty-two per cent of the aircraft did not return from such raids.'

The aircraft roared at six hundred kilometres an hour across the North Sea. The weather was filthy. There was a violent storm over Jutland and as they raced at five metres height across the Baltic spray drenched their windscreens, leaving a thin layer of salt that hampered visibility. By the time the aircraft neared Copenhagen the pilots' range of vision had been reduced to little more than the width of a matchbox cover, a circumstance which was to have tragic consequences. But the low-flying tactic succeeded. There was no interference from German fighters or guns. Crossing Zealand the Mustangs increased speed and flew ahead to engage possible fighters, anti-aircraft batteries and the guns of the *Nürnberg*. At eighteen minutes past eleven the first wave thundered in over Copenhagen. Skimming the rooftops south of Søndermarken Park, the force veered left over the railway freight depot. Then came tragedy. Wing-Commander Kilboe, flying on the port side of the first box with his vision impaired by the salted-up windscreen, hit a searchlight mast. His aircraft, severely damaged and out of control, continued on towards Frederiksberg Allé. He broke radio silence to say that he would try to make a forced landing in Frederiksberg Gaarden park, but his luck was out. He lost height and crashed on to the French School, where the children were at their morning lessons. His bombs exploded, spreading an inferno of blazing oil and petrol.

'The first box pressed on towards Shellhus, turned over the New Theatre and went in for the attack,' Truelsen said. 'They dived low over Sankt Jørgens Lake and at about a hundred metres from the target released their bombs. At twenty minutes past eleven the first six tons burst on the Gestapo headquarters. The second box, following immediately, saw ahead a building almost hidden by the smoke and flame from Kilboe's crashed aircraft and mistook it for Shellhus. They released their load too soon and the bombs hurtled down on the French School, destroying almost the whole of Frederiksberg Allé. When, after their return to base, the crews heard what they had done, they were horrified, but it was one of those terrible accidents which happen in wars. They were not to blame.

'Over Copenhagen the force lost two Mosquitoes and a Mustang hit by the guns of the *Nürnberg*. On the way to Nykø-bing another Mosquito was hit and went into the sea. A fourth was hit near Samsø and crashed into the Kattegat. In that air-craft was an architect who had been active in the Norwegian Resistance before he escaped to England and joined the RAF. I knew him well. Our total losses in the raid were four Mos-quitoes, two Mustangs, and ten brave men.'

The attack took the Germans completely by surprise. When their air-raid observers saw the fighters and bombers flying in over the city at rooftop height, they mistook them for Luftwaffe aircraft on a training flight and gave no warning. When the sirens were sounded at last, it was on the orders of the Danish civil defence. By that time the bombs were raining down on the Gestapo headquarters.

Police-Inspector C. Lyst Hansen said: 'It was my hard luck to be on the sixth floor when the raid began. I should have been transferred that morning to Frøslev but I was taken down too late to catch the car. I was escorted up to my cell again, and since I had to occupy myself until the car returned for me at one o'clock, I found a book and lay down on my mattress to read.

'Suddenly I heard the sound of aircraft and the rattle of machine-guns. I jumped up hastily. I remembered what had happened at Aarhus University and I had no doubt what we, immediately under the roof of Shellhus, could expect. The machine-gun bullets were hammering on the walls; then two

planes roared down in a power-dive and there was a long-drawn
screaming sound, followed by two violent explosions. The whole
building shook and there was such a shower of dust that I
couldn't see from one side of the cell to the other. My bed shot
across the floor and I was covered with broken plaster. I had
one thought—to get out, fast. I banged desperately on the door
with my fists, but nobody came to open up. I took a heavy
stool, swung it over my head and flung it at the door. To
my amazement it shattered the panel. That damned door was
made of ordinary plywood, and for months we'd thought it was
an impregnable barrier to freedom! In less time than it takes
to tell, I'd yanked out the panel and was out in the corridor.

'Our guard, a middle-aged SS man, was standing pressed up
against the wall, shaking with fright. His face was as white as a
sheet. I rushed at him and shook him by the shoulders, yelling:
"The keys! Give me the keys to the cells." He looked at me
dazedly. Plane after plane dived on the building, bombs exploded on the floors beneath us, and we were both covered in
plaster dust. The chap was absolutely paralysed. He was staring
up at a big hole which one of the bombs had torn in the roof
and kept repeating, as if in a trance: *"Es geht schön ... Es
geht schön..."* Again I shouted for the keys, and he handed
me a pair of nail-scissors. I searched his pockets and found the
keys, and in no time I'd freed the first of my comrades. They
started to splinter other cell doors with a fire-extinguisher and
those they couldn't manage I opened with the keys. Aage
Schoch was in the last cell I unlocked. I said: "Come on, Schoch.
We're going home." In a remarkably short time everybody
from cells 6 to 22, towards Kampmannsgade, was out. It was
impossible to get to cells 1 to 5. They were towards Nyropsgade
and just around the corner a bomb had made a gigantic hole
in the floor. We couldn't jump across it. It was a sheer miracle
that the man in No. 6 was alive; a bomb had taken away all
the outer wall and half the cell with it. But there was no time
for reflections of that sort. From my trip downstairs earlier in
the morning I knew exactly where the stairs to the back yard
were, and in a moment a whole procession was rushing down
that way. Everybody was gone when I got to the ground floor

with Schoch and Mogens Fog. We ran to the open door in the barbed-wire fence at the end of the yard and emerged into an alley flanked by more fences. It led to Vestre Farimagsgade and at that end, too, the door was open. We plunged through thick clouds of smoke and dust out into the street. Not a soul was in sight. The German guards had been killed or had bolted. We could hear shooting on the other side of the building but we walked calmly across the pavement and through the barbed-wire entanglements. I say "through" because the wire had either been cut or had been blown clean outside the open door.

'We hurried up Vestre Farimagsgade to Jarmersgade. As we neared the corner somebody shot at us and we took cover behind the Technological Institute. At Jarmers Plads I said good-bye to my two companions. I brushed down my clothes as well as I could and went into a stairway for shelter, for the raid was still on. Just then a bomb burst on the Technological Institute and for about the tenth time I felt as if all the air had been sucked out of my lungs.

'I watched the Hipo cars and German army vehicles racing towards Shellhus, which was now burning fiercely. Shortly afterwards the all-clear sounded and I started off down Studiestræchet. At the corner of Nørregade I met Fog and Schoch again. Like me, they were still white with plaster dust, but happy. They'd taken refuge in an air-raid shelter until the raid ended. Schoch said: "You were in Frøslev. How on earth did you get here to set us free?" The intelligence service on the sixth floor was very good and everybody knew I'd been booked for transfer to the camp; but the bombs had started falling before word could get around that I'd missed the car.'

Eight prisoners died in the raid. Twenty-seven got safely away. More than a hundred Germans were killed but because a military funeral had been taking place at eleven o'clock the Gestapo chiefs were not in Shellhus when the attack took place. One of Hoffmann's assistants was heard to say that it was a pity Hoffmann had not gone through the floors to the basement with his five office safes.

On the morning of 22 March 1944, *Information* reported:

The grim reality of war came to Copenhagen yesterday. The RAF with its precision-bombing of Shellhus gave a helping hand to the Danish Resistance in their final battle against the Germans in Denmark. Many were killed or wounded and we will honour the memory of those who died that Denmark may live. We will meet with gratitude those pilots who destroyed the monument to the Gestapo terror in the heart of Copenhagen. During the raid many Germans and their collaborators were killed and incredible quantities of documents were destroyed—documents which have put or in the very near future could have put Danish freedom fighters in prison or against the execution wall.

This raid, which the Copenhagen people have long hoped for, came now because the German terror had reached a climax. General Lindemann's 'stricter course with the Danes' recently cost the lives of thirty-four good Danes in front of the execution squads and at the same time torture in German prisons and interrogation rooms, especially in the now defunct Shellhus, has been put into operation so that torture now takes place at nearly all interrogations. Among the many Danes, some of the best people in the Resistance, who escaped because the RAF bombed with almost terrifying precision, are witnesses whose reports would shock the civilised world. The gratitude of these men to the RAF is shared by the Danish people who yesterday, while Shellhus went up in smoke and flames, felt that in this final struggle the invisible Danish front and the victorious armies of the free world fight together.

Unfortunately, many Danes were killed far away from the centre of the raid, especially many children in the French School in Frederiksberg Allé, because a British aircraft after having collided with a searchlight mast on the goods train terrain loosed bombs in two places at Frederiksberg and finally crashed on the school. For the parents who lost their dearest, there can be no consolation. We can only express our deepest condolences.

From the beginning of 1942 one of the main objectives of Denmark's four biggest illegal organisations—the Communist party, *Dansk Samling*, *Ringen* and *Frit Danmark*—was to recruit a secret citizen army who, after training, would remain inactive until the landing of Allied troops. In this endeavour the communists and *Dansk Samling* made effective use of their party officials and members, while the non-political *Ringen* and *Frit Danmark* worked through their connections with the illegal Press, sports clubs, cultural societies, and the professional associations of doctors, schoolteachers and clergymen. In every city, town and hamlet reliable people were contacted and persuaded to form groups of six to ten men to be trained as fighting units as weapons became available.

On direct orders from General Gørtz, moves to create a similar force had been made even earlier by army intelligence officers, among them Major (now Lieutenant-Colonel) N. B. Schou.

'In 1940 I was a captain in the Second Field Artillery, stationed at Holbæk,' he said. 'My commanding officer was Colonel C. D. O. Lunn, a fine soldier who was well known outside Denmark. In 1918, he had been a delegate of the Red Cross in Germany, repatriating Allied prisoners-of-war. He afterwards became a member of the border commission in Syria and in 1936 he headed the non-intervention commission for the Spanish border. He was a man of very broad vision and modern democratic ideas and I liked him very much. After I became his aide-de-camp in 1938 I worked at week-ends, with his consent, for the general staff's intelligence section, headed by Colonel E. M. Nordentoft and Captain V. L. U. Gyth. Gyth and I were from the same school and though he was three years my senior we were good friends.

'On 9 April 1940, when the invasion came, our garrison was ordered not to resist the Germans. We didn't like that but we had to obey. I heard there was a rumour in Holbæk town that Colonel Lunn had committed suicide. When I told him, his reaction was characteristic. He went to the stables, took out his white horse and rode down the main street and back again; then he continued his exercise in the riding-ground of the barracks. I was standing outside the door of my office when the Germans arrived, a reconnaissance company in cars and on motorcycles. The colonel had also seen them. He handed the reins of his horse to an orderly and went straight to the *pissoir*. I went over to the German major in command of the company and he asked for the garrison commander. I took him to the *pissoir*, an old wooden shack roofed with tar-paper, and there Colonel Lunn received him. Nothing could have been more humiliating for the man.

'Though Colonel Lunn was certain the Germans couldn't win the war he could take no overt action against them. He was bound by his oath of allegiance. Like all senior regular officers he had sworn loyalty to the king, whereas I and other young officers like me had sworn to adhere to the constitution, which was quite another matter. We felt less committed to the government and were determined to do everything we could to carry on the fight.

'Our first move was to commandeer a supply of hand-grenades. The Germans were already sealing our magazines but I knew of some grenades in Ringsted which had been marked out in the books but which hadn't been used. On 11 April, with the colonel's permission, I went to Ringsted barracks with my subalterns and staff-sergeants and retrieved them. As an artillery officer I was wearing a blue uniform with red stripes, which in Germany are staff insignia, and the Germans, who were behaving very correctly, dared not question my authority. I told the Danish sergeant in charge of stores that I knew certain boxes contained grenades which had been taken out of the accounts. We went to the magazine with a German non-com. and, while he was kept busy by the stores sergeant, loaded the grenades into my car. We drove back to our barracks and put the boxes in the cellar beneath my quarters.

'After the fall of France I was kept busy reporting on

Wehrmacht movements to Colonel Nordentoft. The Germans
had been withdrawn from the Holbæk garrison and for the
purpose of training our conscripts we were allowed to go on
exercises and make reconnaissances. I travelled around the district in uniform, quite openly, and got a great deal of information about such operations as the construction of a battery
at Sjællands Odde. Good friends among the civilian population
also supplied us with news of interest to the intelligence section.
Gyth visited us regularly from Copenhagen and told us what
was happening there, and we in turn kept our battalion commanders posted about what was going on in Denmark, Germany and the outside world. We knew quite a lot. Our intelligence service was extremely good.

'Colonel H. A. V. Hansen started a movement, backed by the
war ministry, to foster relations between civilians and the
armed forces. We formed a group in Holbæk and toured community houses, schools and the headquarters of different clubs
and societies. After Colonel Lunn had given a short talk we
showed a film about the army and navy and then answered
questions from the audience. We were out at least once and often
twice a week during the winters of 1940, 1941, and through into
1942, contacting at least ten thousand people in north-western
Zealand. We made friends with the farmers, schoolmasters,
priests, and other important members of the small communities
and told them what we knew about the situation in Denmark,
Britain and France, news they couldn't read in their heavily-
censored newspapers. For example, we were able to explain to
the farmers that when they got good prices for their pigs it
was the Danish National Bank who paid, not the Germans.
They hadn't all realised that. Those talks were a big factor in
building morale and a valuable preparation for a later change
in public opinion about the feasibility of resistance. At the same
time I made many valuable contacts with people who could
give me useful information. All this was done quite openly. The
Germans had no idea of what was going on under their noses.
They couldn't speak Danish and they didn't understand the
Danish way of thinking.'

The rigid loyalty which General Ebbe Gørtz, chief of general

Special issue of *De Frie Danske*, April 1945, commemorating the fifth
anniversary of the German occupation

Police-Constable Frank Zorn on guard at Sorgenfri Castle in 1944

Fighting at Amalienborg Castle on the morning of 5 May, 1945, in which two of the police guard were killed

The Police and the Royal Life Guard change guard at Amalienborg Castle, 10 June, 1945; a month after the liberation. Below: The same occasion; 250 police march away from Amalienborg after almost two years as guards to the royal family

Above: Montgomery arrives in Copenhagen, May 1945.
Left: 'Germany has capitulated', 'Denmark is free at last', say the headlines of the *Berlingske Tidende*. Three Copenhagen freedom fighters read the news.
Bottom: 5 May 1945: happy girls parade through Copenhagen

staff and from 1941 Commander-in-Chief of the Danish army, gave to the legal government and its edicts sometimes laid him open to public criticism and suspicion (as when, rather than saddle one of his officers with the disgrace, he attended the parade in connection with *Frikorps Danmark*'s departure for the Russian front). Colonel Schou is in no doubt where the general's real sympathies lay.

'I have in my possession Z-orders dated 6 November 1940,' he said. 'Z-orders were orders for calling up conscript classes for part-mobilisation. They were always kept ready for issue. On 6 November 1940, we in Holbæk were instructed by Gyth to go through them secretly and prepare them for use in case of emergency. I'm quite certain General Gørtz knew and approved of that. Such an order couldn't have been given without the knowledge and approval of the chief of general staff. It must have been made with his full consent, which changes the accepted view of Gørtz's attitude quite considerably.

'I was in sole charge of the operation in that region of Zealand. I received the Z-orders and sorted them out. In all parishes in Denmark there's a man whose job it is to keep a register of all men liable to military service. I drove to every parish in the region, went through the orders with the registrar and sometimes with his wife and discussed every man on the list. We weeded out all known German sympathisers or possible sympathisers, together with men unsuitable for any other reason. Every approved Z-order was stamped with the letter "P". Our aim was to prepare a force of good, reliable soldiers who in an emergency could get to Holbæk, equipped with uniform and weapons, within two or three hours. There would be no formal mobilisation; a courier would be dispatched secretly to call every man to action. I covered the whole of north-western Zealand during the first months of 1941. When the job was done I handed the Z-orders to Colonel Lunn for safe-keeping.

'Other officers were making similar surveys throughout Denmark, so as early as the spring of 1941 we had established the nucleus of an underground army, the so-called *P-styrke* (P-force). Gyth visited me one day and showed me an armband which could be distributed if there weren't enough uniforms for our fighting groups. It was the blue band with red and white stripes which later was to become the badge of the Resistance movement.'

Schou was promoted major in January 1941, and in November he was given command of a battery. A year later he was posted to the staff of the general-inspector of artillery.

'As I was working in Copenhagen but still living in Holbæk, the general let me go home at week-ends,' he said. 'That turned out to be a very useful concession.

'Colonel Lunn was a close friend of Colonel Helge Bennike, commanding officer of the Fourth Infantry Regiment and commander of the Roskilde garrison. The Germans were in the Roskilde barracks but there were still large stores of Danish weapons, uniforms, and all kinds of gear. At the beginning of 1943 the Danes were ordered to clear out of Roskilde because the *Wehrmacht* wanted the barracks to themselves. Colonel Bennike didn't see why they should have the equipment as well, so he compiled false registers of the contents of the stores. He and Lunn had already found places on four neighbouring estates and in summer-houses near Roskilde where supplies could be hidden.

'Bennike got Harald Kjær, who owned a timber company, to make some boxes. Into these were packed uniforms, steel helmets, boots, underwear, rifles, sub-machine guns, machine-guns, and complete equipment for about seven hundred men. My good friend Otto Madsen, a director of the Ford Company in Holbæk, lent me a lorry and disguised as a workman I drove to Roskilde barracks, where First-Lieutenant Erik Bennike, the colonel's son, helped me to load up. I had a cocked pistol on the seat beside me and Erik also had his gun ready when we drove out past the German sentries, but we weren't challenged. We drove to the places the colonels had chosen, where twelve of the Roskilde officers helped us to hide the boxes. Later, with some officers from Holbæk, we got further loads. Altogether we took away complete equipment for four companies: uniforms, weapons, half a million rounds of ammunition, and two or three thousand hand-grenades. All the work was done on Saturday and Sunday mornings, the only times I had free.

'In July 1943, I was given another battery of mobile 75mm guns, manned by engineering students in training as officer-cadets. I was with that battery on 29 August, the day Denmark's military forces were disarmed and interned. Since I couldn't get hold of any explosive to blow up the guns, I gave orders to split the breeches. We handed the battery over to the *Wehrmacht* in that condition. We also drained the oil from our vehicles, so that as soon as the Germans tried to use them, the engines seized.

'Officers and men were separated for internment, and we discussed among ourselves how we should behave towards our guards. I argued that we should pretend to be friendly. We had no weapons; the only thing left to us was to try to break their morale. We had a civilian-type radio and we organised a rota to talk to the German officers, telling them what we'd heard from the BBC. In September news came of a big German defeat and retreat in the Caucasus. We played on that and shook them badly. We were absolutely convinced they were going to lose the war and we rubbed it in at every opportunity.'

Gradually the Danish army was disbanded and sent home—first the conscripts, then the non-commissioned officers, and finally the officers.

'In October, after several moves, I was sent to Fredensborg,' Schou said. 'The day before I was due to be released an *Abwehr* officer, Heinrich von Grone, questioned me about weapons which the Germans had found in North Zealand. I said I'd heard about them while I was in internment. He then asked me about Harald Kjær, who, I gathered, had been arrested. I denied knowing him, although I had his business card in my pocket. Grone was polite enough but I sensed that he didn't believe me. He went off to make a telephone call and while he was away I ate the card. I've never been sure that he didn't deliberately give me that opportunity. He was a decent soldier, not a Nazi. When he returned he said he was very sorry but he had to take me to Copenhagen. There he escorted me to Dagmarhus and handed me over to the Gestapo. That evening I was sent to Vestre Fængsel. I wasn't charged but I was interrogated for four or five days. The Gestapo got nothing out of me and at

last they gave up. After I'd signed a statement promising that
if I heard anything further about the hidden weapons I'd
inform the German authorities, I was released.

'At the end of October I began to organise new fighting
groups. One evening I was told that Colonel C. F. Løkkegaard
at Roskilde wanted to talk to me. I had to go to Ringsted to
meet some officers, so, since it was on my way, I got off the
train at Roskilde. The colonel warned me that the Germans
knew the part I'd played in taking and hiding the military
stores. I returned to Copenhagen, went straight to the war
ministry and saw Major P. V. Hammershøy, who was one of
the leaders of our organisation. I told him that I'd been "blown"
and asked what I should do. "Get out at once," he said. That
same evening, 4 November 1943, I crossed the Øresund from
Christianshavn in a police patrol boat.

'Shortly after my arrival in Sweden Nordentoft called me to
Stockholm to create a counter-espionage branch of the intelligence service, and in cooperation with Ronald Turnbull of SOE
and Major Frederick R. Stevenson of SIS we organised a field
security police force. We collected information from all parts
of Denmark about *stikkers*, collaborators, Schalburgmen and
other traitors and I was personally responsible for keeping
Danforce free from Nazi infiltrators. My sub-section was also
responsible for keeping the British informed about Gestapo and
Abwehr activities and I think we did a good job.'

The existence of two separate 'waiting' forces—the military
groups and those of the communists, *Dansk Samling*, *Ringen*
and *Frit Danmark*—posed difficulties, not least in the equitable
division of the supplies arriving from Sweden and Britain. The
situation was complicated further by the existence of groups
scattered about the country unconnected with either the
military or the four civilian organisations. To bring order into
the confusion and to organise all the groups under a single
command, the Free Council established in December 1943, the
so-called *M-udvalg* (military committee), composed of men with
long experience in illegal work and in close touch with every
branch of the Resistance Movement. Its first members were Stig
Jensen and Ole Geisler (SOE), Svend Wagner (communists),

Jørgen Staffeldt (*Dansk Samling*), and Aage Højland Christensen (army), succeeded in February 1944, by P. V. T. Ahnfeldt-Mollerup. Their job was to contact existing groups throughout Denmark, to form new groups, to bind them all together into one efficient force, and to regulate the reception, storage, transport and distribution of weapons and exposives. In Jutland this work was undertaken by Flemming Juncker.

The country was divided into six regions, each with its own independent command: 1, North Jutland; 2, Mid-Jutland; 3, South Jutland, including Varde and Kolding; 4, Funen; 5, Zealand and Lolland-Falster; and 6, Copenhagen. Later in the year Bornholm was designated as a separate, seventh, region. To facilitate communication between *M-udvalg* in Copenhagen and the peninsula, a joint commanding authority was established to co-ordinate the three Jutland regions. In the provinces authorities for counties and towns were set up under the regional commanders, and in Copenhagen there were seven sectional commanding authorities under which the groups usually combined in companies. The commanding authorities everywhere comprised at all levels representatives of the active Resistance organisations, supplemented by regular officers of the army and navy. The regional commanders kept in touch with *M-udvalg* by means of couriers and direct radio communication was established with SHAEF.

Recruiting proceeded vigorously and by July 1944, the underground army had attained a strength of at least twenty-five thousand men drawn from every section of the population, from factory hands and farm labourers to merchants, doctors and priests. They were of all ages from callow youth to white-haired maturity. Some had only the sketchiest training in the use of weapons; others had already gained valuable experience as conscripts or professional soldiers and sailors. The original intention was that the force should be held in waiting until the time came to join Allied troops in a final show-down with the Germans but many of the younger men chafed against the inactivity and, with the approval of *M-udvalg*, began increasingly to take part in sabotage. Indeed, practically all the railway sabotage in Jutland, to which the Allied high command attached great importance, was carried out by units of the underground army.

In a recent scholarly treatise* the military value to the Allies of the Jutland railway sabotage is somewhat unfavourably re-assessed; but even if it were true that the operations had less strategic relevance than earlier historians had claimed, an opinion very much open to question, the immense importance of the work in strengthening the morale of the Danes and in harassing the German occupying forces cannot be denied.

The object of railway sabotage was to delay German transport of troops, war materials, fuel and food over the main and branch lines of the Danish railway network, and in particular, over the north-bound and south-bound trunk lines in Jutland, the Germans' main link with Norway. To this end, in more than eight thousand actions the saboteurs destroyed thirty-one bridges, eight engine-sheds, eighteen water-towers, twenty-five switch installations, and fifty-eight locomotives, and derailed one hundred and nineteen trains. For good measure, on a night in February 1945, all the machine-tools in the four Danish factories making switches for the state railways were wrecked.

Most of the actions were of a minor character. It was sufficient for the saboteurs to blow up a section of rails and sleepers. The Danish maintenance gangs, many of whom were saboteurs in their off-duty hours, could be relied upon to take from half a day to several days to carry out the necessary repairs.

At first the saboteurs aimed at exploding their charges under the trains, thus damaging the permanent way and the freight wagons while avoiding serious harm to the locomotives, which usually carried Danish drivers and firemen. The Germans retaliated by putting 'Ascension squads' of Resistance prisoners from Frøslev in the first wagons as hostages, but this move was counteracted by timing the charges to explode on the line just before the arrival of the train.

The attitude of the railwaymen generally towards the increased hazards of their jobs was expressed by a Jutland

---

* *Jernbanesabotagen i Danmark*, by Aage Trommer, Odense University Press, 1971.

engine-driver. He said: 'One day I had to take a German troop train from Tønder to the camp at Oksbøl, near Varde. Shortly after we pulled out saboteurs blew up two water-towers, two block-posts in Esbjerg and the big signal box at Bramminge station. For a couple of days the lines to and from Esbjerg were completely blocked. Very often similar incidents meant that we had to work overtime for three or four hours or even longer, and naturally, since we're only human, we'd blast those saboteurs fervently, but just the same, they had our sympathy.'

The reaction of the Germans to the disruption of their transport was predictably violent. Many saboteurs, including some railwaymen, were executed, and counter-terror was tried —for the first time on 8 October 1944—with the blowing up of several civilian passenger trains. These brutal tactics had no more effect than the vain attempt to conceal the routes and schedules of trains by permitting the Jutland traffic controllers to inform the subordinate railway officials of movements only at the last possible moment. During the winter of 1944–5, when the campaign was at its height, the Germans were forced to place sentries at intervals of fifty to seventy-five metres along all the most important stretches of track, but even that was not enough. The sabotage intensified month by month and there are well-authenticated stories of daring groups planting their charges almost between the legs of the guards.

There were light-hearted episodes. When on 24 January 1945, Colonel-General Georg Lindemann, an infantryman, replaced Hanneken as German Commander-in-Chief in Denmark, *Information* suggested that the Jutland railway saboteurs should make him live up to his title, *general zum fuss* (general on foot). Accordingly, every time he left his headquarters in Silkeborg the line was blown up in front of his train. When in March 1945, his train was derailed near Struer, he was so furious that he ordered his men to burn down the nearest farmhouse, a stroke of bad luck for the farmer, who had nothing to do with the sabotage. In similar exuberant vein, the railway saboteurs celebrated Hitler's last birthday with an explosion every fourth minute.

By the end of April 1945, the underground army numbered

more than forty-three thousand men. They were never called upon to prove themselves in battle, but after the capitulation they performed useful service in collecting and guarding German weapons and war materials, maintaining order in the towns and cities, and assisting Danforce and Allied detachments in border control.

Colonel Schou also ended his war on the Jutland border. He said: 'I arrived back in Copenhagen on the evening of 5 May and billeted myself in the Grand Hotel on Vesterbrogade, where a number of rooms had become suddenly vacant. There was fighting in the street at about noon on Sunday, 6 May, and some of my bullets are still lodged in a wall of Vesterport, opposite the hotel. Friends in Holbæk arranged for my wife and daughters to come to Copenhagen on the Monday morning, so that we could be reunited after one and a half years. We had only a few minutes together before I was ordered with Major Frederick Stevenson to Second Army headquarters to inform the staff about the situation in Denmark and to arrange for the repatriation of the German troops. It was agreed that they should march out of the country through two channels: Aabenraa-Krusaa and Tønder-Sæd. About half the field security police were sent to the border to screen them and we got to Krusaa on Tuesday night.

'We had just finished dinner on the following evening when I was told that a hospital train had arrived at the nearby Padborg station. The Danish engine-crew didn't want to take it any further. I drove over to see what I could do. The train was standing in the station with about eight hundred wounded aboard. I ordered it to be cleared. That was one of the things in my life I shall always regret. The wounded were brought out, some of them in a very bad way. We searched the train and I found that many of the soldiers were carrying Danish money. That had to be stopped. I issued an order that no German could keep more than one ten-kroner note; the rest had to be left at the station. The troops were searched and we put all the Danish money into a sack. Then we had to get the train away. I didn't want to have eight hundred wounded on our hands; we simply couldn't feed and nurse them. I found some

Germans with another locomotive and forced them to couple it to the train. Next day another train arrived and we searched and got rid of that one, too. We collected millions of Danish kroner and handed them over to a representative of the National Bank. I never saw a man look more astonished.

'One day that week I was standing with Major Stevenson at a road junction near Krusaa when we saw a small German motorised column approaching. As they passed us I saw in the leading car Heinrich von Grone, the *Abwehr* officer who'd arrested me in Fredersborg. I ordered the vehicles into a field to dump all their equipment. Then, pointing to Grone, I said to a field security policeman: "Arrest that man."

'That gave me great personal satisfaction.'

INDEX

Aarhus Echo, 83
Af Petersén, Maj. C., 37
Ahnfeldt-Mollerup, P. V. T., 288, 309
Akselbo, Peter, 205
Albertsen, Viggo, 43
Albret, J. (Matthew), 60
Algreen-Petersen, Christian (Christian), 112-17, 128, 138-41, 143-7
Algreen-Petersen, Mrs, 113-14
Alsvold, Gunnar, 165
Anders And, see Larsen, Maj. F.
  Busenius
Andersen, Ejnar, 155
Andersen, Erik, 106
Andersen, Gøtrick, 59
Andersen, Henning, 271-2
Andersen, Martin Villiam, 173
Andersen, Niels, 131-2
Andersen, Pastor Otto, 285
Arbejderbladet, 83, 169
Auschwitz, 120
Axel, Prince, 38, 103

Bæklund, Max, 194-5, 228
Bakman, Cato, 104
Bang, A. C., 103
Bangsbøll, Comdr F. C. S., 45
Barandon, P. G. L., 245
Barfod, Egil, 210-11
Barfoed, Sigurd, 125
Bateson, Gp-Capt. Bob, 297
Beckmann, Kaj (Bruhn), 174
Bendtsen, Ole Bjørn (Ole Skevsbo), 142
Benedicte, Princess, 240
Bennike, First-Lt. Erik, 306
Bennike, Col. Helge, 306
Bergh, J. (Cain), 60
Berlingske Tidende, 9, 13, 29, 147, 155, 160
Bertelsen, 214-15
Bertelsen, Agnes, 227-8
Bertelsen, O. B., 211, 226, 227, 232, 236
Berthelsen, 138
Best, Dr Werner, 87, 108, 245-6
Bierberg, Elkan, 105

Bingham, Com. Brian (Brian Russell), 8, 47, 50
Binney, Sir George, 46-7
Birkedal-Hansen, Ib, 144
Bisquit, see Jacobsen, J.
Bjarnasson, Jørgen, 194
Blixenkrone-Møller, O., 45
Blum, Leon, 32
Bohr, Harald, 35
Bohr, Mrs Niels, 35, 36
Bohr, Prof. Niels, 32-7
Boje, Jørgen, 270
Boje, Mrs, 270
Bomhoff, Gunnar, 211, 243
Bomhoff, Helmer, 232, 238, 240, 241-3
Bomhoff, Liz, 232-3, 238, 240, 242-4
Bonnesen, Edith (Lotte), 8, 70-80, 147
Bopa, 9, 10, 19, 26, 64, 72, 157, 158, 169-91, 193, 209, 210, 212, 213, 240-241, 251, 257
Borking, Capt. Poul, 288
Bornholm, 124
Borup, Peer, 207
Bothildsen-Nielsen, 105, 153, 247
Bovensiepen, Otto, 109
Brandt, Børge, see Thing, Børge
Bredkær, Troels, 104-5
Brøchner, Henning, 270
Brøndum, Henning, 153, 247
Brooke, Gen. Alan, 43
Bruhn, see Beckmann, Kaj
Bruhn, Dr. Carl Johan, 55, 56
Brüun, Poul, 288
Buchenwald, 24, 248
Buhl, Vilhelm, 19, 170, 173
Bunch-Christensen, Erik, 100-1, 104-5
Bundesen, H., 45, 46
Bunke, Dr Erich, 144, 243-4, 287

Cain, see Bergh, J.
Capra, Frank, 258
Caprani, 148
Chadwick, Prof. James, 33-5
Cherwell, Lord, 36
Chievitz, Prof. Ole, 83, 84-5
Christensen, Aage Hojland, 309
Christensen, Axel, 105-6

Christensen, Ellen, 219-25
Christensen, Ernst, 94, 157-8, 165, 168
Christensen, Ib Mogens Bech (Knud), 8, 134, 156-68, 179-80
Christensen, Nygaard, 125
Christensen, Mrs, 196-7
Christensen, Mrs Ernst, 94, 157, 165, 168
Christian, see Algreen-Petersen, Christian
Christian X, King, 8, 12, 14, 18, 23, 36, 38, 92, 109, 245-52, 253, 303
Christiansen, Gunnar (Mat), 59, 60
Christiansen, Hans (Leif), 138-9
Christiansen, L. H., 288
Christiansen, Werner, 125, 128, 144
Christiansen, Lt.-Comdr Christian Hassager, 30-1
Christophersen, Henry, 83, 84
Christophersen, Sigfred, 18, 54-5, 124
Christophersen, Thorbjørn, 124
Churchill, Sir Winston, 36
Churchill Club, 15, 168, 261-9
Citronen, see Schmidt, Jørgen Haagen
Clapham, Sqn-Ldr Peter, 296-7
Clausen, Fritz, 93, 254
Clausen, Comdr Børge, 288
Close, Stanley, 50-1
Coningham, Sir Arthur, 295
Crone, Erik, 105, 288

Dachau, 106, 219, 288
Dagmarhus, 63, 65, 66, 70, 71, 72, 98, 104, 129, 142, 164, 196, 200, 209, 211, 215, 231, 232, 236, 238, 287, 307
Danforce (Danish Brigade), 40-2, 43, 47, 210, 266
Danish Brigade, see Danforce
Dansk Hjælpetjeneste, 119, 126, 154
Dansk Samling, 14, 15, 81, 82, 196, 210, 211, 270, 302, 308, 309
Dansk Ungdomssamvirke, 15-16, 82
Dansk-svensk Flygtningetjeneste, 119, 126, 131-2, 134, 143, 147, 148, 155, 163
Dardel, Gustav von, 293
Darket, H. Uffe, 261-6
Darket, Sven Juul, 261, 266-9
Davidsen, Oscar, 201
De Frie Danske, 9, 70, 82-3, 84, 85, 121, 192

Delbo, Hedvig, 201-2, 204-6, 209
Denham, Capt. H., 29, 43-4
Dessau, Einar, 121-2
Dessauer Ufer, 105
Dewing, General, 41
Dibnah, Dick, 51
Dierlich, Poul, 142
Døssing, Thomas, 83, 84-5, 290
Drescher, Fritz, 148
Drescher, Major, 71-2
Duckwitz, G. F., 8, 108
Dyrberg, Gunnar (Herman), 210, 213, 215-17, 230, 234-40

Ehrenswärd, General, 41
Ekstrabladet, 121, 122
Ellerman, 47
Elpert, 287
Elstrøm, Arne, 154
Embry, A.V.M. Basil, 295-7
Eriksen, F. Ahlgreen, 275-8

Færdrelandet, 283
Fauerschou-Hviid, Bent (Flammen), 8, 146, 161-2, 197-9, 204, 205-6, 213, 215, 220-1, 223, 226-44
Feilberg, Lt. Leif, 260
Ferryman, Brig. Mockler, 274
Fiil, Gudrun, 271
Fiil, Marius, 270-2
Fiil, Niels, 271-2
Finn, see Lillelund, Jens
Fischer-Holst, Tage (Joseph), 60
Flammen, see Fauerschou-Hviid, Bent
Fog, Prof. Mogens, 58, 83, 84, 288, 290, 300
Folkets Camp, 83
Fortsæt, 163
Foss, Erling, 43
Frandsen, Erik, 273-5
Frederik, Crown Prince, 38, 250, 251
Frederiksen, Kjeld, 105
Frederiksen, Svend Aage, 270
Freedom Council, 23-4, 25, 41, 43, 85, 91, 119, 132, 137, 141, 155, 170, 174, 182, 196, 210, 212, 290, 291
Friediger, Chief Rabbi M., 120
Fries, Christian, 105
Frihedsraadets Bladudvalg, 91
Frit Danmark, 83, 85, 156-8, 257, 289, 302, 308

Frøslev, 147, 210, 211, 259-60, 268, 277, 288, 298, 300, 310
Fyhn, Ole, 113, 116
Fyhn, Peter, 102, 105-6, 113

Gamst-Pedersen, Lt. Knud, 210
Geisler, Ole, 144, 147, 196, 270-3, 308
Gemysen, see Østergaard, Bent Hoegsbro
Gersfelt, Grete, 227
Gersfelt, Jørgen, 227
Gert, see Jensen, Holger
Gilbert, 221
Gjerløv, Hans, 10, 253-6, 257
Glavind, Johannes, 171
Goering, Hermann, 253
Gørtz, Gen. Ebbe, 194, 302, 304-5
Gottschalch, Hans-Henrik, 165, 168
Graae, Jutta, 28, 31, 33, 43
Gregersen, Lt. H. P., 288
Grone, Heinrich von, 307, 313
Grunnet, Niels, 88
Gry, 84
Gudme, Peter de Hemmer, 89
Gustav V, King—of Sweden, 36
Gustav Adolf, King—of Sweden, 36
Gyberg, Werner, 124, 154
Gylding-Sabroe, A., 154
Gyldmark, Sven, 256
Gyth, Capt. Volmer L. U., 28, 29, 31, 32-8, 40, 43, 55, 302, 304, 305

Hæstrup, Dr Jørgen, 10, 17, 82, 274
Hagens, Dr Erik, 180-1
Hambro, Sir Charles, 30
Hamburg, 105
Hammer, Mogens, 55-8, 70
Hammer, Svend Erik, 70
Hammerich, RA Carl, 288
Hammershøy, Maj. P. V., 45, 308
Hanneken, Gen. Hermann von, 20, 194, 209, 245-6, 272, 311
Hans, see Sand, John Georg
Hansen, Arne Egon, 173
Hansen, Christian Ulrik, 196, 197, 199-200, 273, 286
Hansen, C. Lyst, 288, 298-300
Hansen, Erik Frost, 254
Hansen, Gunnar 'Nu', 254
Hansen, Hans, see Sandbæk, Pastor Harald
Hansen, H. C., 91, 109

Hansen, H. Kj. Duus (Robert), 60
Hansen, Ib Birkedal, 247
Hansen, Johan Kjær, 271-2
Hansen, Johannes, 30-1
Hansen, Lorens Arne Duus (Napkin), 8, 18, 34-5, 44, 53-69, 72-3, 76, 79-80
Hansen, Nedermark, 247
Hansen, Poul, 193, 196
Hansen, Col. H. A. V., 304
Hansen, Mrs Lorens Arne Duus, 63-5
Hartmann-Schmidt, Tage, 288
Haslund, Peter Emil Vilhelm, 184
Haubirk, Ejler, 102, 105
Haussen, Per Albin, 41
Hedtoft, Hans, 41, 109
Heilesen, Claus, 111
Heister, Hans, 288
Helweg, Ole, 124, 125, 128-9
Hendil, Leif B., 121-6, 129-32, 138-9, 147-8, 163, 258
Hendriksen, Carl Næsh, 89
Henningsen, Capt. Poul, 249
Henriques, Carl Otto, 131
Henriques, C. B., 109
Heøgh, Prof. Carsten, 164
Herman, see Dyrberg, Gunnar
Hermannsen, Hans, 287-8
HH, see Petersen, Poul
Himmler, Heinrich, 109
Hitler, Adolf, 10, 12, 13, 17, 18, 21, 23, 30, 108, 167, 287, 311
Hoffman, Dr Karl Heinz, 259, 287-8, 293, 300
Holbach, J. (Jonas), 60
Holdsworth, Capt. C. R. W., 49
Holger Danske, 10, 19, 21, 64, 77, 115, 127, 147, 158, 161, 175, 187, 192-212, 213, 214, 228, 229, 234, 237, 240, 242, 251, 257, 273
Hollingworth, Lt.-Comdr R. C., 69
Holmboe, Ebbe, 105
Holst, Thorkild, 170
Horserød, 101, 111, 112, 114, 127, 158, 219, 260
Houmann, Børge, 83, 84, 169
Husfeldt, Prof. E., 141
Hvalkof, Lt.-Col. F. L., 39
Hygom, Hakon, 105

Ingeborg, Princess—of Sweden, 36
Informatión, 18, 24, 86-90, 144, 148, 292, 301, 311

Isak, *see* Jepsen, Willy
Isberg, Hagbart, 165
Iversen, Albert Carlo, 271-2

Jacobsen, Henry, 173
Jacobsen, J. (Bisquit), 60
Jacobsen, Romeo, 105
Jakob, *see* Martens, Jens
Jakobsen, Frode, 119, 211, 291
Jakobson, Prof. Malte, 48
Jarset, Mogens (Bob), 194-5, 228
Jelgren, Poul (Sam), 60
Jens, *see* Mehl, Victor Behring
Jensen, Erik, 144, 147
Jensen, Herta (Melukka), 90
Jensen, Holger (Gert), 190
Jensen, Karl V., 83, 84
Jensen, Knud Børge (Spræng Schmidt), 193, 213-4
Jensen, Peter, 270
Jensen, Robert (Tom), 124-6, 128-35, 138, 143-7, 154, 159-60
Jensen, Søren, *see* Petersen, Harald
Jensen, Stig, 273, 275, 308
Jensen, Pastor Kjelgaard, 111
Jepsen, Willy (Isak), 60
Jerichow, Herbert, 121, 131-2, 147
Jespersen, Jørgen (KK), 175-7, 240
Jessen, 287
Jessen, Jess, 254
Johannesen, Johannes, 8, 117-19, 122, 126, 154
Johannesen, Johannes Poul, 56-7, 59
Johansen, E. Borch, 58
Johansen, Hans, 190
Johansen, Kaj, 89, 121, 148
John, *see* Nielsen, Svend Otto
Jonas, *see* Holbach, J.
Jørgen, *see* Muus, Flemming
Jørgensen, A. J., 280
Jørgensen, Arne, 105
Jørgensen, Jørgen, 292
Jørgensen, Robert, 89
Jørgensen, Selmer, 148
Jørgensen, Sven (Terkel), 188-9, 191
Jørgensen, William, 288
Jørgensen, Capt. Fritz, 288
Jørgensen, Lieutenant, 46
Jørgensen, Mrs, 116
Joseph, *see* Fischer-Holst, Tage
Juncker, Flemming, 196, 270, 272-3, 309

Kampmann, Ove, 288

K-Committee, 24
Keiser-Nielsen, Dr H., 193
Kerteminde, 112
Kiær, Lt. Erling, 155
Kiding, Hans Christian, 226
Kieler, Flemming, 197
Kieler, Jørgen, 197, 206, 207
Kiilerich, Ole, 83, 84-5
Kilboe, Wing-Commander, 297
Kis, *see* Kisling, Christian
Kisling, Christian (Kis), 211, 215, 239
Kjær, Harald, 306-7
Kjær, Niels Nielsen, 271-2
Kjølsen, Capt. F., 39
KK, *see* Jespersen, Jørgen
Klein, Prof. Oskar, 36
Klinting, 115
Klitgaard, Mogens, 122
Knud, *see* Christensen, Ib Mogens Bech
Knudsen, 266-7
Knudsen—two brothers, 133, 163
Knudtzon, Maj.-Gen. Kristian, 39, 43
Koch, 292
Koch, Peder, 207
Koch, Prof. Hal, 82
Kogebog for Sabotører, 170-2
Køster, Dr, 104
Kraft, Henrik, 121-36, 142-3, 147, 163
Kraft, Mrs Henrik, 122, 128, 130
Krenchel, 162
Kristeligt Dagblad, 286
Kristensen, H. P., 162
Kristensen, Sigvald, 89
Kristensen, Søren Peter, 271-2

La Cour, Vilhelm, 14, 81
Lagergreen, Erik, 147
Land og Folk, 82, 83, 85
Landboen, 91
Larsen, Aksel, 83, 84
Larsen, Eigil, 171
Larsen, Holger, 104
Larsen, Knud, 211
Larsen, Niels, 96-8
Larsen, Victor Imanuel, 173
Larsen, Maj. F. Busenius (Anders And), 45, 79
Laub, Niels, 105
Laursen, Kai Linde, 175-6
Leif, *see* Christiansen, Hans
Leifer, Vilhelm, 232
Lillelund, Ena, 193, 203-4

Lillelund, Jens (Finn), 115, 192-206, 209, 211-12, 214, 228, 233, 241, 285
Lindemann, Col.-Gen. Georg, 301, 311
Liseruten, 119, 126, 155
Little Peter, *see* Pedersen, Peter
Løkkegaard, Col. C. F., 308
Lotte, *see* Bonnesen, Edith
Lüdke, Gen. Erich, 245
Lunding, Capt. H. M., 28, 31-2
Lundsteen, K., 45
Lunn, Lt. J. Chr., 288
Lunn, Col. C. D. O., 302-6
Lysglimt, 148

Madsen, Otto, 306
Malmström, Olaf, 254
Malmstrøm, Dr, 275-8
Malmstrøm, Mrs, 275
Malthe-Bruun, Kim, 8, 102, 105-7
Marcussen, 194-5
Marrow, Johnny, 50
Martens, Jens, 157-8, 168
Martinsen, K. B., 162
Marx, Erik, 124, 128-9, 144
Mat, *see* Christiansen, Gunnar
Matthew, *see* Albret, J.
Mehl, Victor Behring (Jens), 175
Melk-Donau, 104
Melukka, *see* Jensen, Herta
Merved, Kai, 174-6
Mikkelsen, Max, 56
Mildner, Dr Rudolf, 108-9
Moesgaard, Ewald, 194-5
Moesgaard, Poul, 228
Mogensen, Helge, 106
Mohr, O. C., 18
Mølgaard, Lt. N. J., 288
Møller, Aksel, 91
Møller, Frits Blichfeldt, 138-9
Möller, Gustav, 47-8
Møller, John Christmas, 83, 94
Møller, Karl, 113
Möller, P. Rønnelin (Saul), 60
Moltke, Count 'Bobby', 33
Montgomery, F.M. B. L., 9, 23, 45
Mørch, Comdr P. A., 28, 31, 37-8, 40, 41, 43, 47-8
Moses, *see* Nielsen, P.
Mouritsen, Birge, 105
M-udvalg, 308-9
Munch, Dr P., 16
Munck, Børge, 228
Munck, Carl, 192, 228

Munck, Ebbe, 8, 13, 18, 29, 30, 31, 35, 41, 43, 47, 55, 79, 102, 124, 131, 134
Munck, Svend Aage, 147, 155
Munk, Kaj, 22, 94, 256, 286
Munk, Mrs Stubben, 205
Muus, Flemming B. (Jørgen), 58, 62, 72, 76-7, 79, 270-4

Naesselund, Gunnar, 18
Napkin, *see* Hansen, Lorens Arne Duus
Nationaltidende, 83, 86, 89
Nedermark-Hansen, 139
Neuengamme, 84, 104, 105, 106, 207, 210, 219, 248
Nielsen, Aage Julius, 173
Nielsen, Erik, 290
Nielsen, Harald, 173
Nielsen, Jonny, 173
Nielsen, Knud Enver, 173
Nielsen, P. (Moses), 60
Nielsen, Poul Overgaard, 256-7
Nielsen, Svend Otto (John), 8, 196-209, 212, 228
Nielsen-Ourø, Police-Commissioner, 249
Nielson, 93
Niemüller, Martin, 32
1944, 134, 148, 158, 160-8
Noah, *see* Stotz, Thomas Friederich
Nøjgaard, Rev. Dr Niels, 256
Nordentoft, Lt. Bent, 288
Nordentoft, Lt.-Col. E. M., 28, 31, 41, 43, 44, 302, 304, 308
Nordisk Boghandel, 143, 209
Nordisk Nyhedstjeneste, 86, 87
Nørup, Jørgen, 288
Nyborg, 112, 264-5
Nygaard, Erik, 232, 242-3
Nygaard, Mrs Erik, 244
Nyholm, Cmdr Hans, 45, 288
Ny Tip, 84

Office of Strategic Services (OSS), 43, 47
Olstrup, Alf E., 288-9
Olufsen, 65-6
Øresundstjeneste, 155
Ørnberg, Leif, 163
Ørum, Mrs, 115-16
OSS, *see* Office of Strategic Services

Østergaard, Bent Hoegsbro (Gemysen), 239
Østergaard, Mrs Bent Hoegsbro, 239
Outze, Børge, 86-9, 121, 148
Oxlund, Capt. Kaj, 124

Paddy, see Schultz, Patrick
Pancke, Police-General, 248, 251
Parkov, Knud, 130
Patik, Finn, 254
Pedersen, Jens, 196, 198-9, 240
Pedersen, Jens, 261
Pedersen, Knud, 261, 264, 266
Pedersen, Leif, 240
Pedersen, O. G., 288
Pedersen, Peter (Little Peter), 232, 236
Pedersen, Pastor, 261
Peter Group, 23, 267
Petersen, Erik V., 252
Petersen, Ernst, 82, 83, 84
Petersen, Hans, 173
Petersen, Harald (Søren Jensen), 212
Petersen, I. Bruhn, 45
Petersen, J. Palm, 288
Petersen, Poul (HH), 175
Petersen, Dr Thorup, 270
Petersen, Lt. Kjeld, 54
Plambech, Harry Svend, 173
Plovfuren, 91
Polack, Jørgen, 122, 132
Politiken, 89
Porta, 105
Poulsen, Erik Schousboe, 226-32, 238, 240
Poulsen, Lise, 227-30, 232
Preisser, 287
Princes, The, 13, 28-42, 44, 54-5, 57, 59
Prior, Mogens, 289-90
Prior, Gen. W. W., 11
Prip-Buus, Esther, 284-5
Prom, P., 45
Prytz, Rud, 83, 84

Ramsing, Bob, 197-200, 206, 210, 212, 233-4, 240-1
Rasch, Svend, 105
Rasmussen, Børge, 285
Rasmussen, Knud, 102, 106
Rasmussen, Svend Eduard, 123
Ravnbo, Hjalmar, 102
Rehberg, Prof. P. Brandt, 288-93

Reitzel, Erik, 148
Renthe-Fink, Cecil von, 18, 245
Reventlow, Count Ludvig, 106
Ribbentrop, 19, 108
Ringen, 119, 211, 302, 308
Robert, see Hansen, H. Kj. Duus
Rothe, Walther, 232
Rottbøll, Capt. C. M., 56-7, 58
Russell, Brian, see Bingham, Com. Brian
Ryvangen, 106, 168, 173, 208, 272, 288

Sachsenhausen, 84
Sam, see Jelgren, Paul
Sand, John Georg (Hans), 190
Sandbæk, Mrs Harald, 285
Sandbæk, Pastor Harald (Hans Hansen), 8, 279-86
Sandberg, Henrik, 257-60
Sandberg, Oliver, 100-1
Saul, see Møller, P. Rønnelin
Scavenius, Erik, 16, 19, 20, 82, 290
Schacht, Hjalmar, 32
Schafer, Peter, see Schwerdt, Otto
Scheich, Air-Gen. Ritter von, 246
Schiønnemann, Leif, 164-5
Schlichtkrull, Captain, 251
Schmidt, Jørgen Haagen (Citronen), 8, 73, 150, 161-2, 213-25, 228-9, 235-8, 240, 242-3
Schmidt, Spræng, see Jensen, Knud Børge
Schoch, Aage, 288, 290, 299-300
Schou, Maj. N. B., 302-8, 312-13
Schultz, Patrick (Paddy), 234-5, 237, 238-9
Schuschnigg, 32
Schweitzer, 281
Schwerdt, Otto (Peter Schafer), 247
Secret Intelligence Service (SIS), 18, 43, 54, 55, 308
Seidenfaden, Erik, 18
Sejr, Arne, 8, 92-102, 104, 121, 122-3, 156
Sejr, Jørgen, 104
Seybold, 236
SHAEF, 40, 174, 191, 309
Shellhus, 9, 73-80, 84, 89, 146, 158, 163, 164, 204, 221, 257, 268, 286, 287-301
Simonsen, Kaj, 131-2
SIS, see Secret Intelligence Service

Sismore, Squadron-Leader, 296
Skevsbo, Ole, see Bendtsen, Ole
  Bjørn
Slette-Hans, 114-17
Sneum, Lt. Thomas, 18, 54-5
Social-Demokraten, 89
SOE, see Special Operations Executive
Soedermann, Harry, 38
Søndergaard, Josef (Tom), 192-6, 213
Søren, 76-7, 138-9, 143-4, 146, 147
Sørensen, Arne, 14, 290
Sørensen, Axel, 285
Sørensen, Peter Bergenhammer, 271-2
Sørensen, Poul, 288
Special Operations Executive (SOE),
  18, 19, 20, 28, 30, 32, 43, 45, 55-60,
  62, 67, 69, 72, 144, 154, 174, 175,
  193, 196, 198, 210, 236, 240, 270,
  272, 273, 274, 293, 308
Speditøren, 119, 126, 127, 136, 144,
  149-54, 214, 221, 233
Sponholtz, August, 105
Stærmose, Erik, 124, 128-9
Staffeldt, Jørgen, 115, 196, 209-10, 233-
  234, 309
Staffeldt, Mogens, 115, 196-7, 209-10
Stagg, Comdr F. N., 55
Stauning, Thorvald, 12
Steinbeck, John, 94, 156, 258
Steinmetz, Eigil, 89
Stensen, 138
Stenz, Andreas, 270
Stevenson, Maj. Frederick R., 308,
  312-13
Stjernen, 83
Stokes, Capt. David 'Ginger', 8, 50-1
Stotz, Thomas Friederich (Noah), 60
Studenternes Efterretningstjeneste, 83,
  94-6, 101-3, 105-6, 111, 119, 121, 126,
  156
Sundby, 138

Tage, 280-1
Teglers, Hans Edvard, 210-11
Tejsen, Aage V. Ström, 221-2
Terkel, see Jørgensen, Sven
Termansen, Helle Gertrud, 158, 163,
  165, 168
Tesdorph, Edward, 125
Thalmay, Jacob, 104
Theilmann, Dr Jørgen, 219

Thing, Børge (Børge Brandt), 174,
  179-80
Thomas, John Oram, 8, 50
Thomsen, Henry, 226, 228
Thomsen, Svend Aage, 254-5
Thorkild, see Tronbjerg, Svend
Thornsberg, Eigil, 270
Thostrup, Lt. S., 39
Thulin, Else, 142
Thygesen, Dr Paul, 236
Tiden, 84
Tiemroth, Lt.-Col. E. C. V., 288-9
Tillisch, F., 45
Tito, Marshal, 272
Toldstrup, Anton J., 52, 60, 169, 273-
  276, 280
Tom, see Jensen, Robert
Torp-Pedersen, Emil, 36-7, 131
Trods Alt, 83-4
Tronbjerg, Svend (Thorkild), 144-7
Truelsen, Svend, 44-5, 121, 293-8
Tse-Tung, Mao, 26
Turnbull, Ronald, 30, 31, 32, 43, 47,
  55, 308

Vestjyden, 83
Vestre Fængsel, 71, 84, 106, 111, 115,
  139, 147, 156, 158, 163, 173, 193,
  204, 207, 209, 239, 240, 259-60, 288-
  289, 307

Wagner, Svend, 308
Walmsley, Charlie, 49, 51
Wäsche, Dr, 142, 236-7
Wedell-Wedellsborg, Ebbe, 288
Wedell-Wedellsborg, Baron Karl, 288
Weiss, Max, 35
Werner, Kriminalrat, 281-3
West, Benny, 31, 35
Westphal, Dr, 287
Wickmann, Alfred, 149
William, 165
Winkel, Capt. Per, 28, 31, 33, 43
Winkelhorn, Kaj, 47
Winther, Jørgen, 105-6
Wolfhagen, Comdr Ebbe, 288
Wray, Dick, 50

Zimling, 133
Zohnesen, W., 288
Zorn, Frank, 9, 10, 247-52

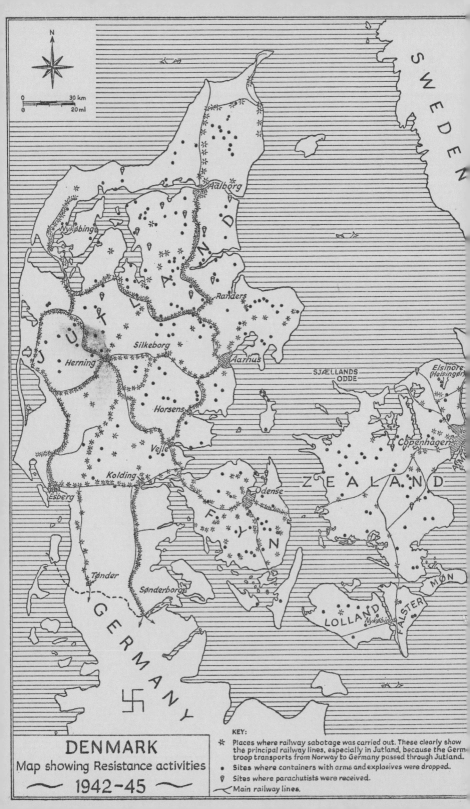

KEY:

*   Places where railway sabotage was carried out. These clearly show the principal railway lines, especially in Jutland, because the German troop transports from Norway to Germany passed through Jutland.

•   Sites where containers with arms and explosives were dropped.

⍭   Sites where parachutists were received.

⌒   Main railway lines.

DENMARK
Map showing Resistance activities
～ 1942-45 ～